TABLE ◇ OF ◇ CONTENTS

DOWNLOAD YOUR FILES

Downloading your files is simple. To access your digital files, please go to the last page of this book and follow the instructions.

For technical assistance, please email: info@vaulteditions.com

Copyright

Copyright © Vault Editions Ltd 2025.

Bibliographical Note

This book is a new work created by Vault Editions Ltd.

ISBN: 978-1-922966-67-4

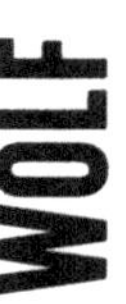

WOLF

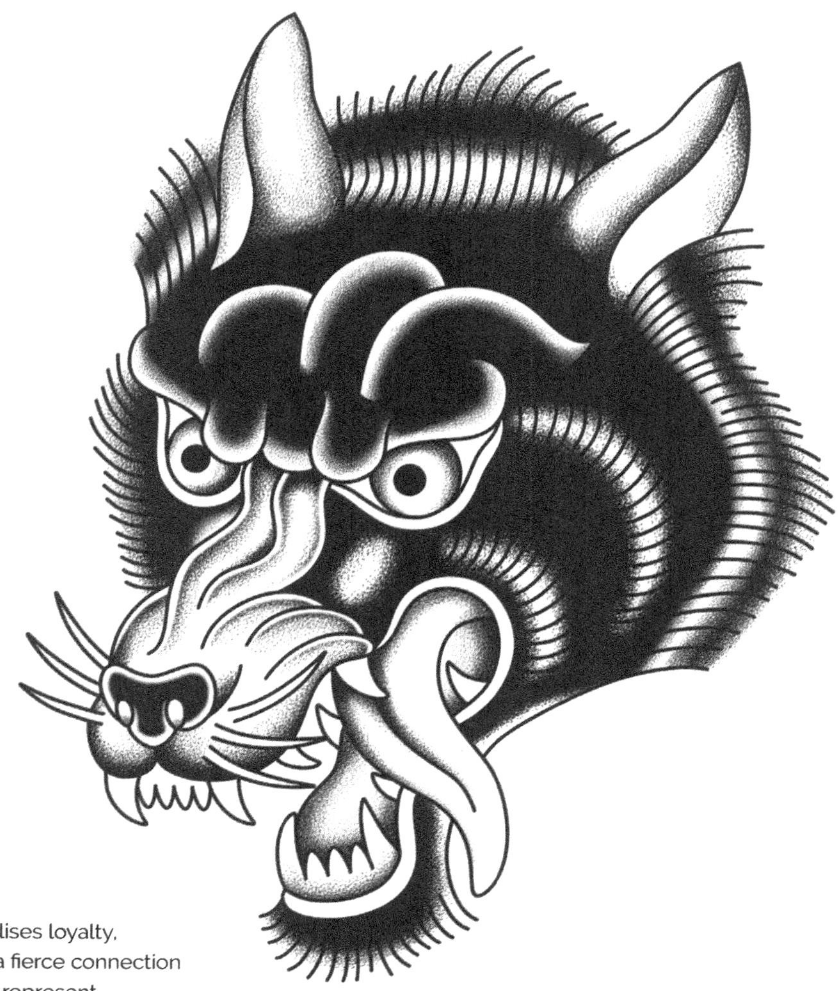

The wolf tattoo symbolises loyalty, instinct, strength, and a fierce connection to the pack. It can also represent independence and resilience in solitude.

01   **02**   **03**

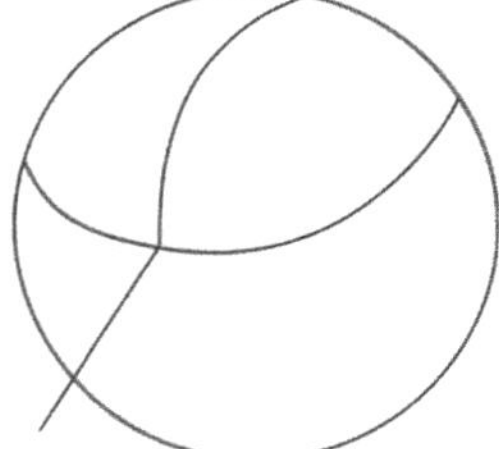

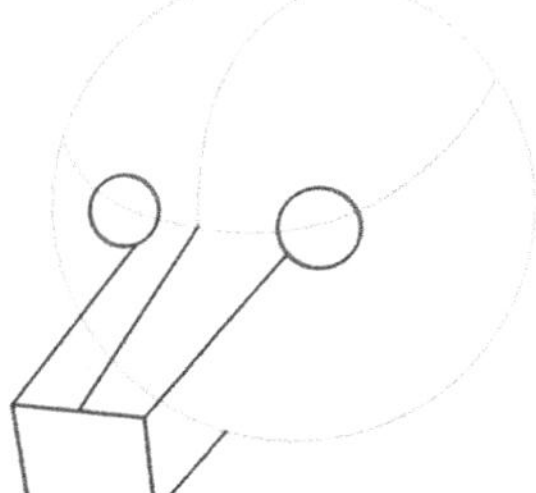

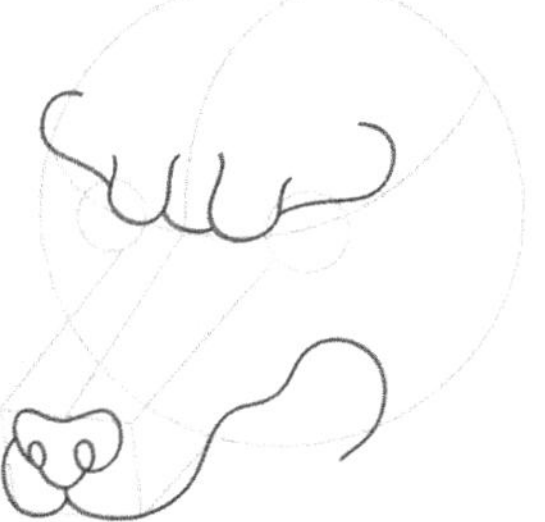

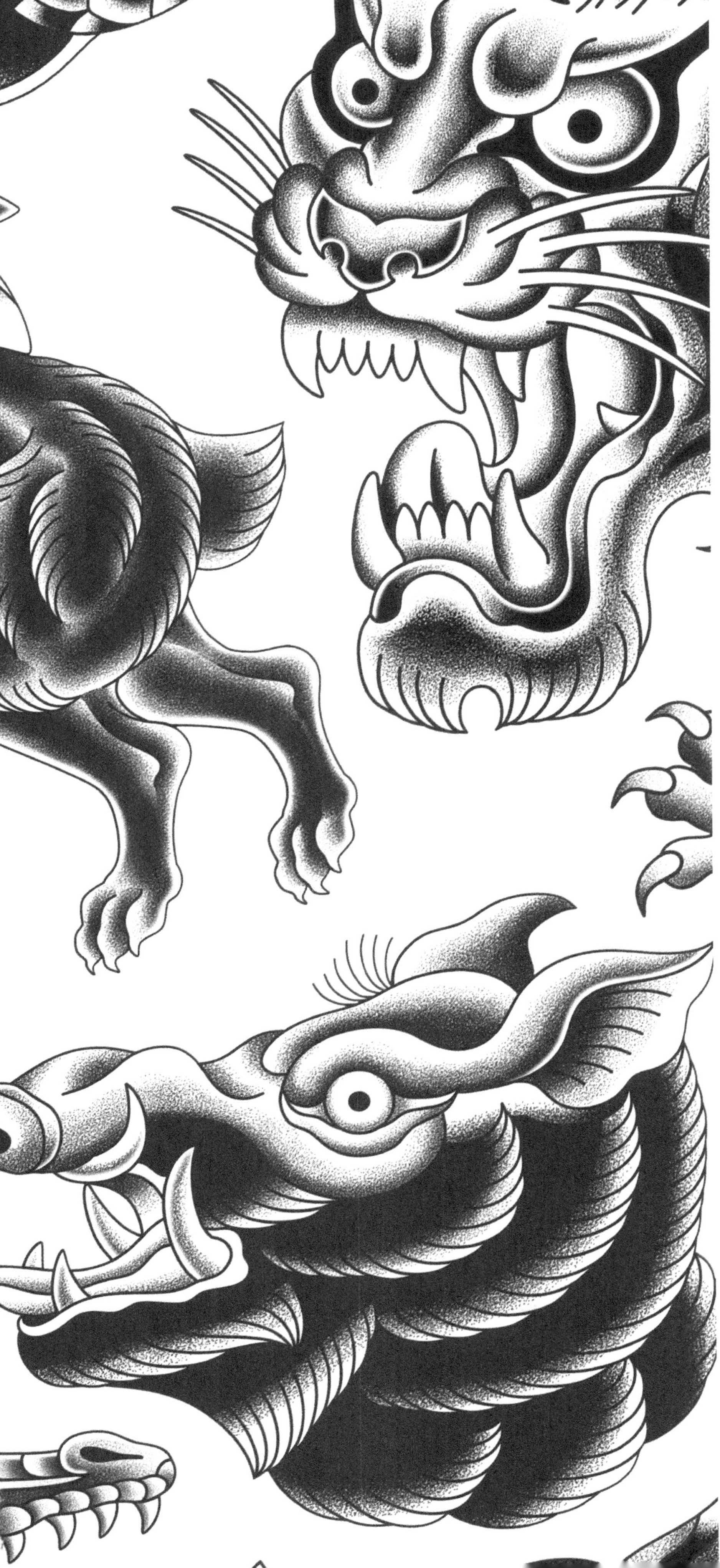

THE VAULT EDITIONS GUIDE TO
MASTERING
THE ART OF
DRAWING

HOW TO DRAW
ANIMAL TATTOOS

A HELPFUL MANUAL FOR
ARTISTS AND DESIGNERS

STEP BY STEP

HAND DRAWN
UNIQUE 40 DESIGNS
BEST QUALITY

EDITIONS
Vault

INTRODUCTION

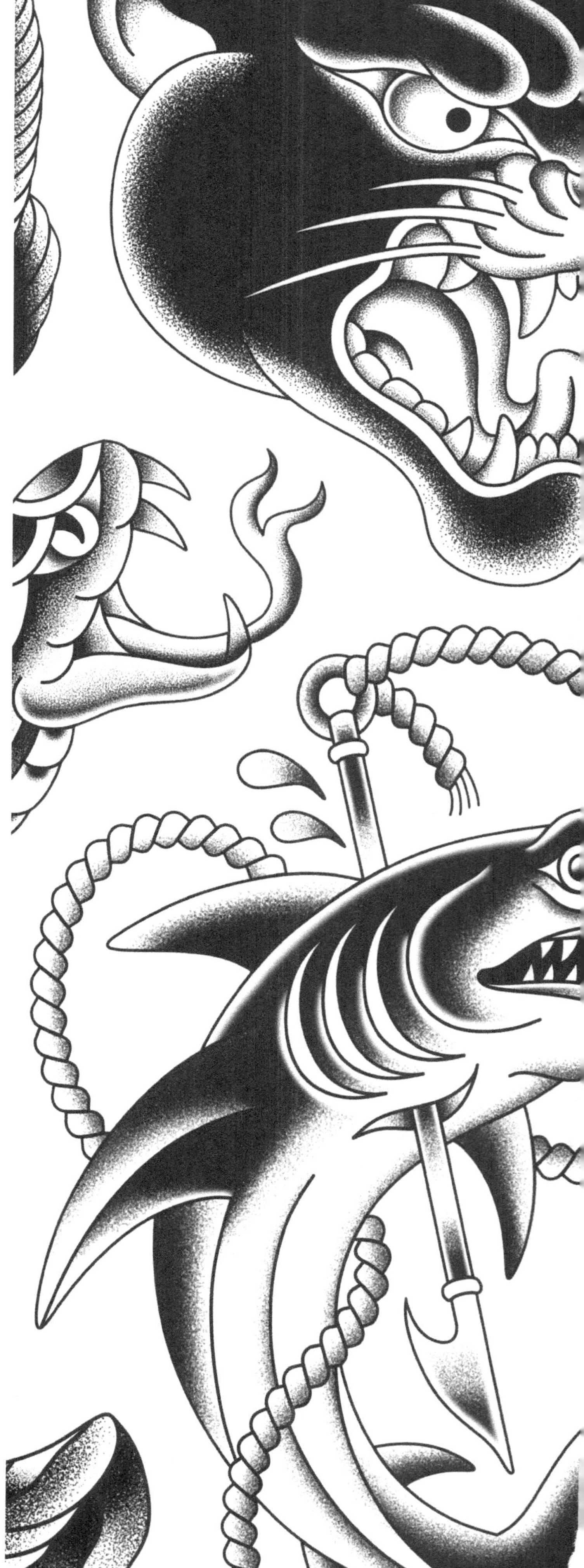

Animals have long been a cornerstone of tattoo design, chosen for their power, symbolism, and striking visual impact. From fierce predators and mythic beasts to loyal companions and sacred creatures, animal motifs represent qualities such as strength, freedom, transformation, and protection. With bold lines, dynamic poses, and timeless appeal, animal imagery remains one of the most popular and enduring genres in tattoo art.

How to Draw Animal Tattoos is a comprehensive step-by-step drawing guide that teaches artists how to create compelling and dynamic animal designs for tattoo application. Using the Vault Editions 12-step drawing process, this book breaks down each subject into clear, manageable stages designed to build confidence, accuracy and technique.

Inside, you'll find 40 iconic animal designs, each selected for its symbolic meaning and visual strength, including snakes, tigers, wolves, eagles, panthers and more. Every illustration was created by Abrom Rose, a skilled artist known for his clarity in visual instruction, making each step accessible and engaging for artists of all skill levels.

Whether you're a tattoo apprentice, illustrator or creative looking to develop your design skills, this book offers a structured and inspiring path into the world of animal tattoo design.

04

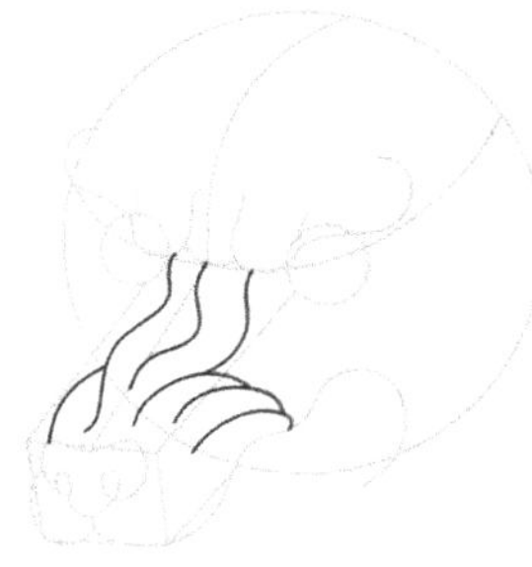

05

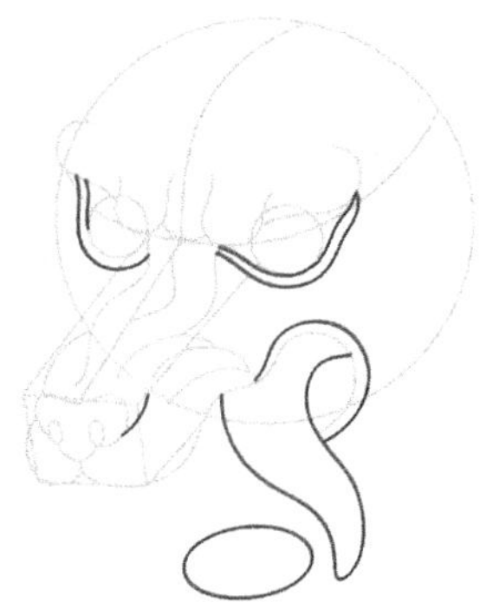

06

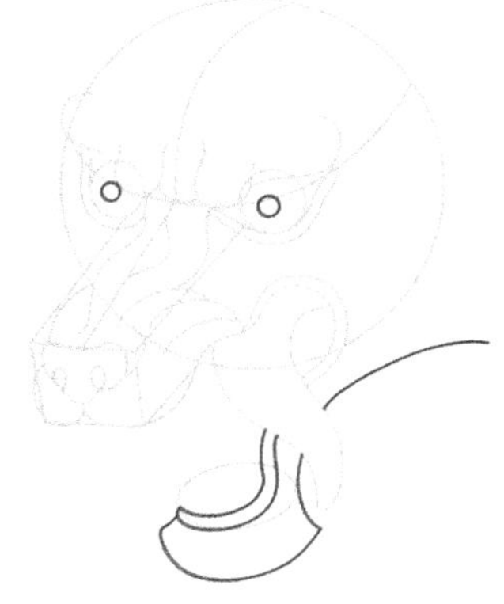

07

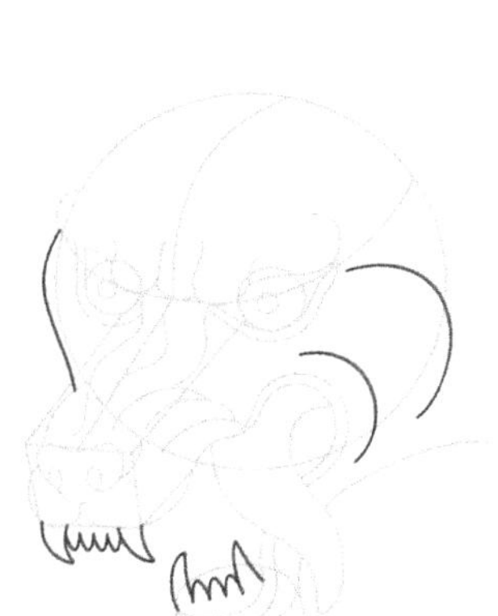

08

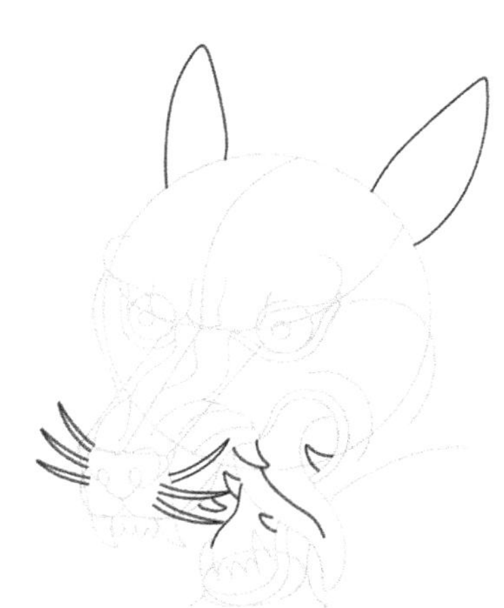

09

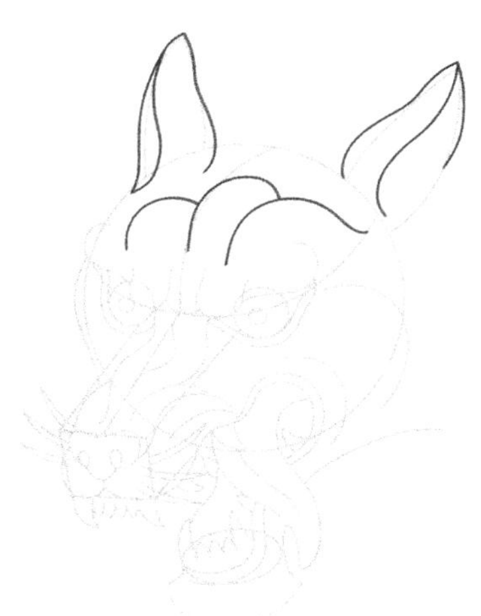

10

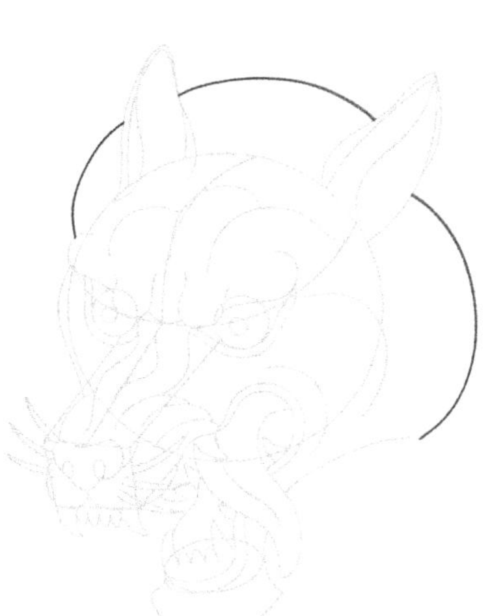

11

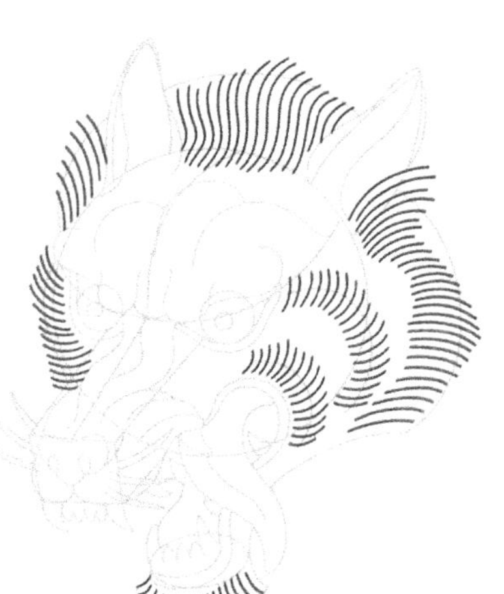

12

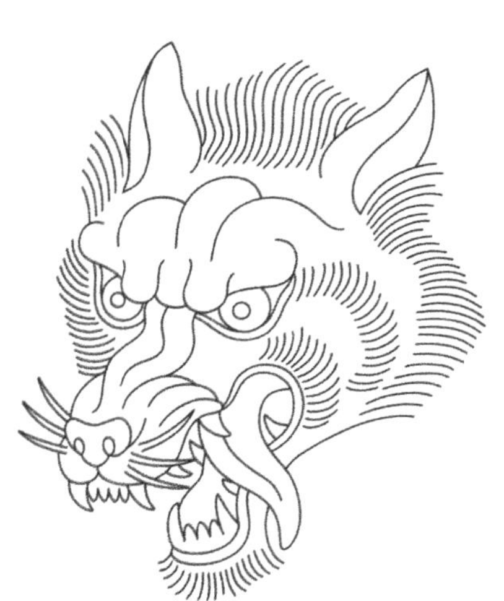

ANIMAL TATTOOS

PANTHER

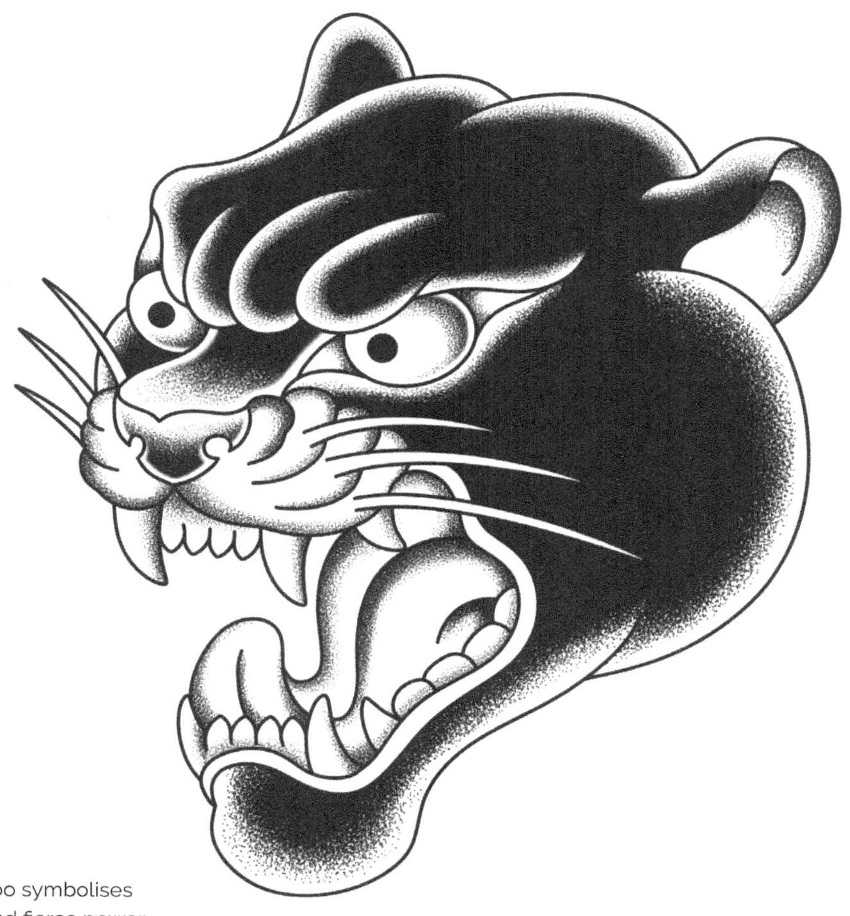

The panther head tattoo symbolises courage, protection, and fierce power. It's a classic motif representing stealth, strength, and unyielding spirit.

01

02

03

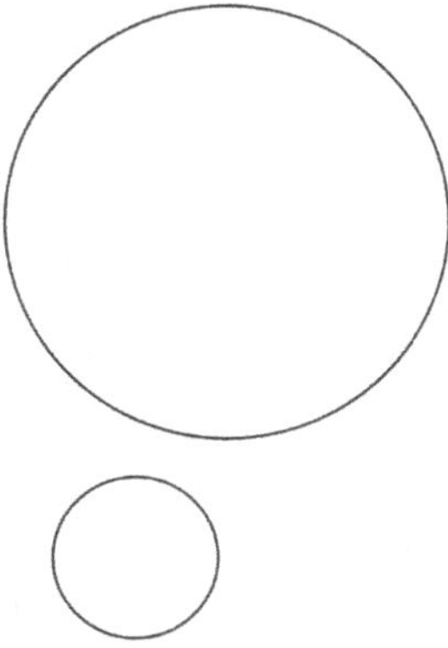

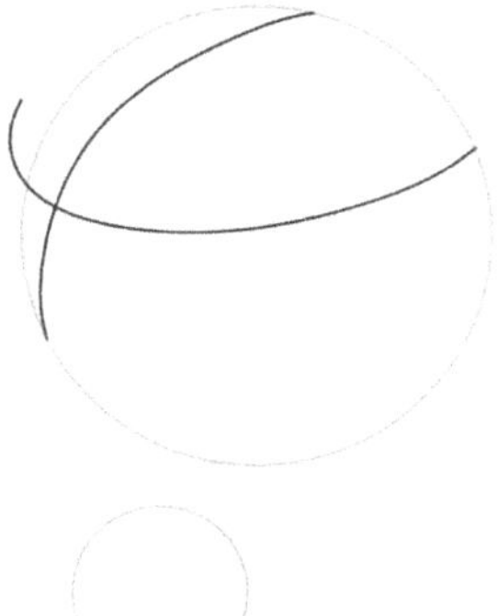

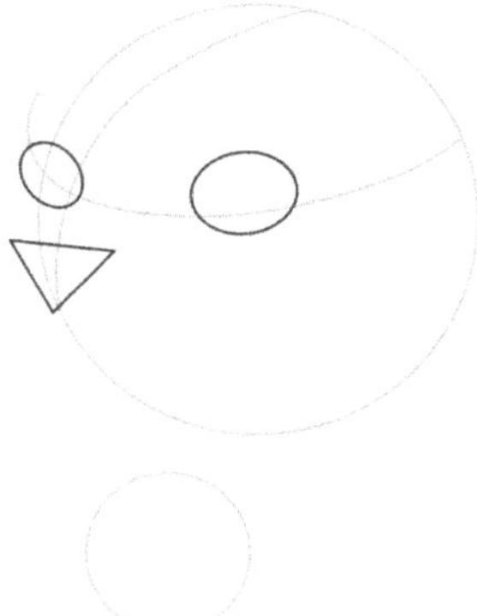

04

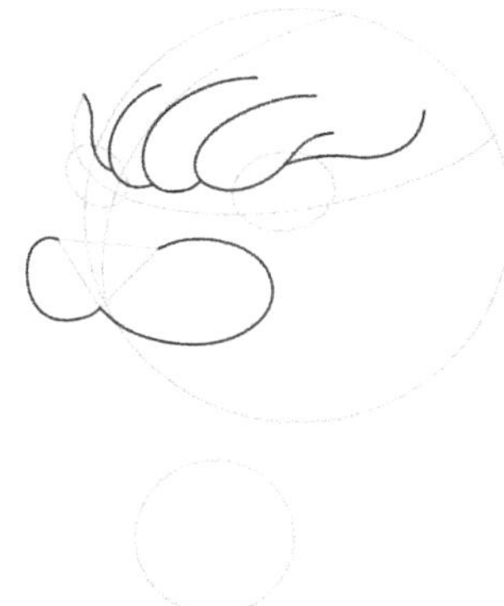

05

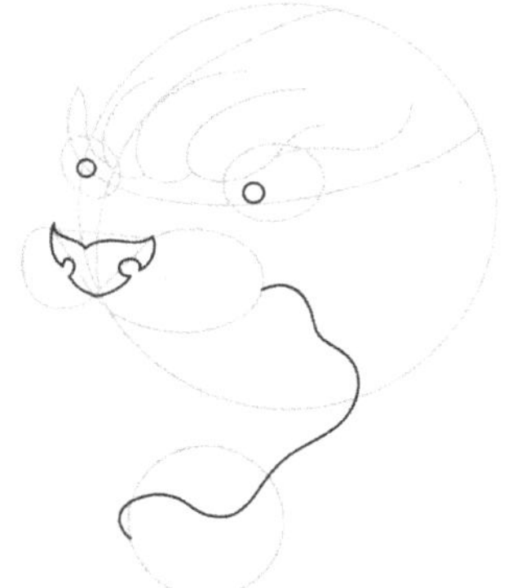

06

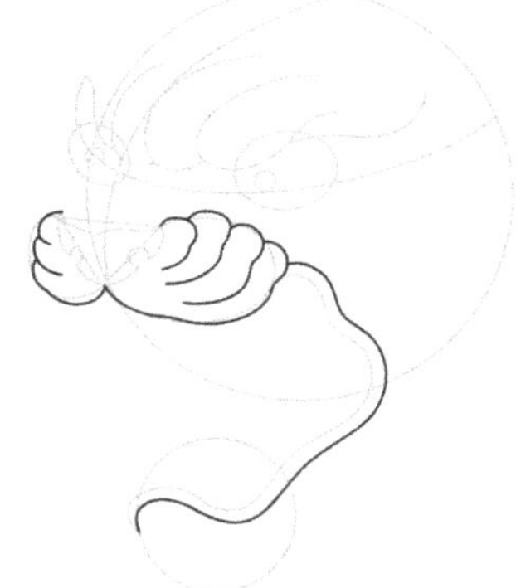

07

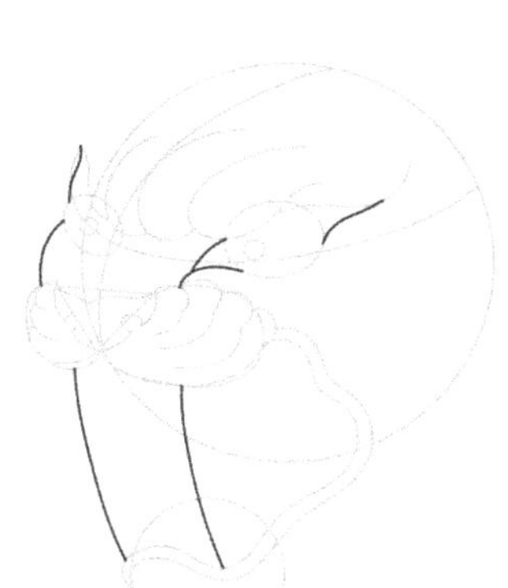

08

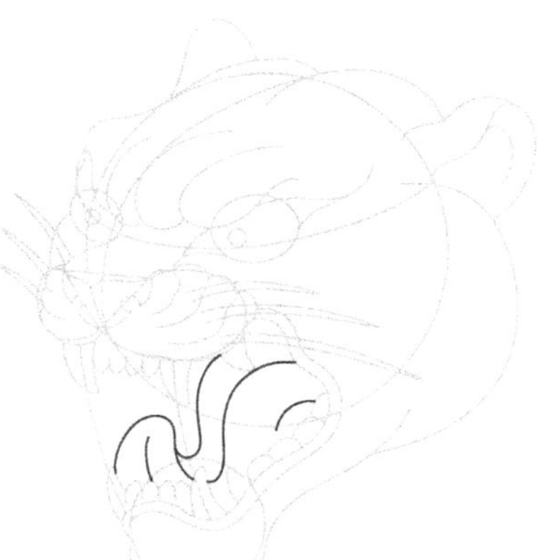

09

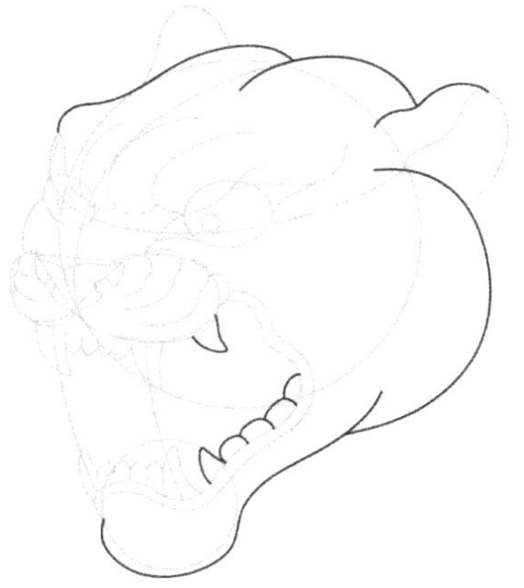

10

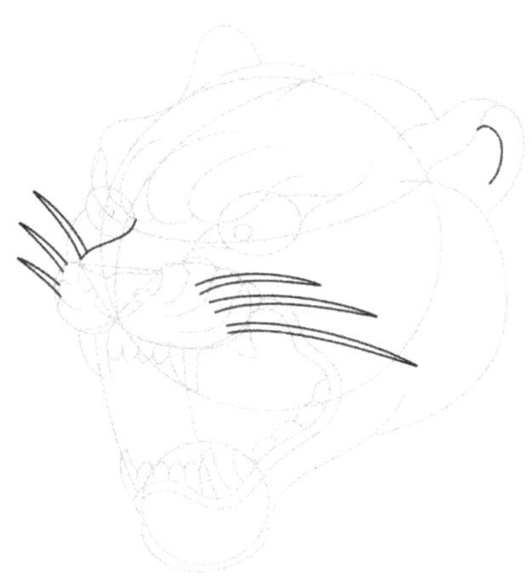

11

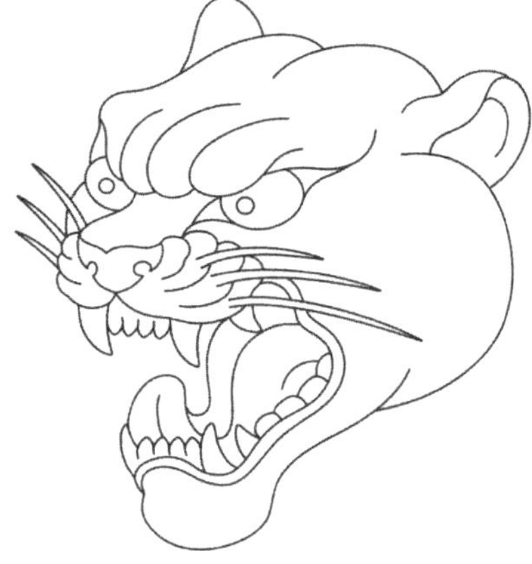

12

ANIMAL TATTOOS

LEOPARD

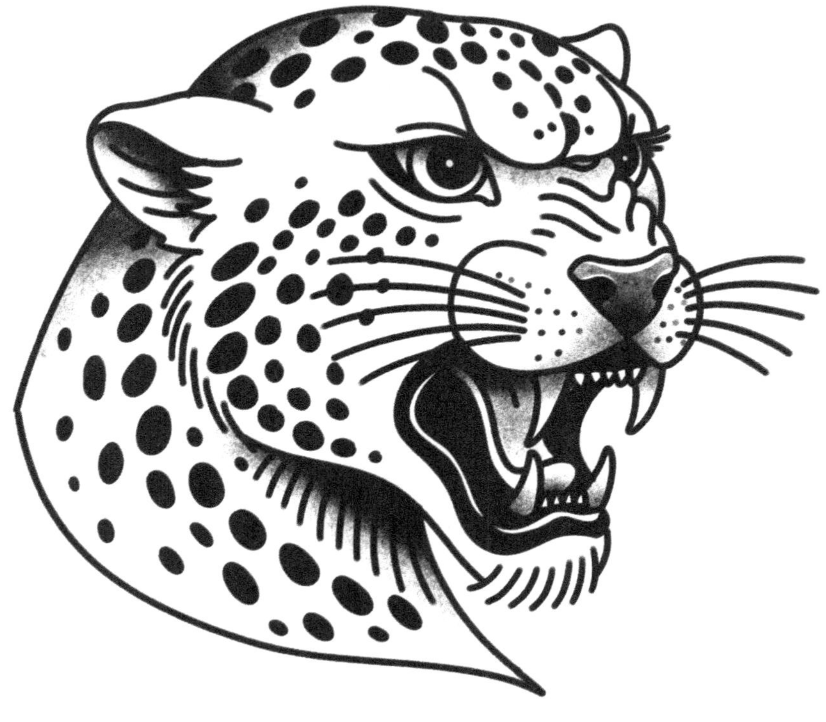

The leopard head tattoo symbolises agility, precision, and silent strength. It often represents cunning, speed, and a fierce, untamed nature.

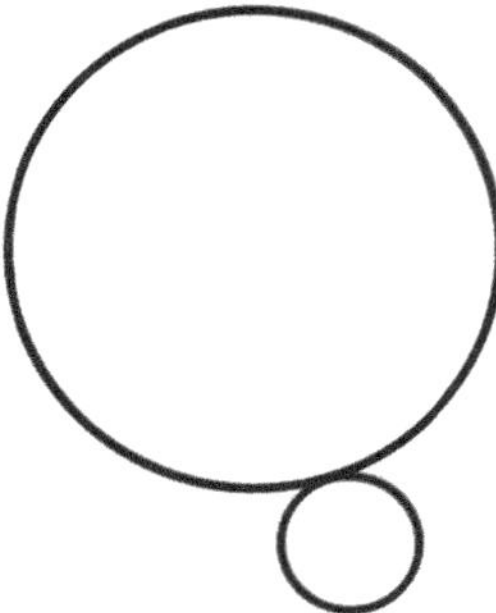

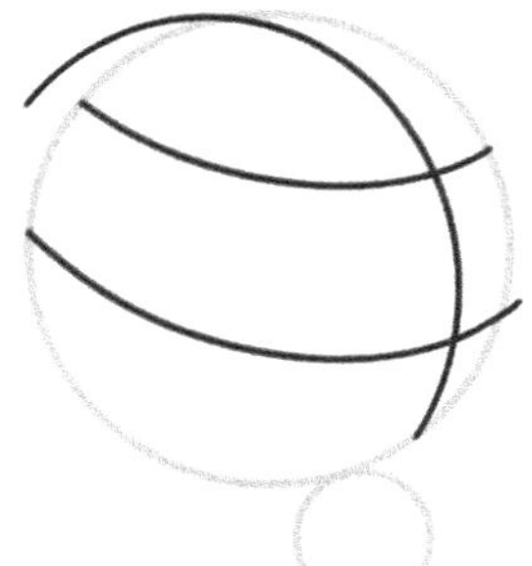

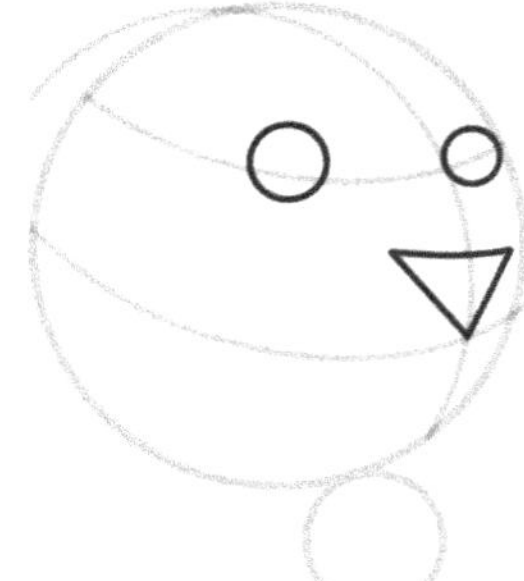

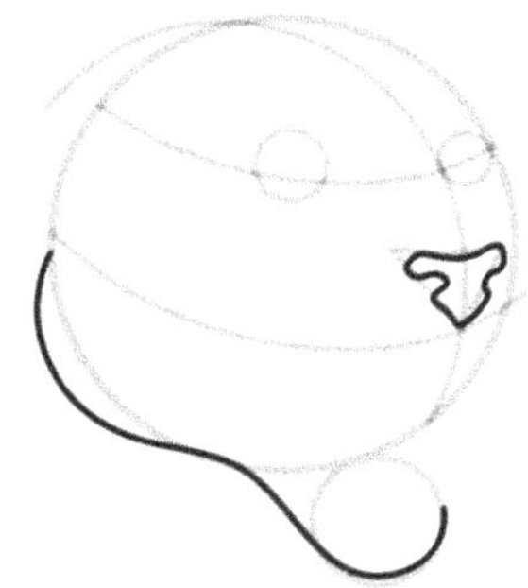 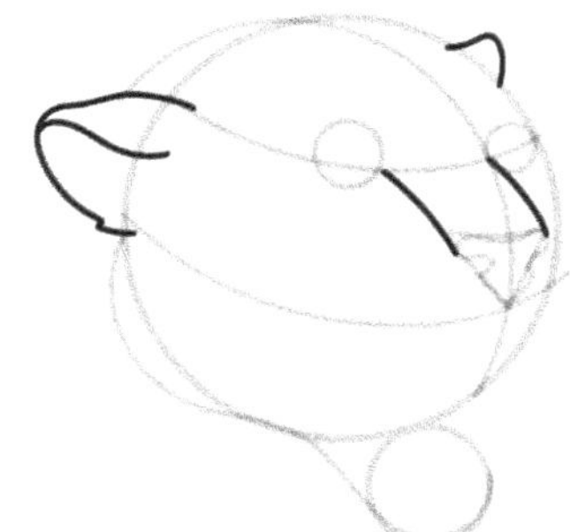 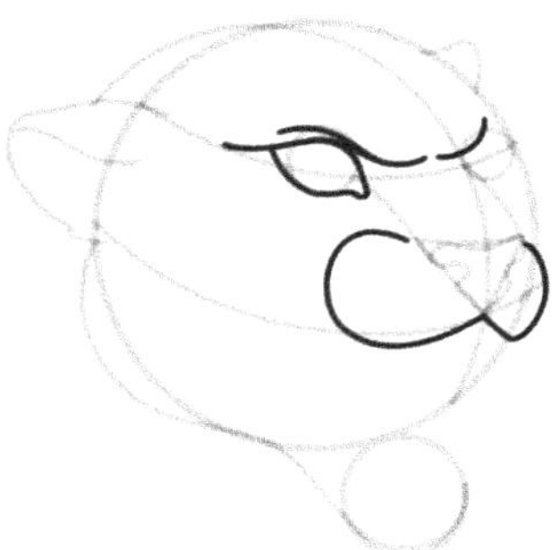

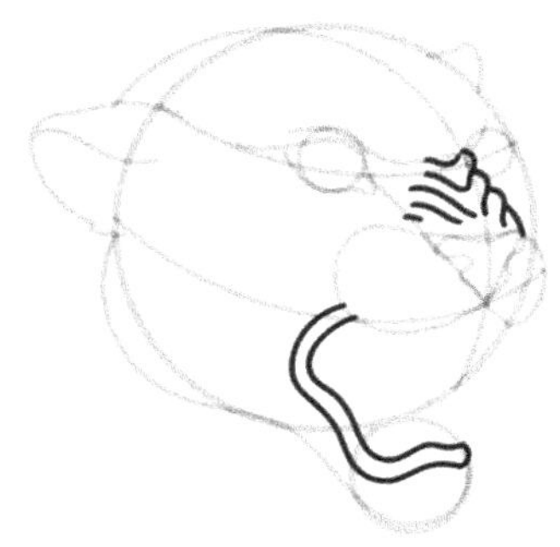 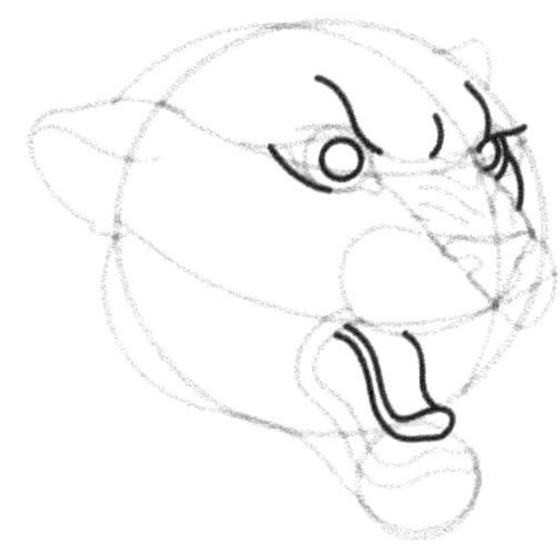 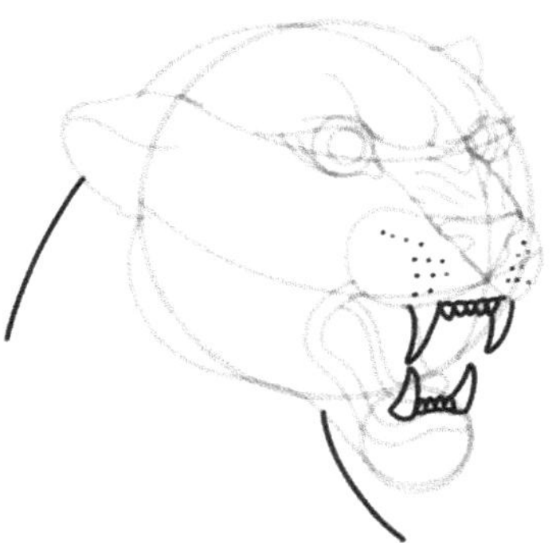

ANIMAL TATTOOS

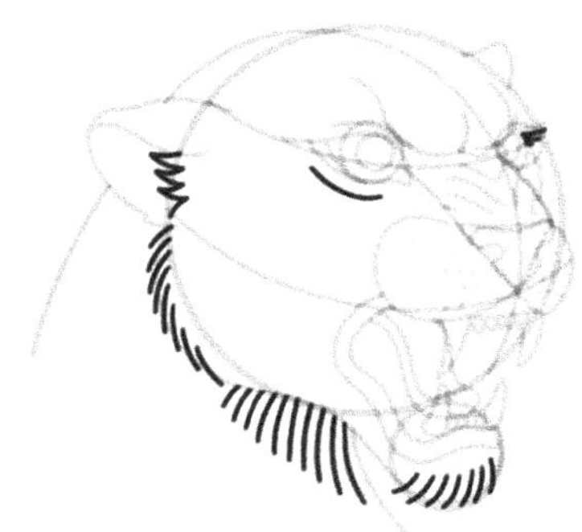 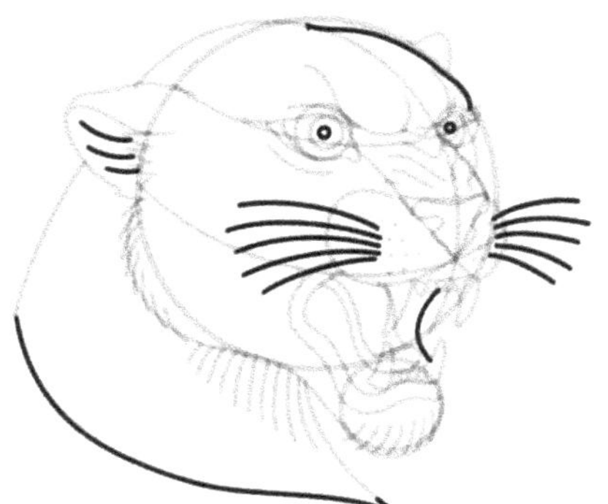 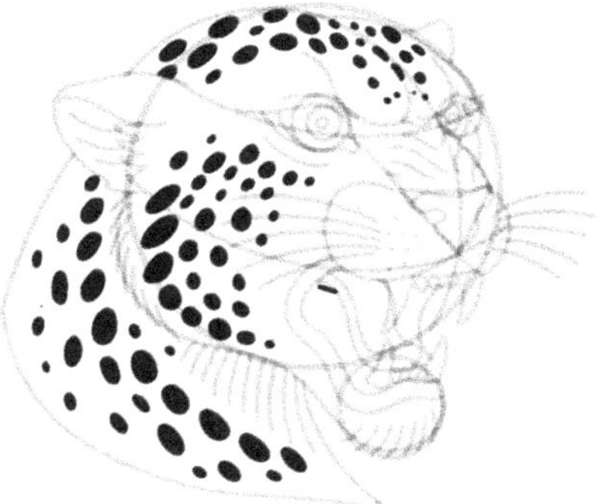

BAT

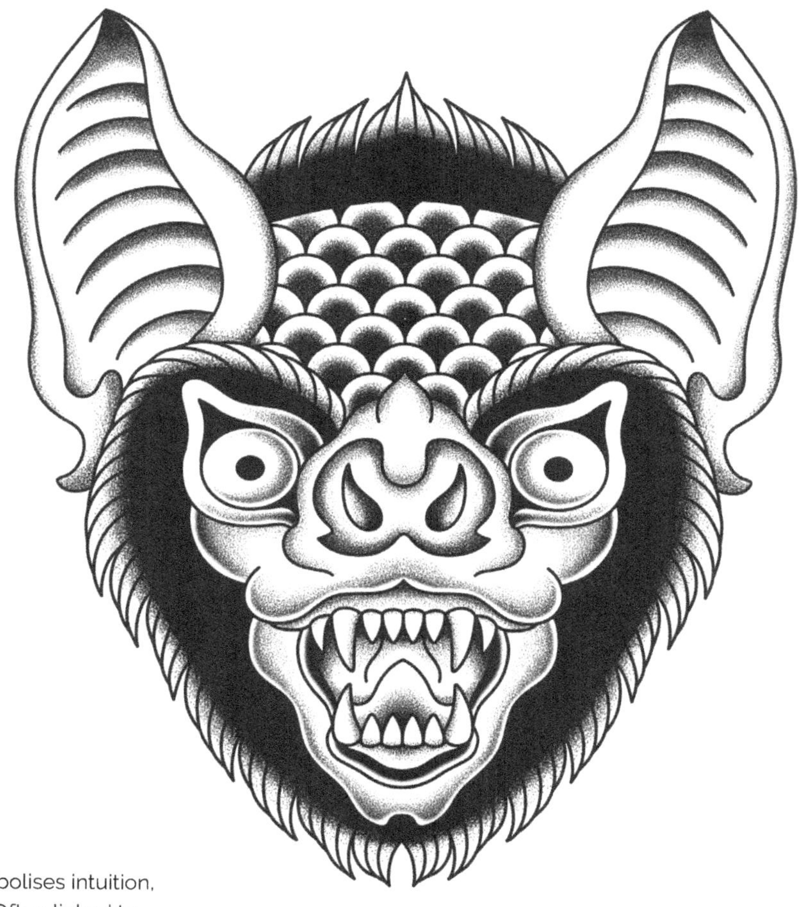

The bat head tattoo symbolises intuition, rebirth, and the unseen. Often linked to night, it represents mystery, transition, and navigating through darkness.

01   02   03

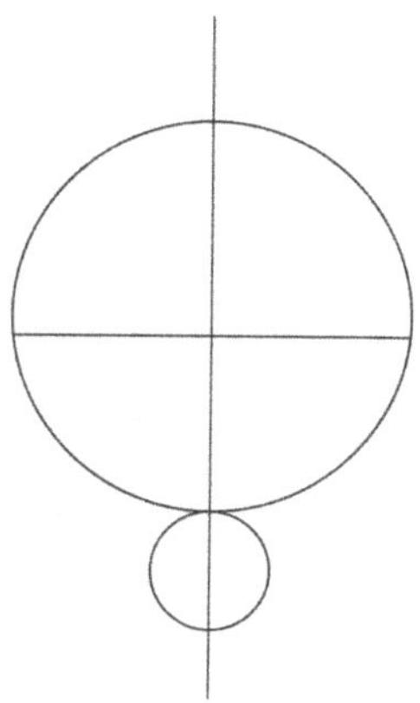

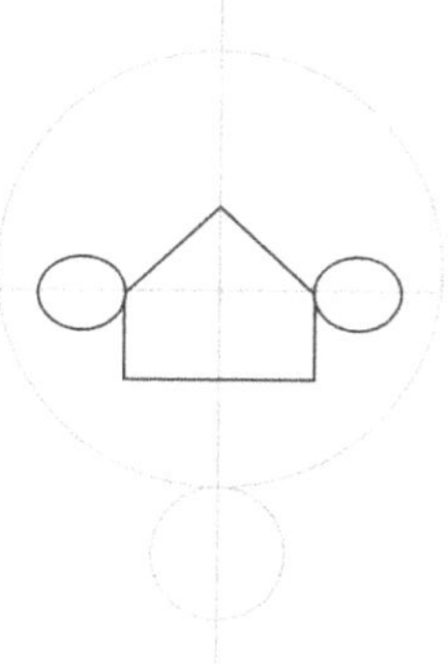

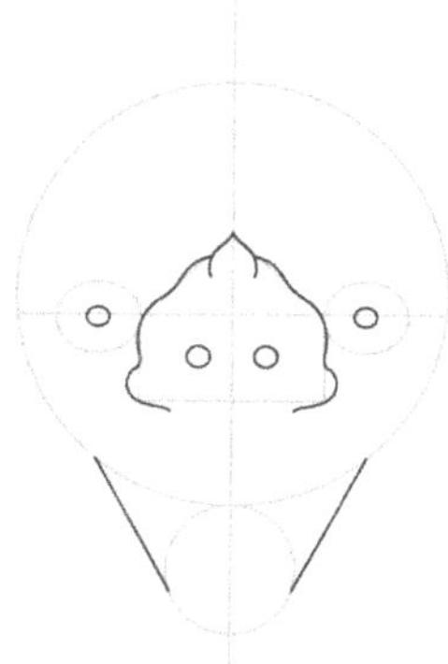

04

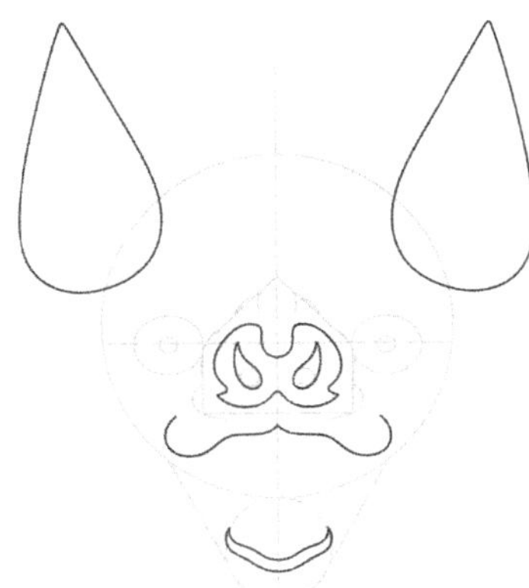

05

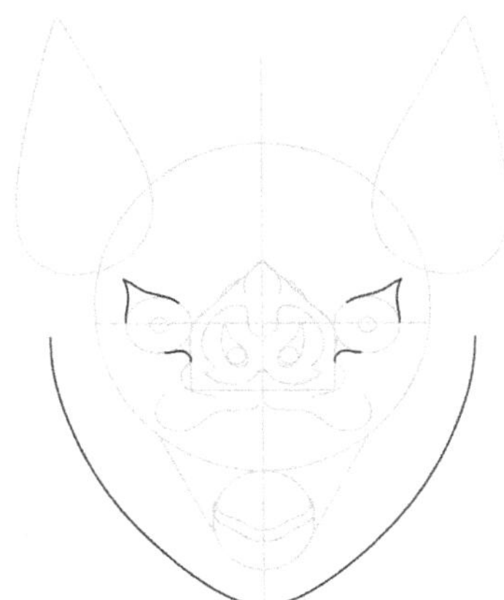

06

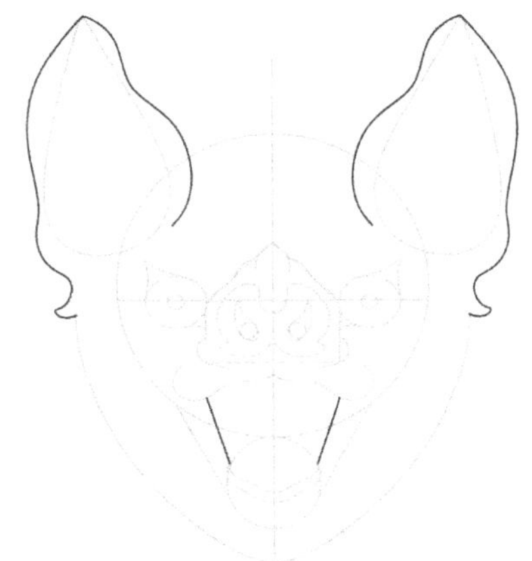

07

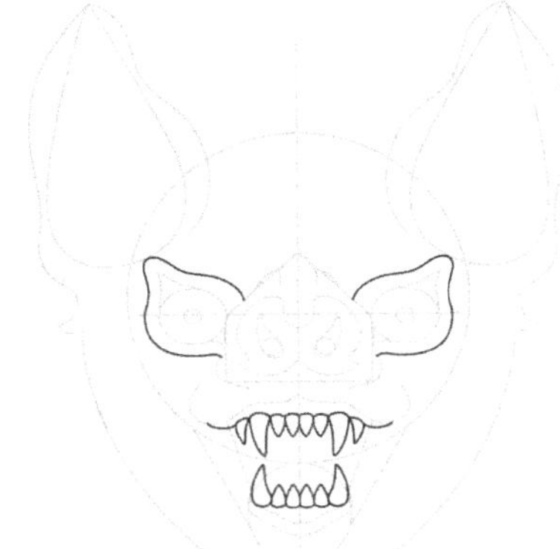

08

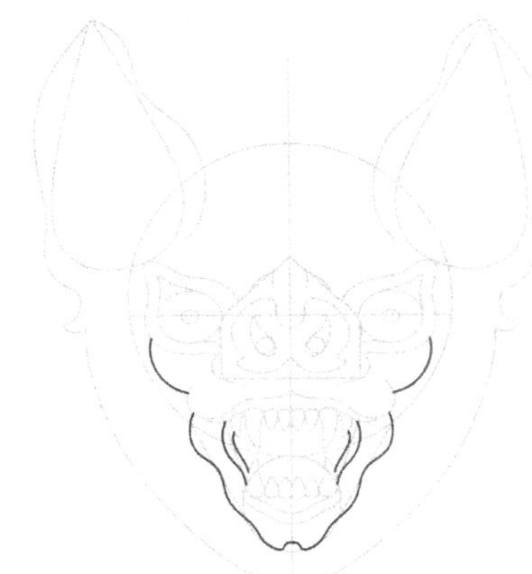

09

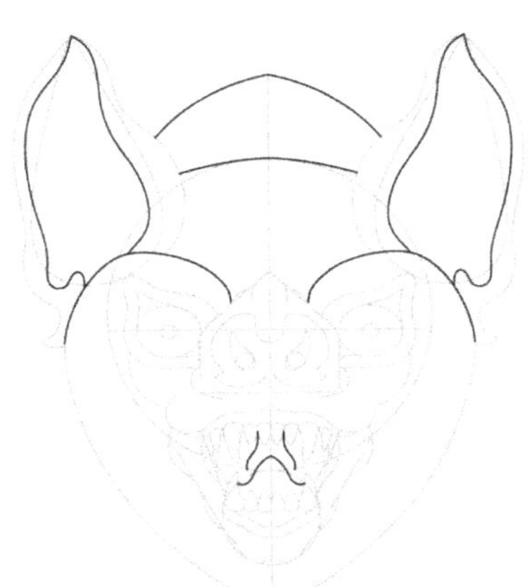

ANIMAL TATTOOS

10

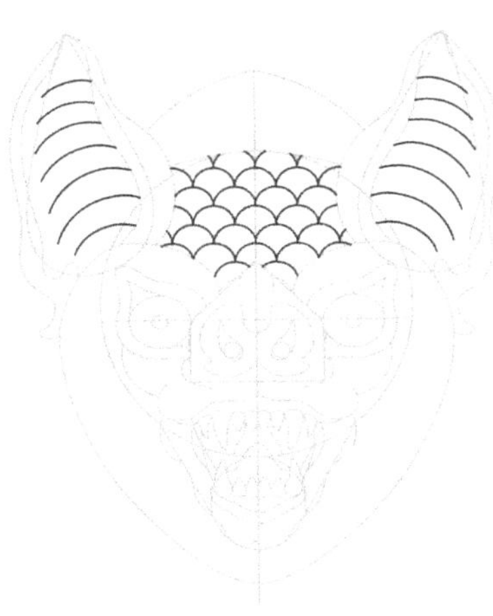

11

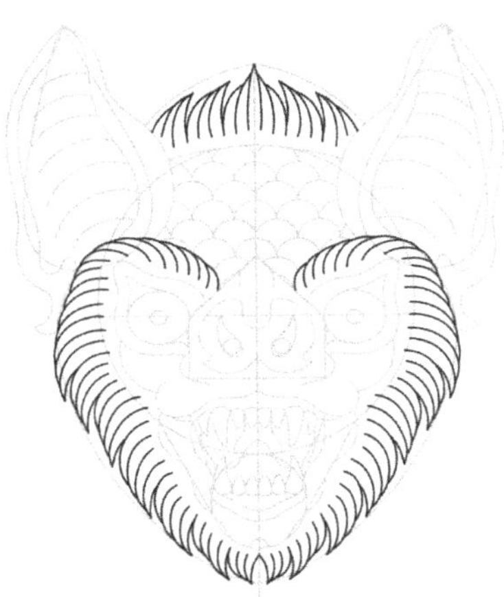

12

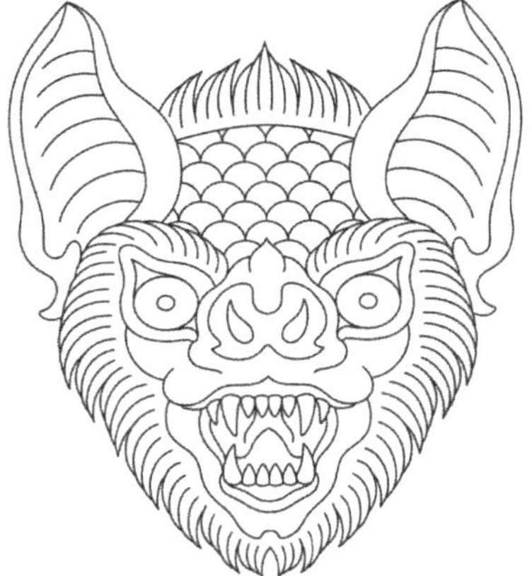

TIGER

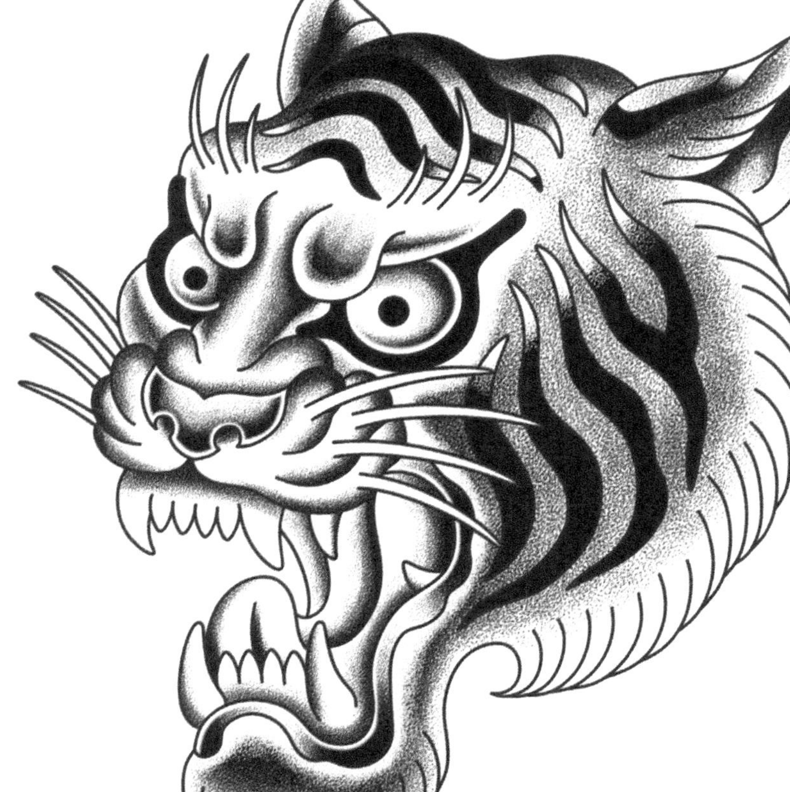

The tiger head tattoo symbolises raw power, courage, and dominance. It embodies fierce will, primal instinct, and the relentless spirit of a warrior.

01

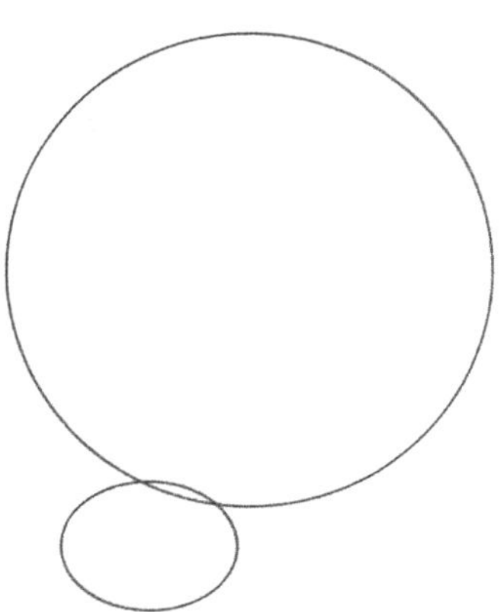

02

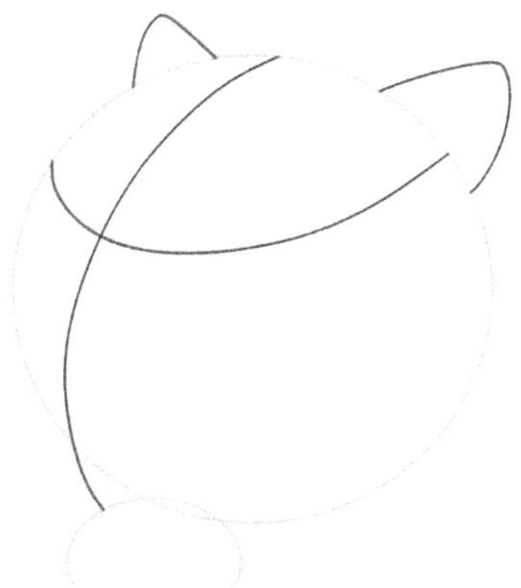

03

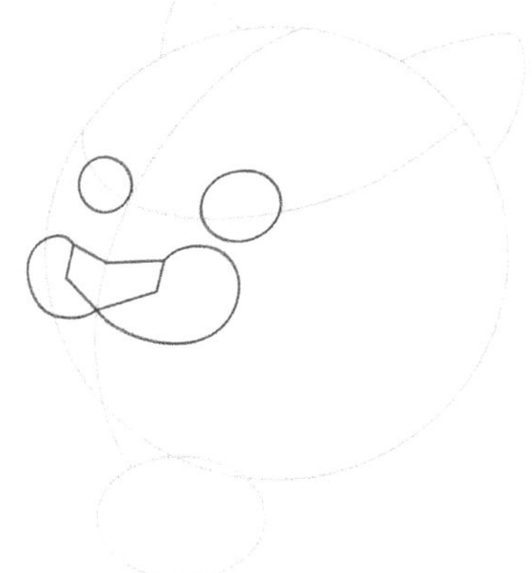

04

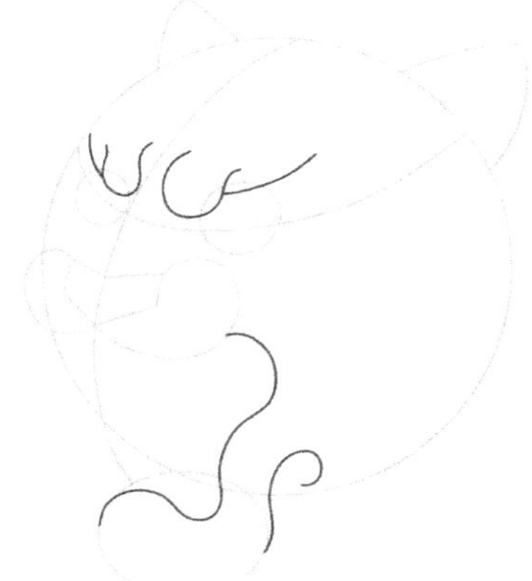

05

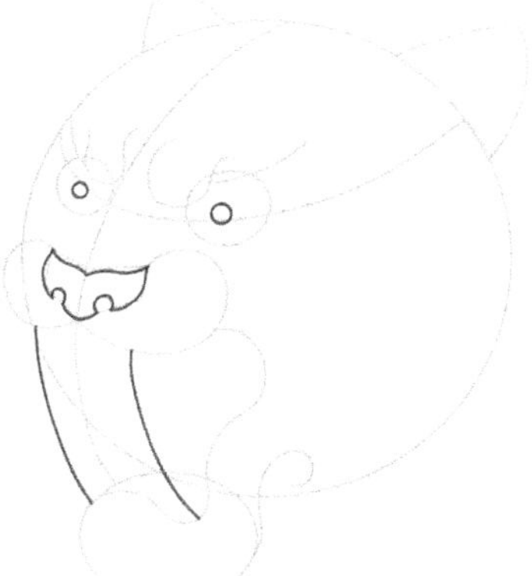

06

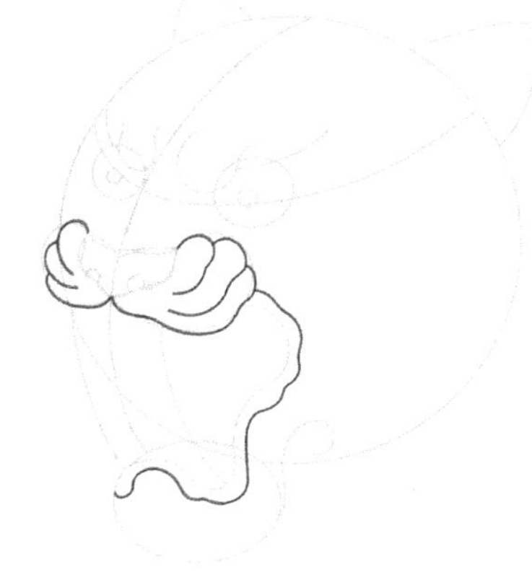

07

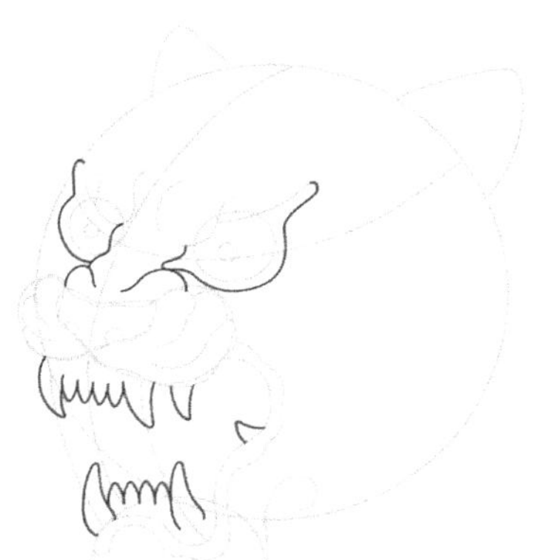

08

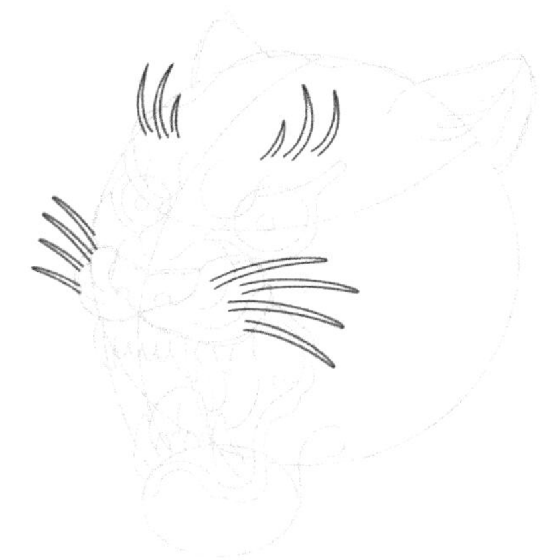

09

10

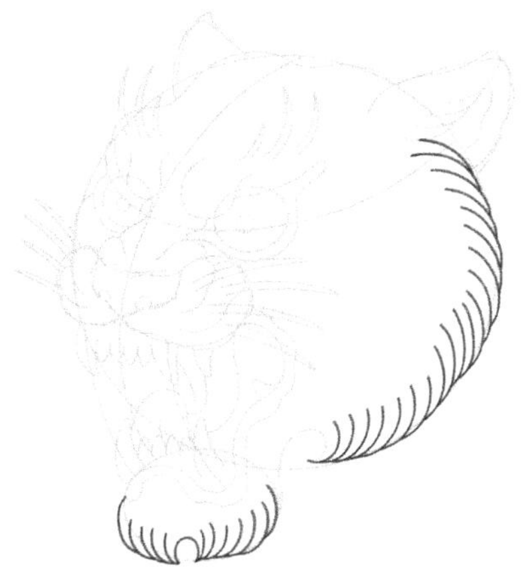

11

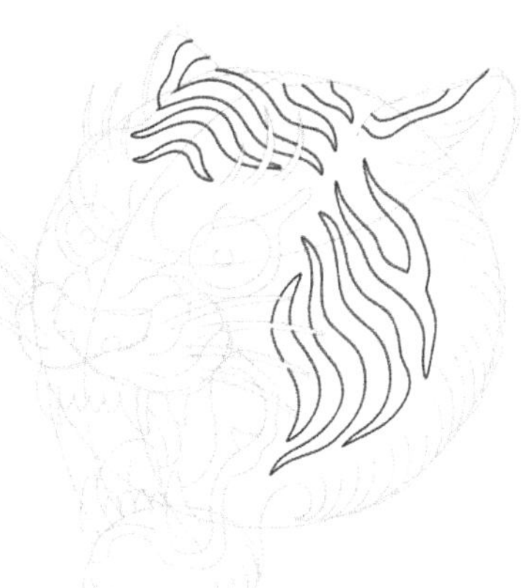

12

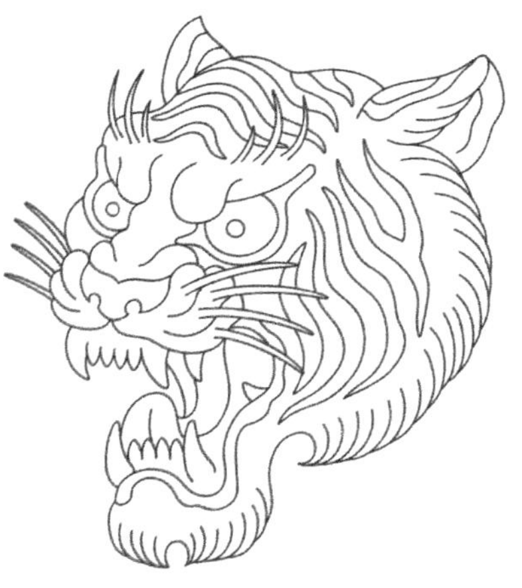

ANIMAL TATTOOS

BEAR

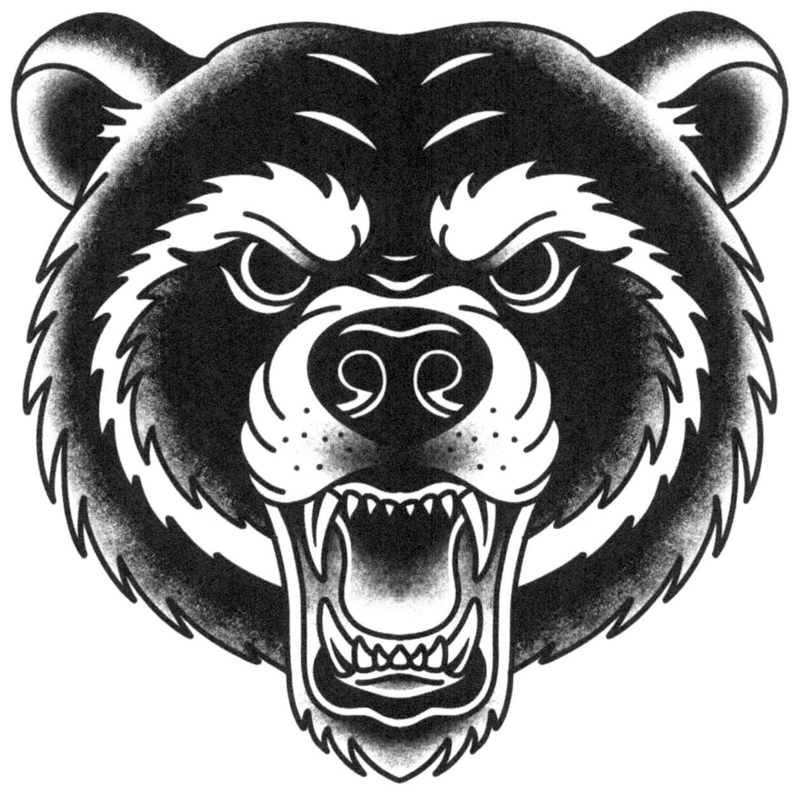

The bear tattoo symbolises strength, protection, and introspection. It represents resilience, courage in solitude, and a deep connection to nature.

01

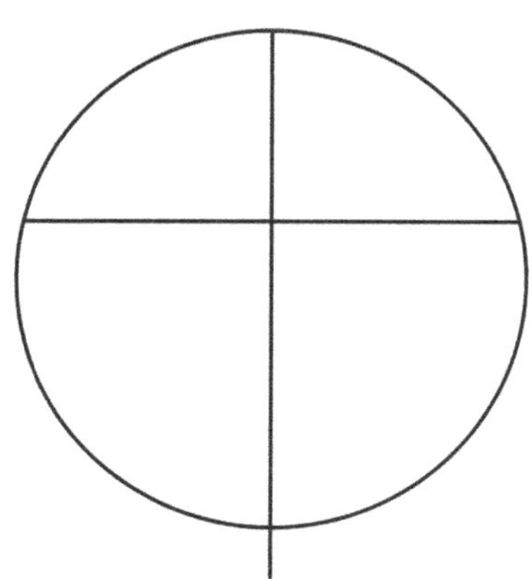

02

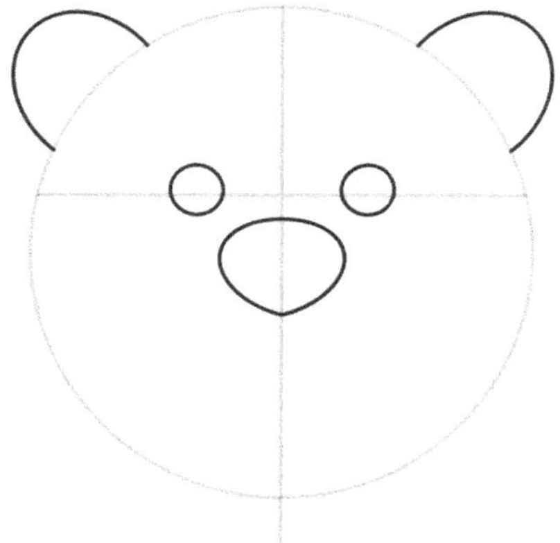

03

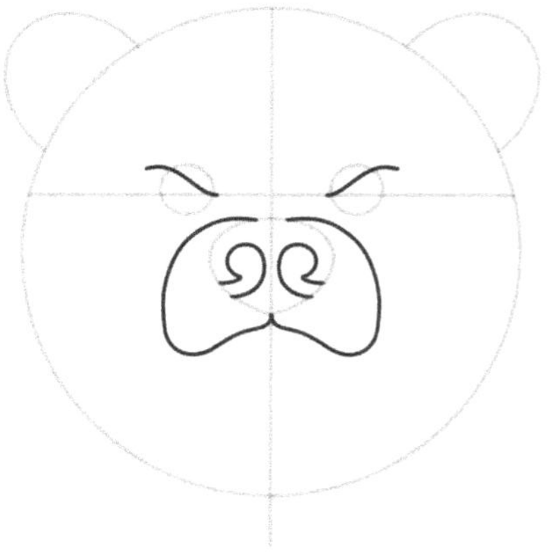

04

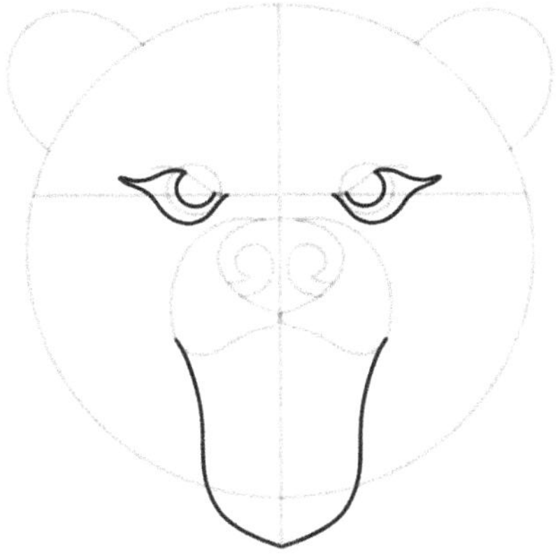

05

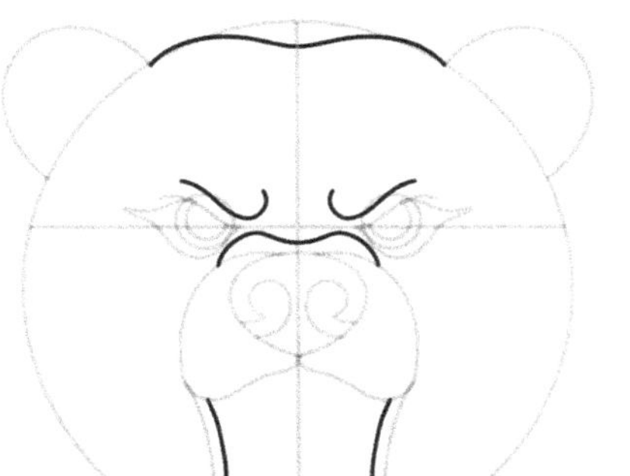

06

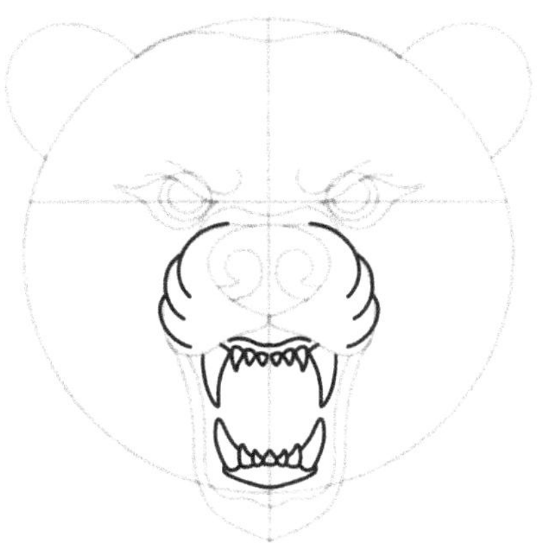

07

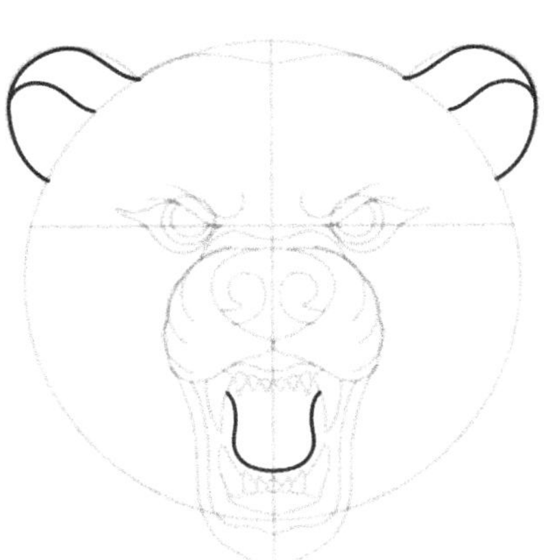

08

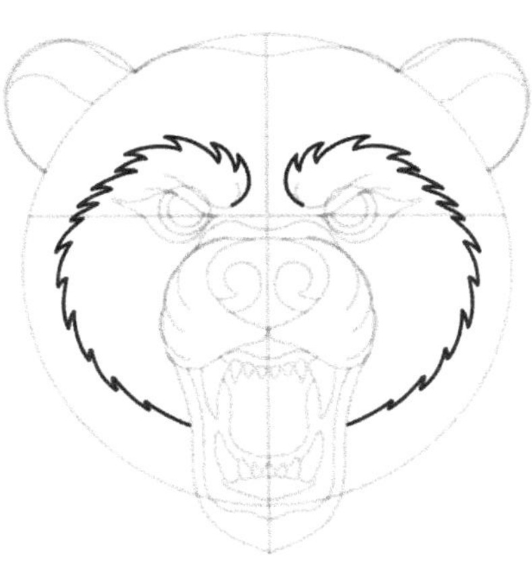

09

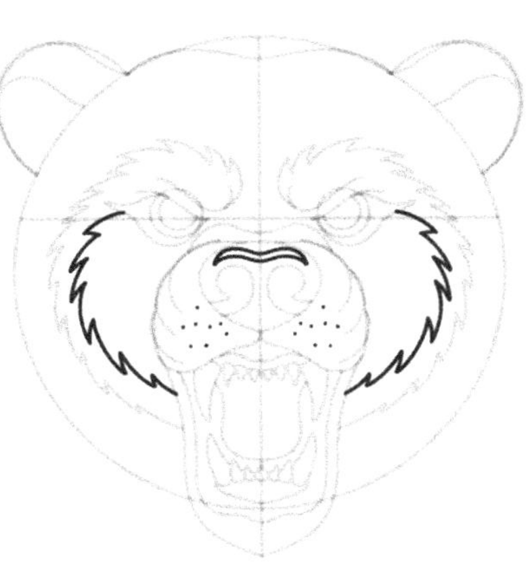

10

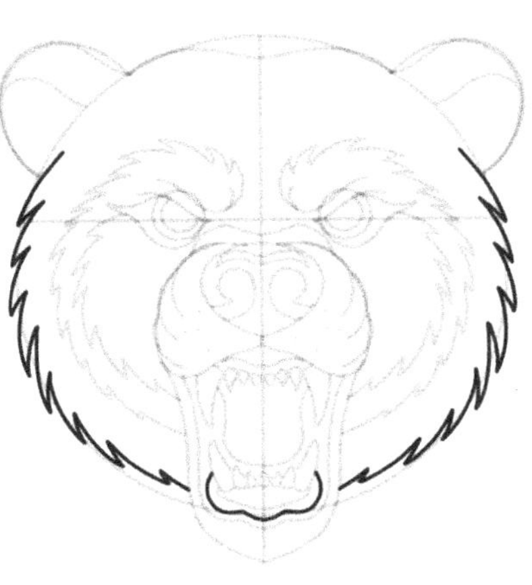

11

12

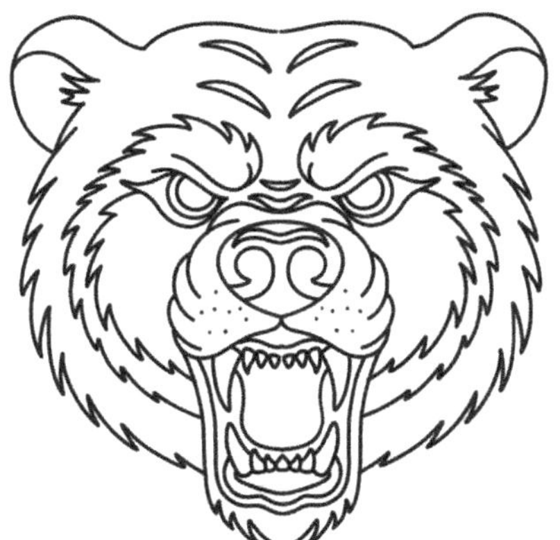

ANIMAL TATTOOS

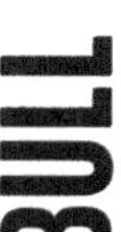

BULL

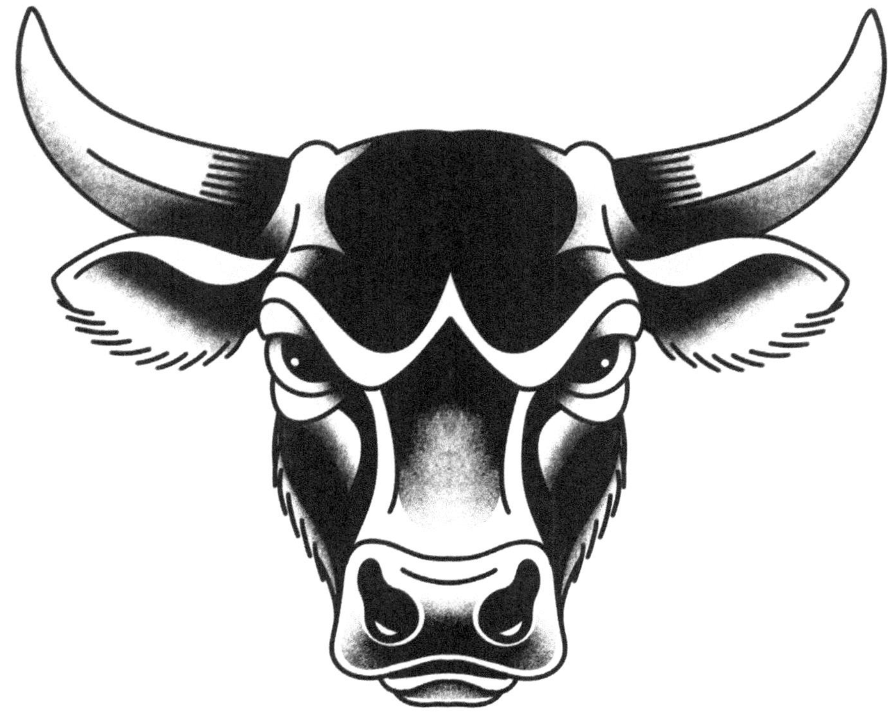

The bull head tattoo symbolises strength,
determination, and stubborn will.
Often linked to virility and protection, it
represents raw power and endurance.

01

02

03

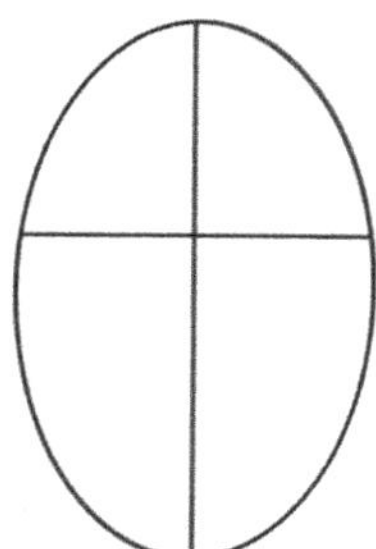

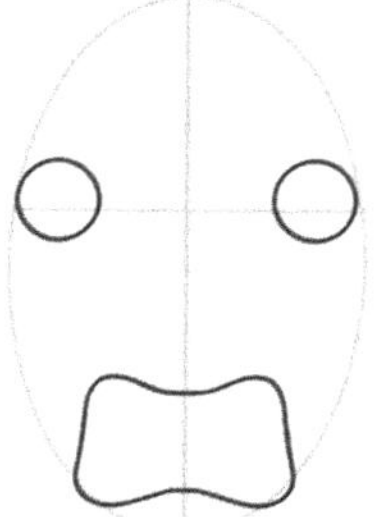

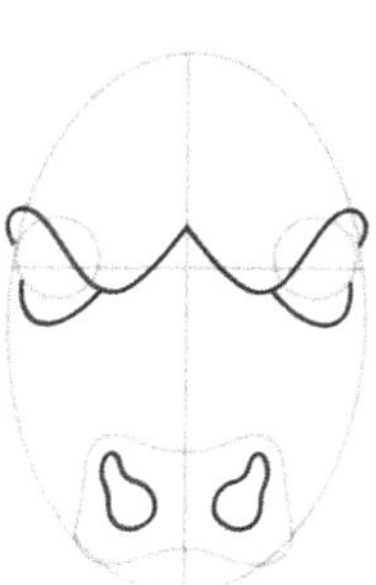

04

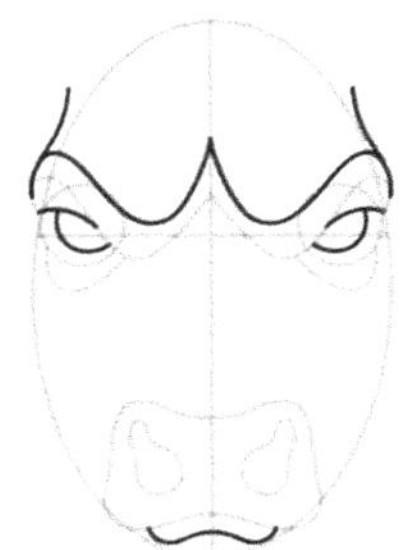

05

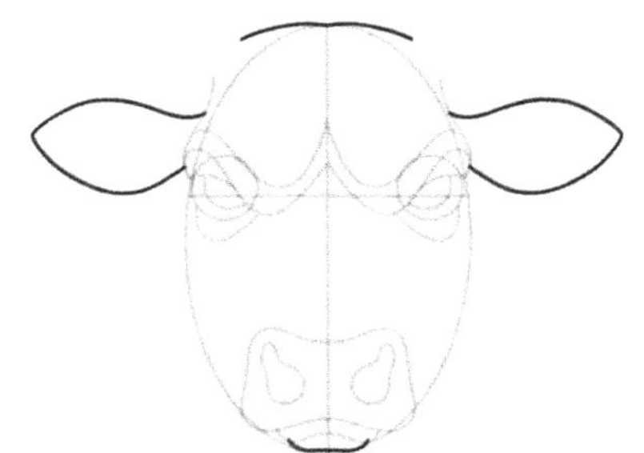

06

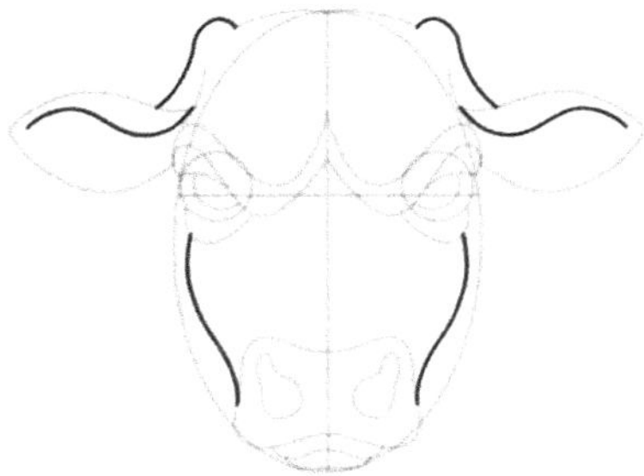

07

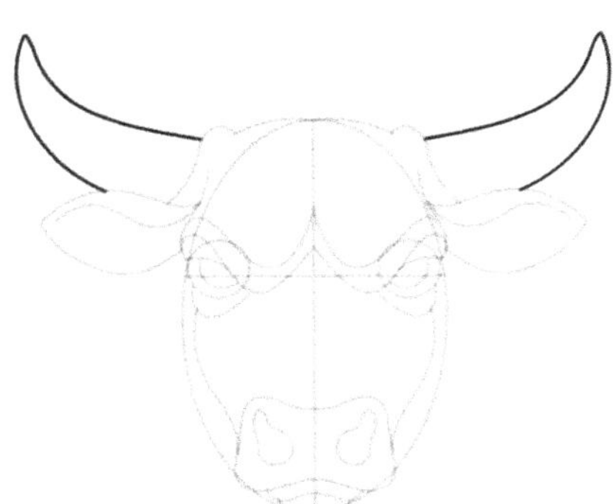

08

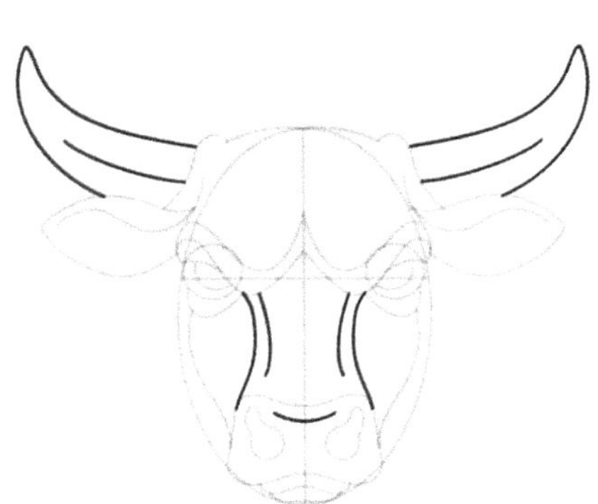

09

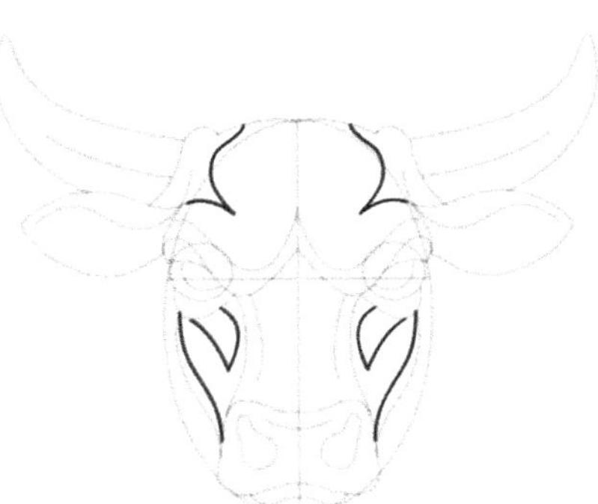

ANIMAL TATTOOS

10

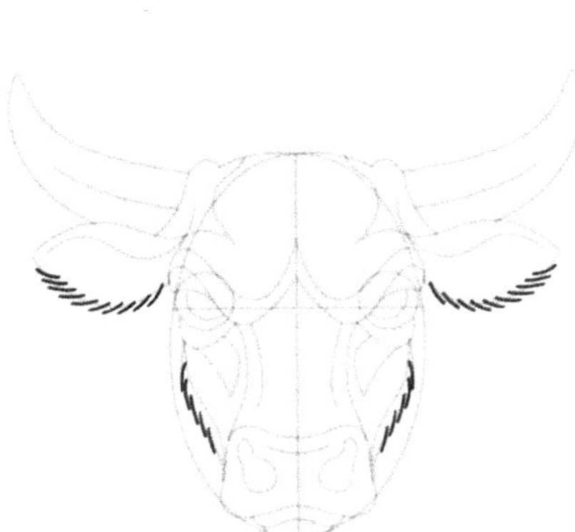

11

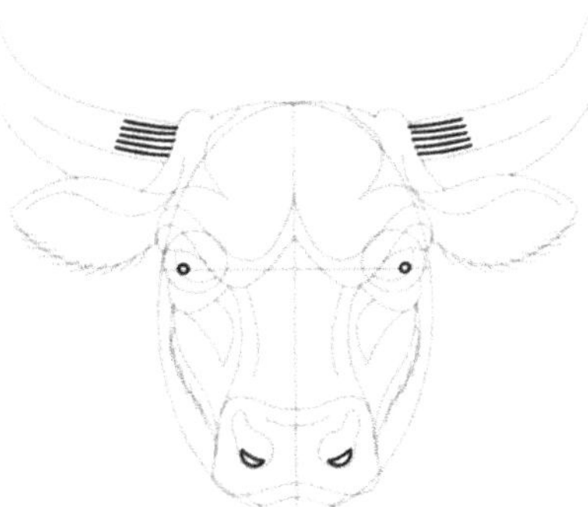

12

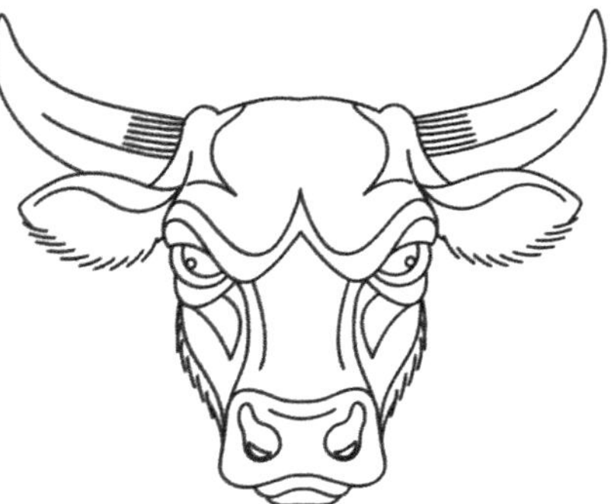

DOBERMAN

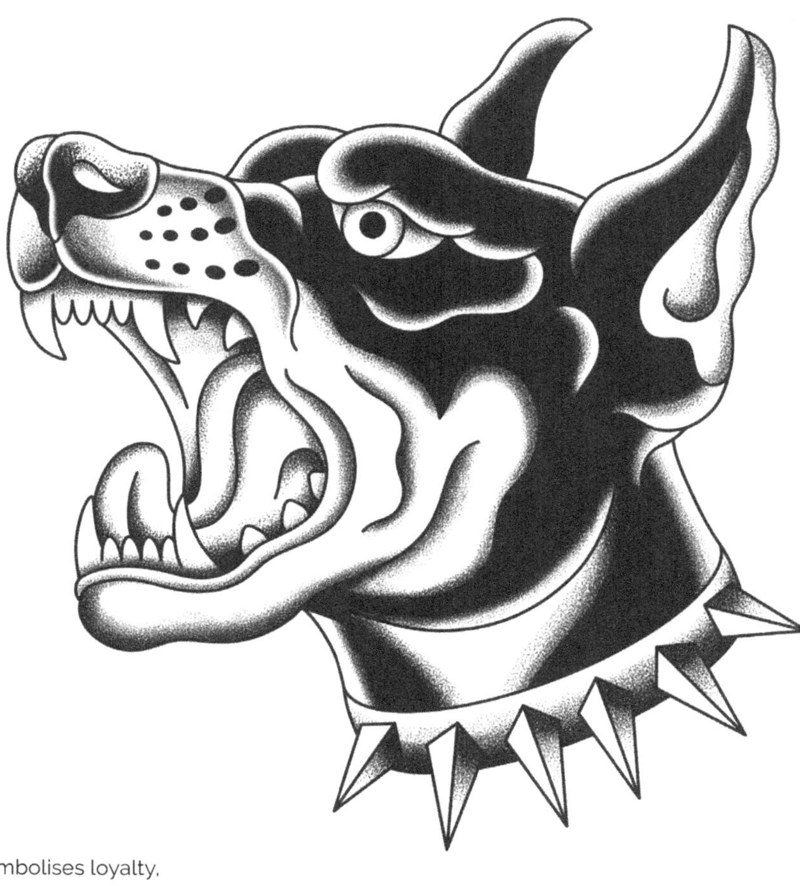

The doberman tattoo symbolises loyalty, alertness, and fearless protection. Known for its strength and intelligence, it also represents vigilance and devotion.

01

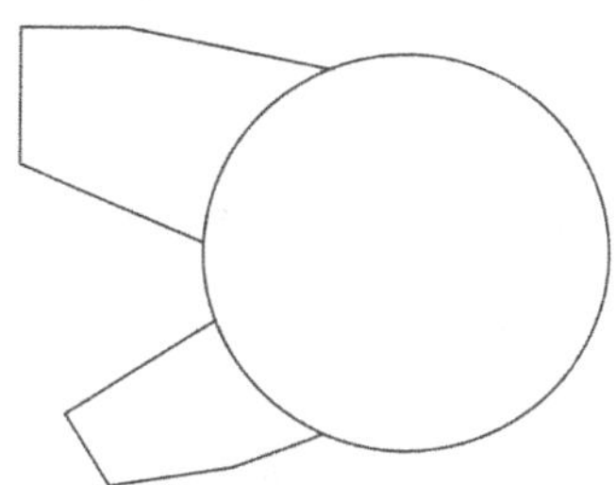

02

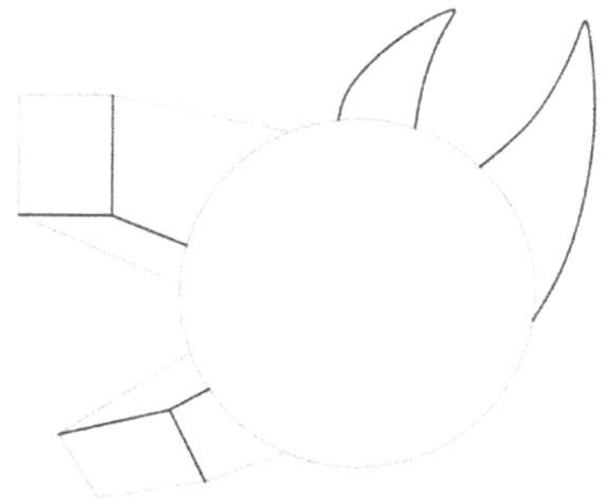

03

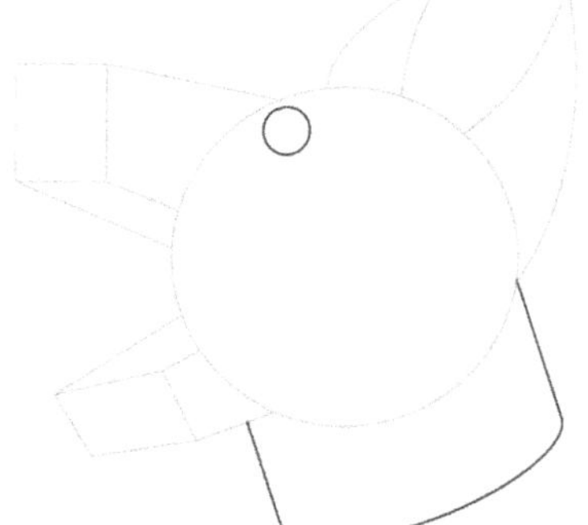

04

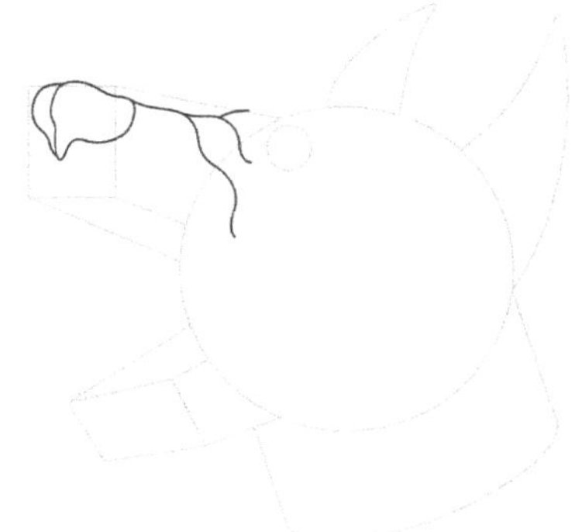

05

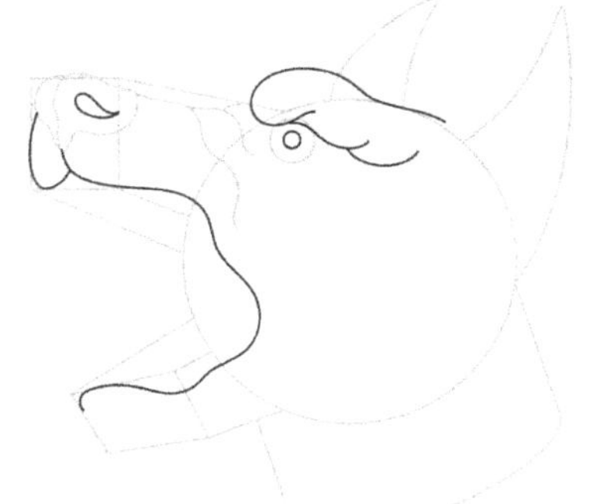

06

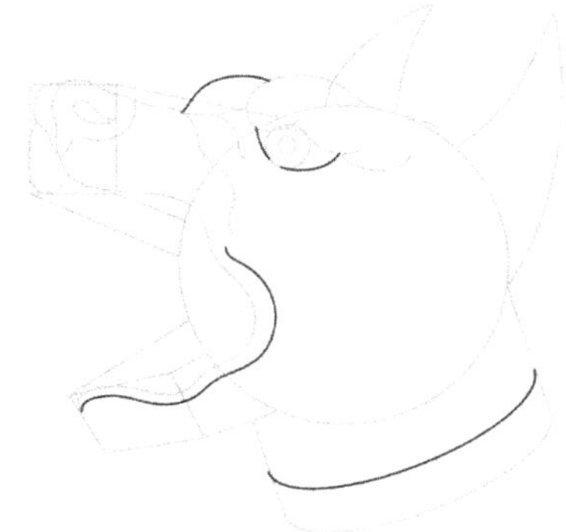

07

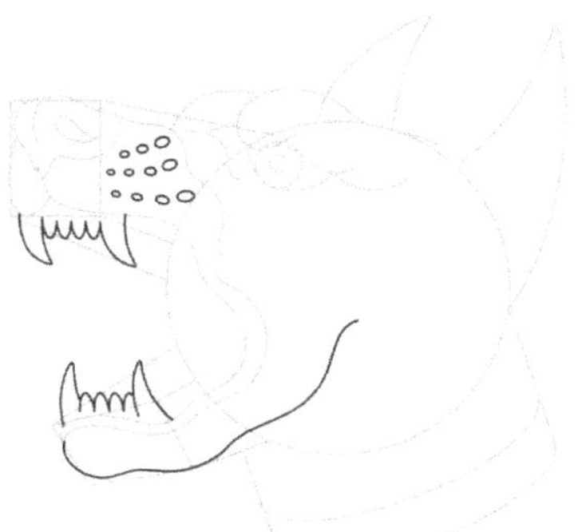

08

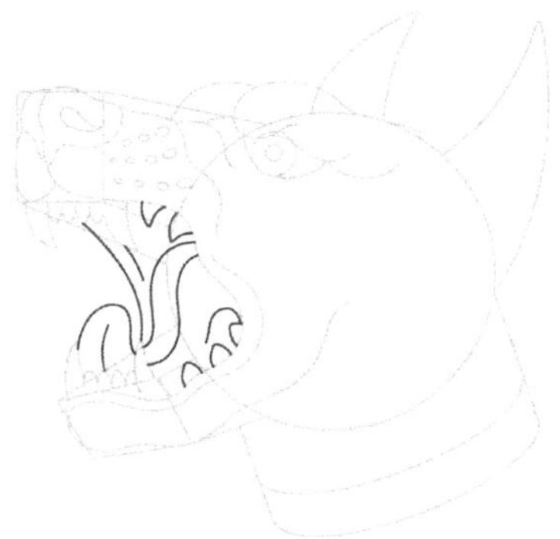

09

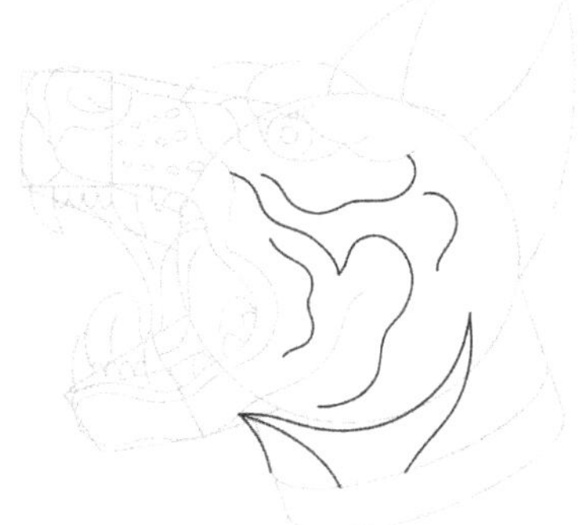

10

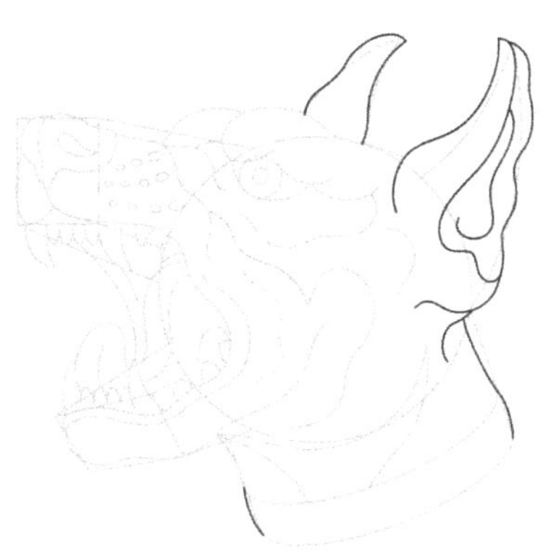

11

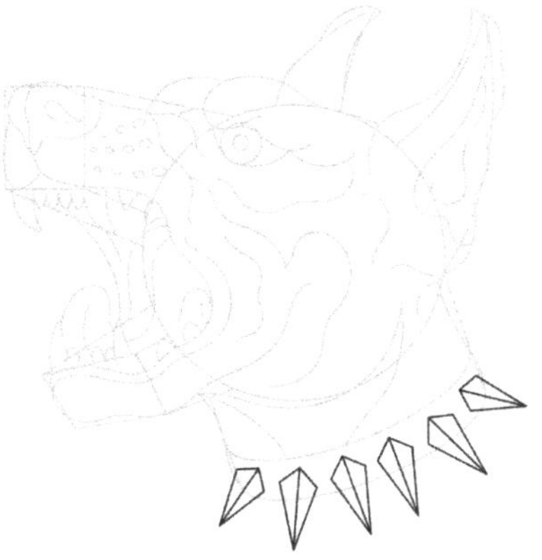

12

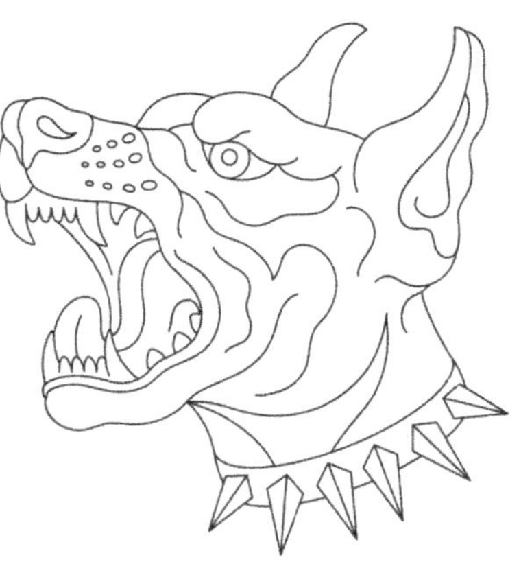

APE

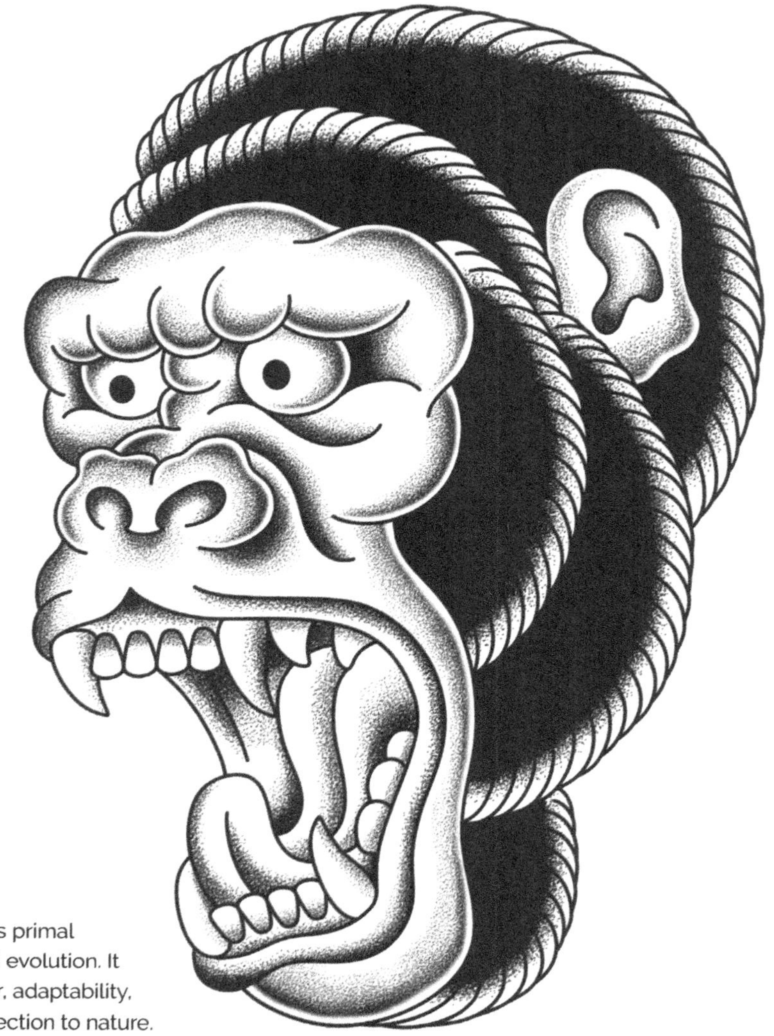

The ape tattoo symbolises primal strength, intelligence, and evolution. It can represent inner power, adaptability, and a raw, untamed connection to nature.

01   **02**   **03**

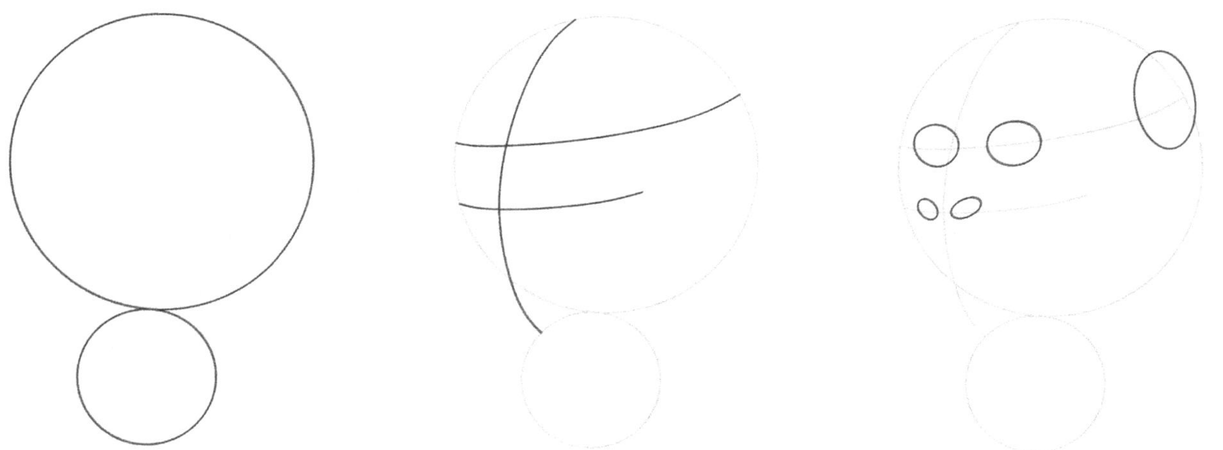

04

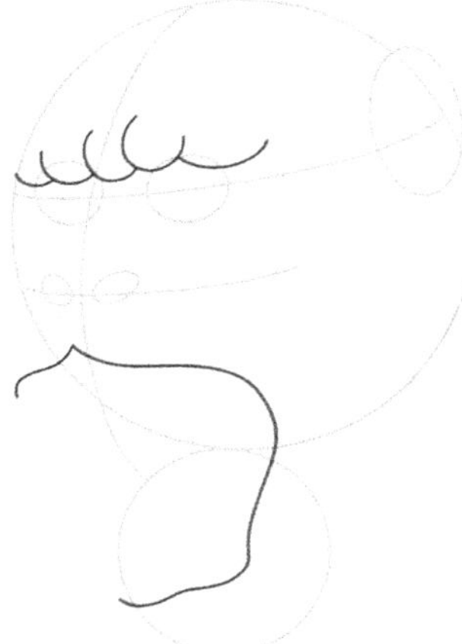

05

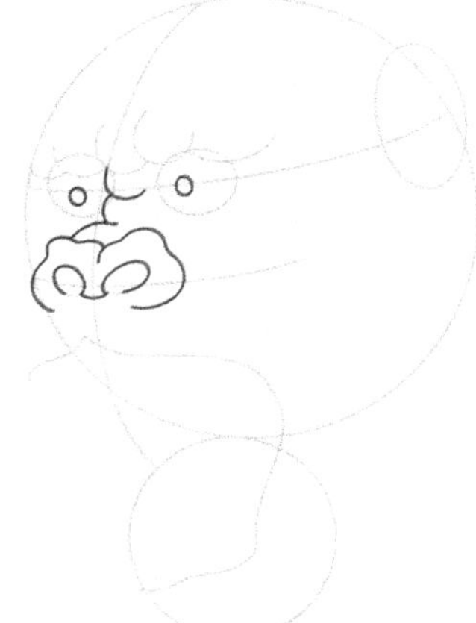

06

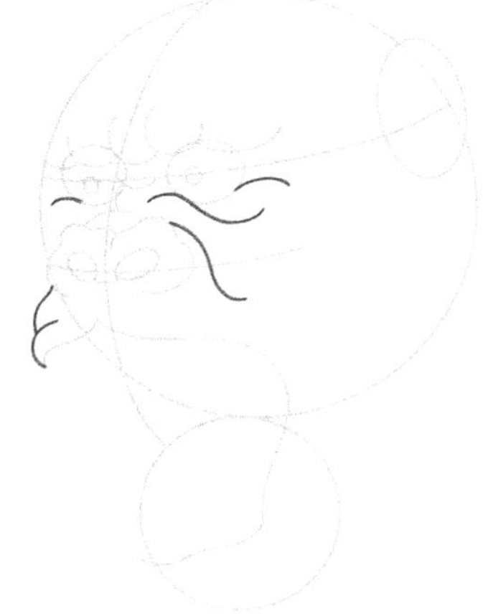

07

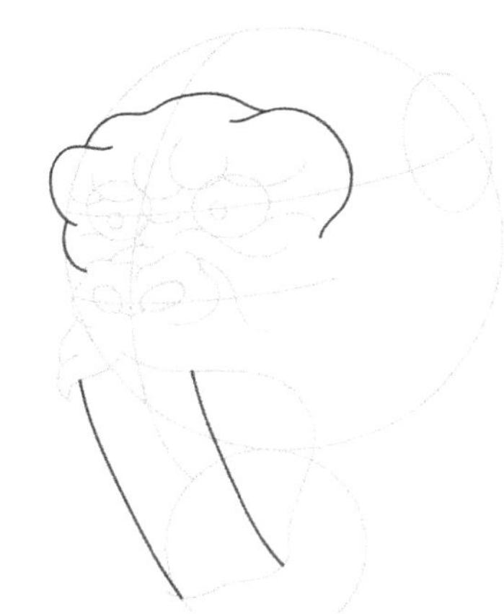

08

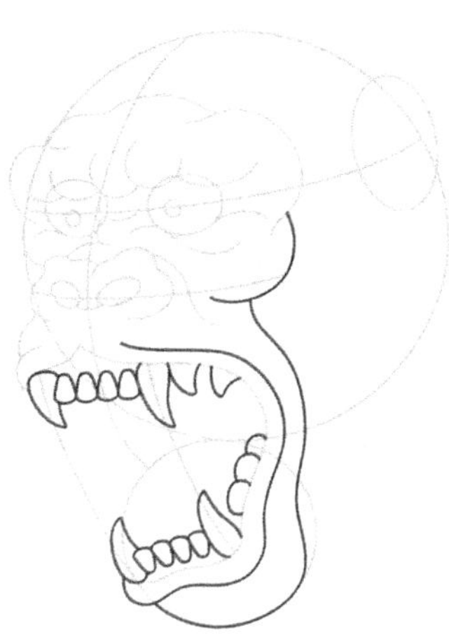

09

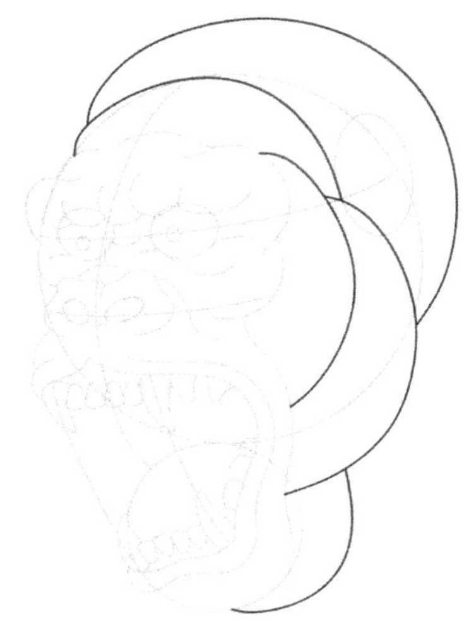

10

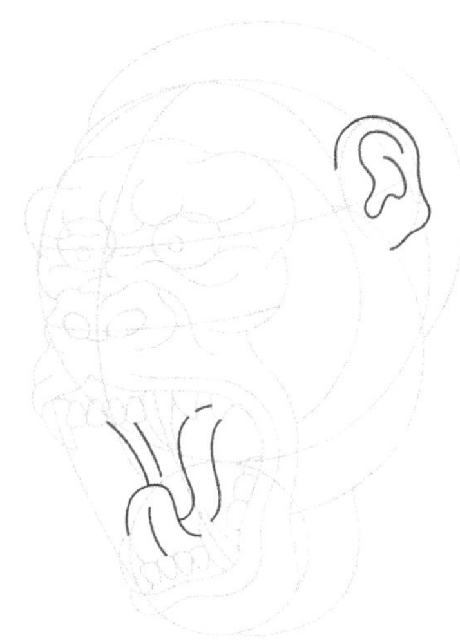

11

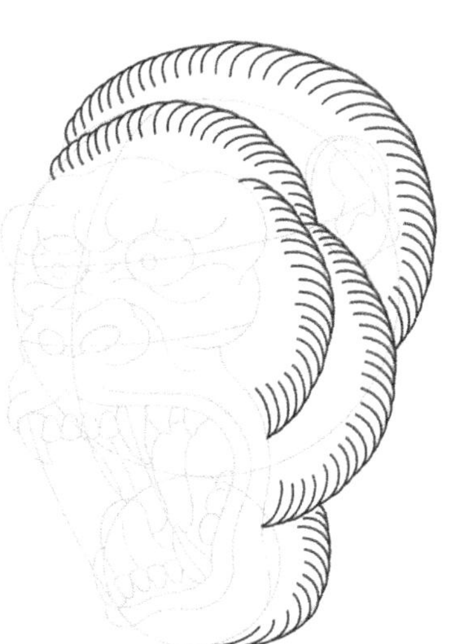

12

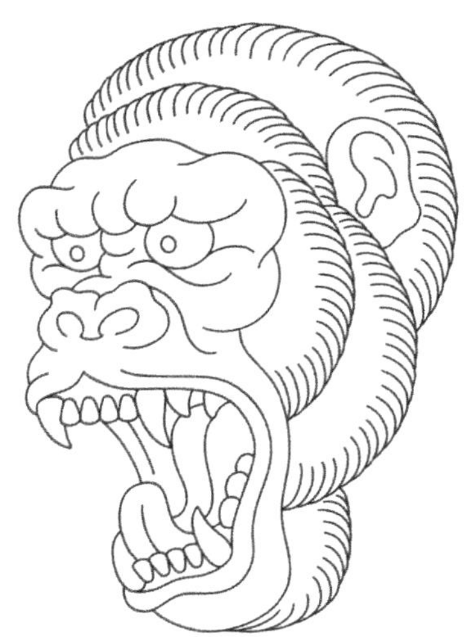

ANIMAL TATTOOS

LION

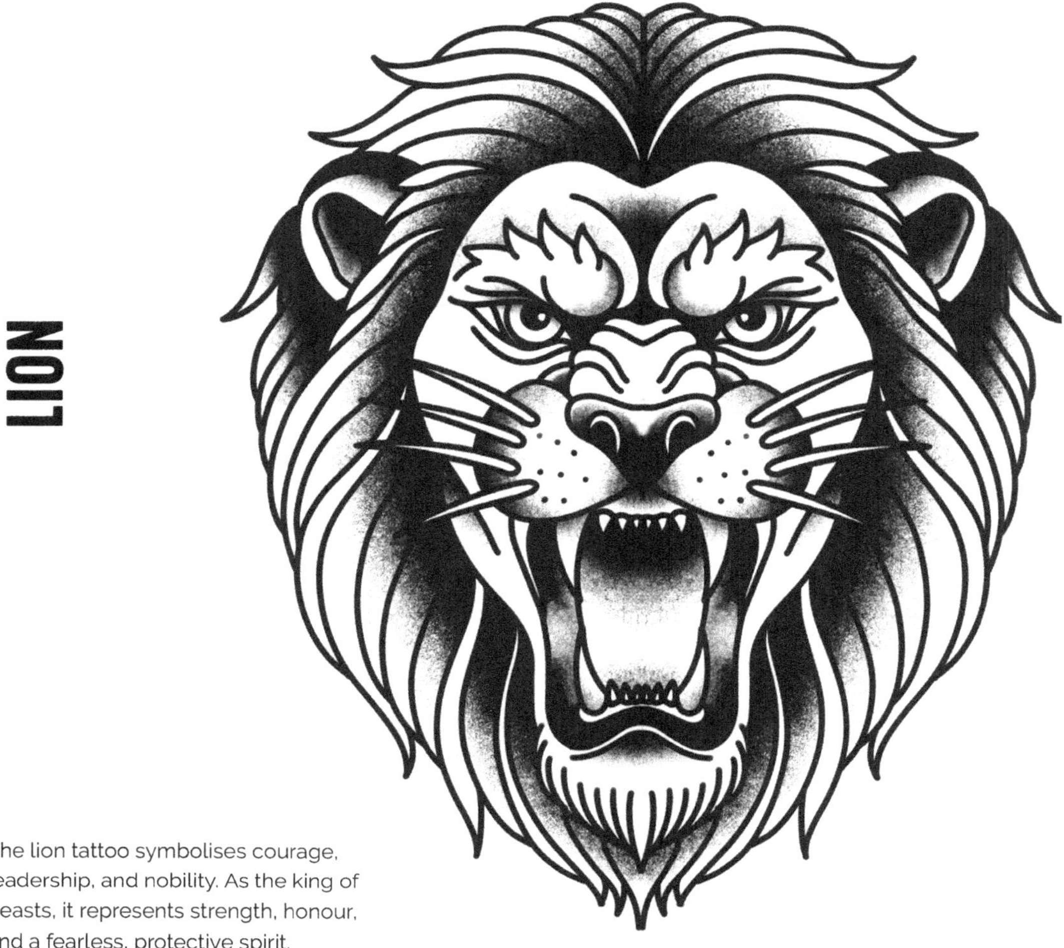

The lion tattoo symbolises courage, leadership, and nobility. As the king of beasts, it represents strength, honour, and a fearless, protective spirit.

01

02

03

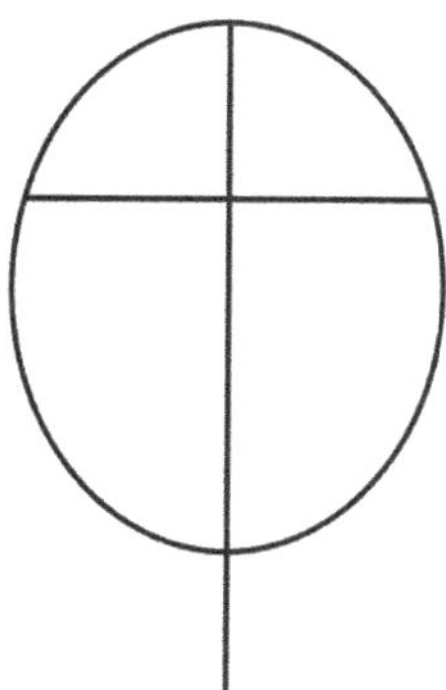

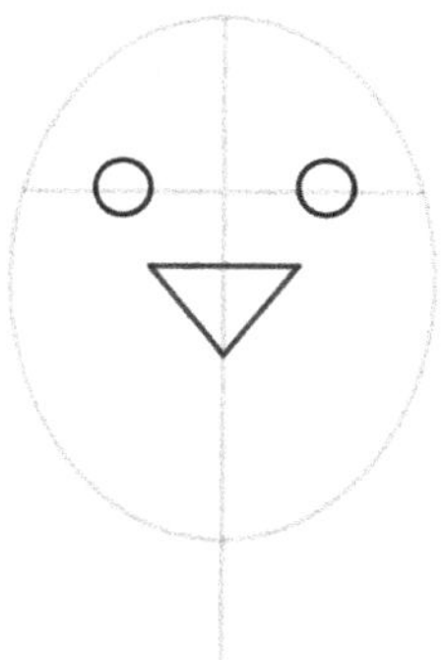

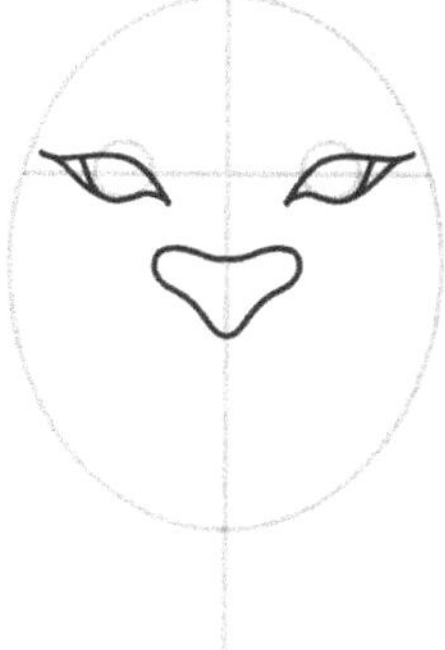

04

05

06

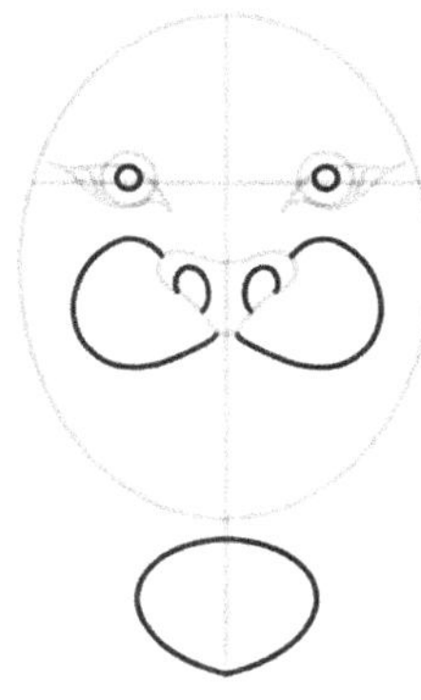

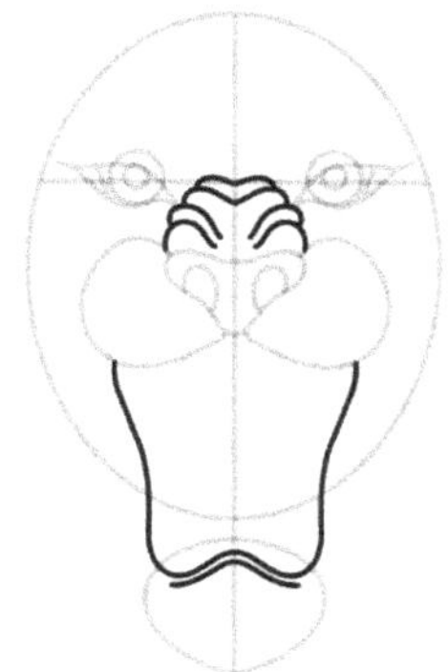

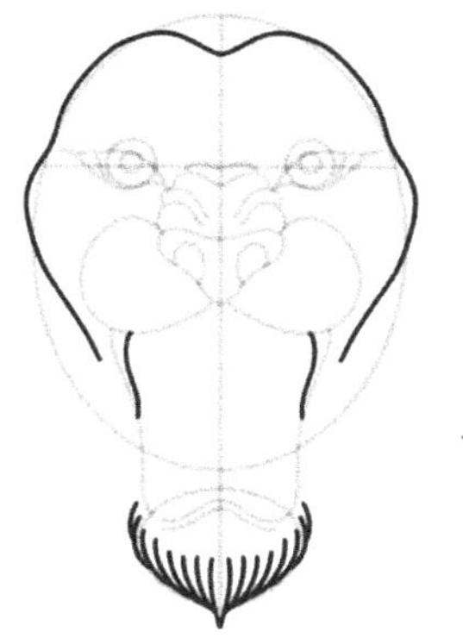

07

08

09

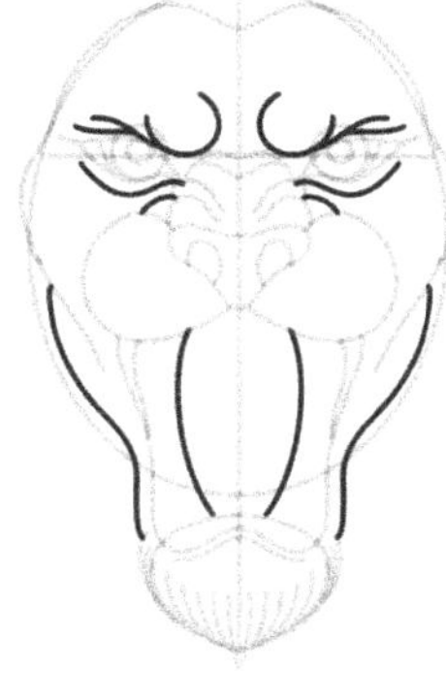

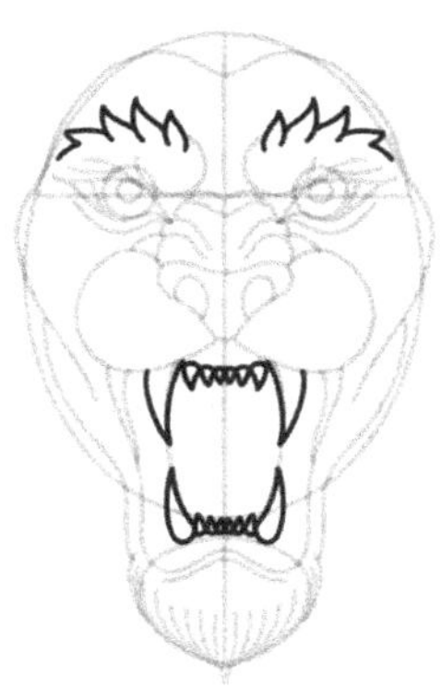

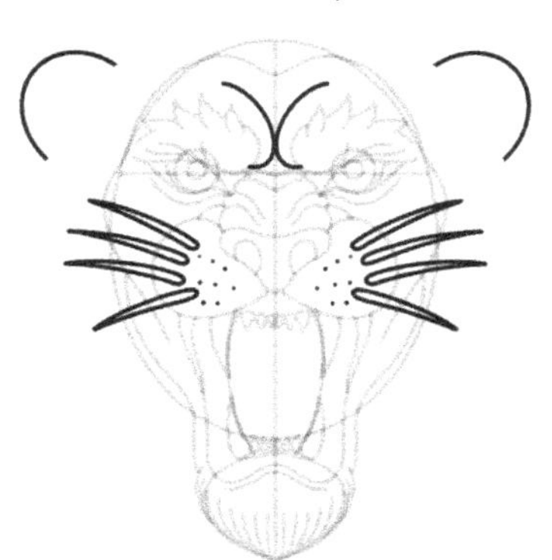

10

11

12

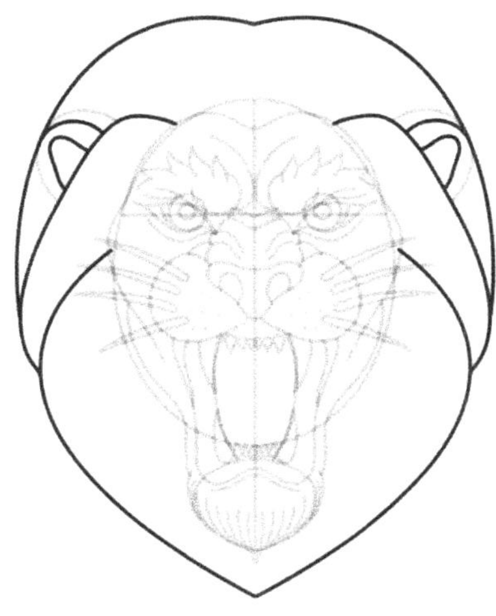

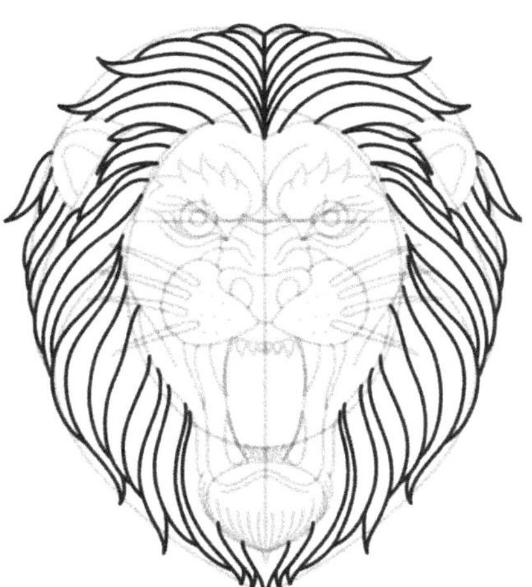

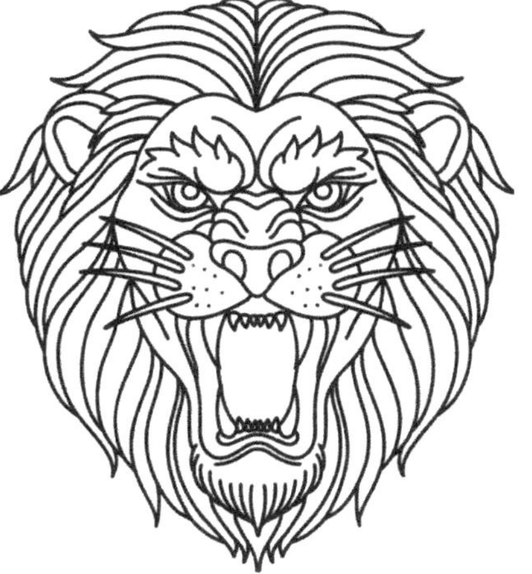

ANIMAL TATTOOS

COCKEREL

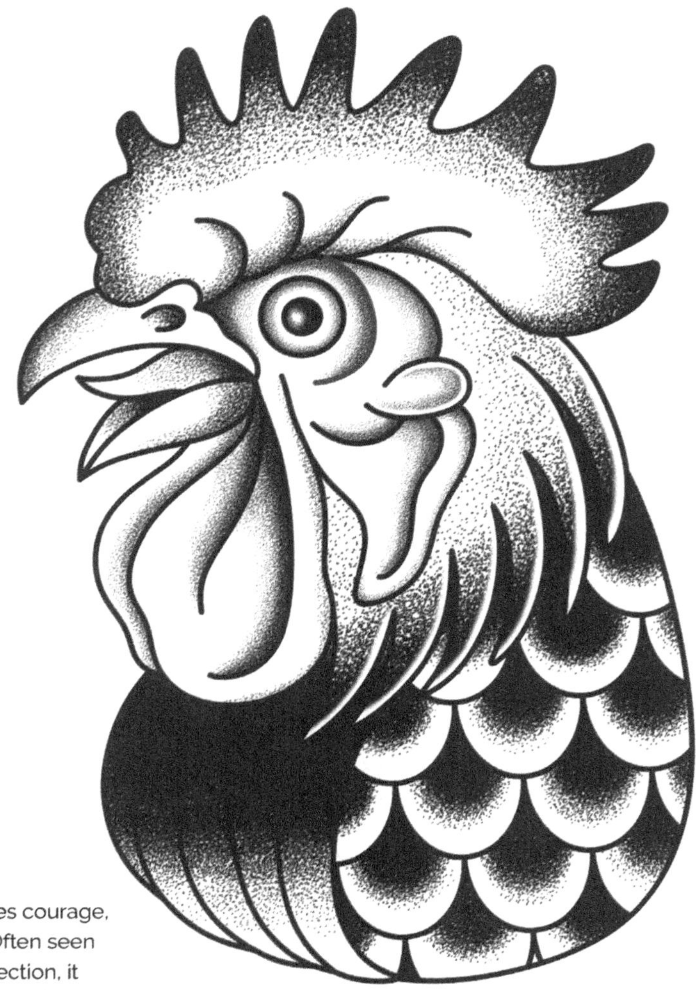

The cockerel tattoo symbolises courage, vigilance, and fighting spirit. Often seen as a symbol of pride and protection, it represents readiness and bold defiance.

01

02

03

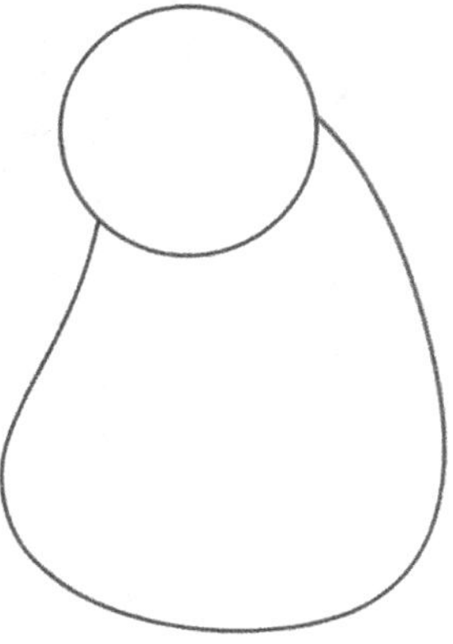

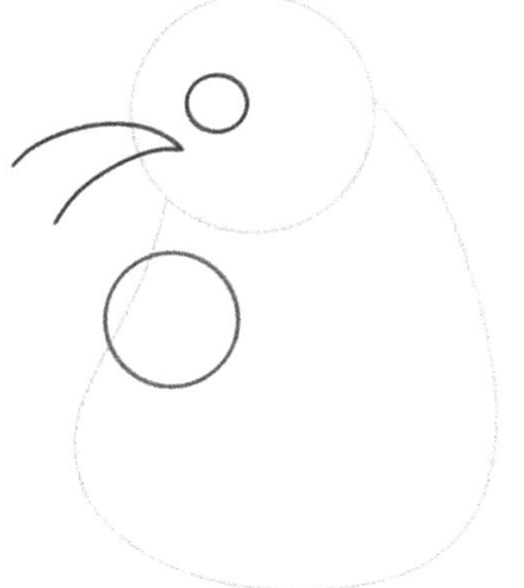

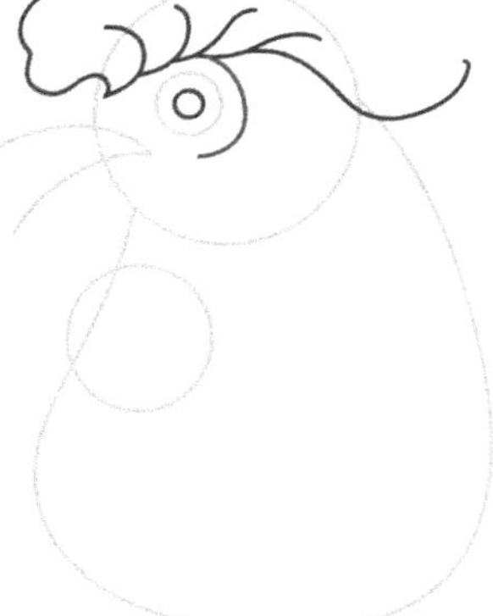

04

05

06

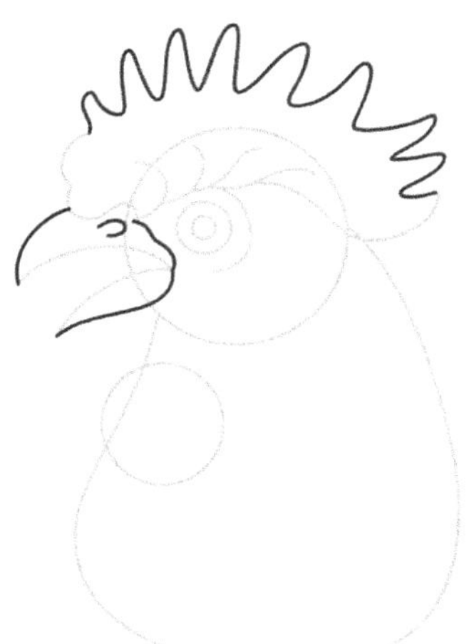

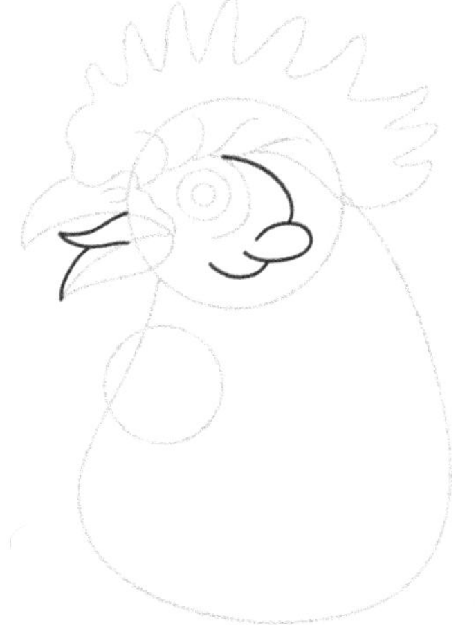

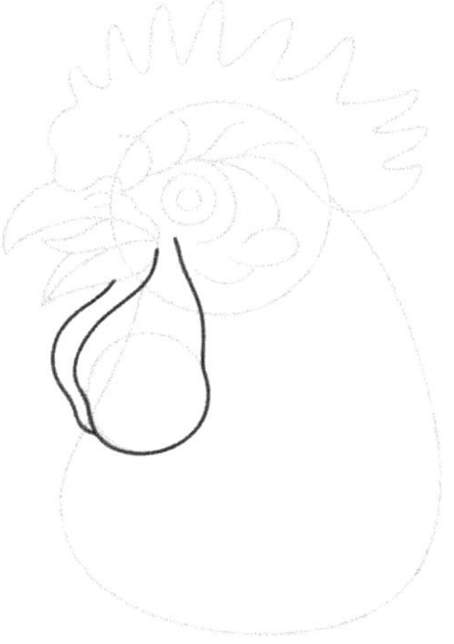

07

08

09

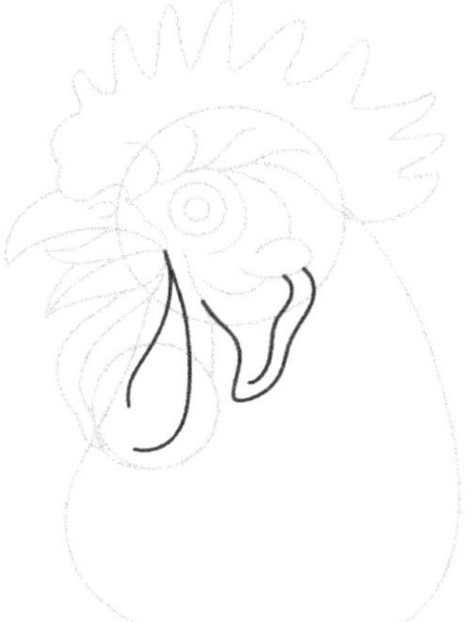

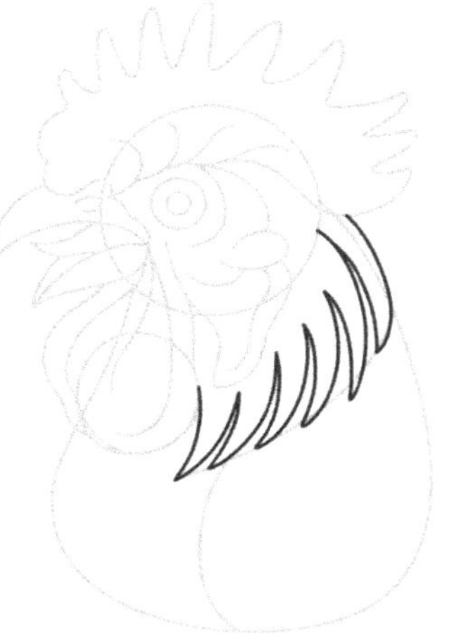

10

11

12

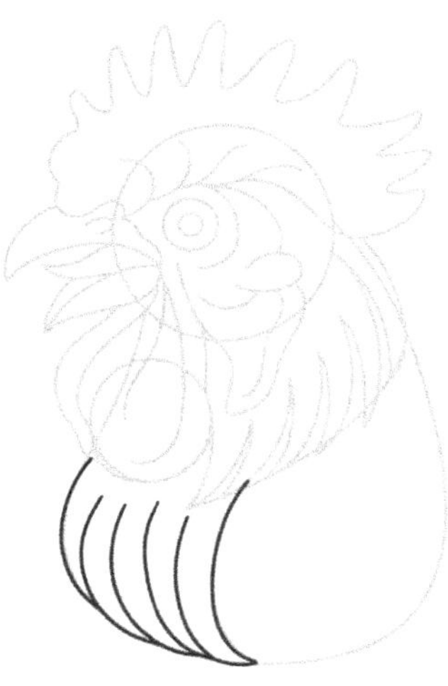

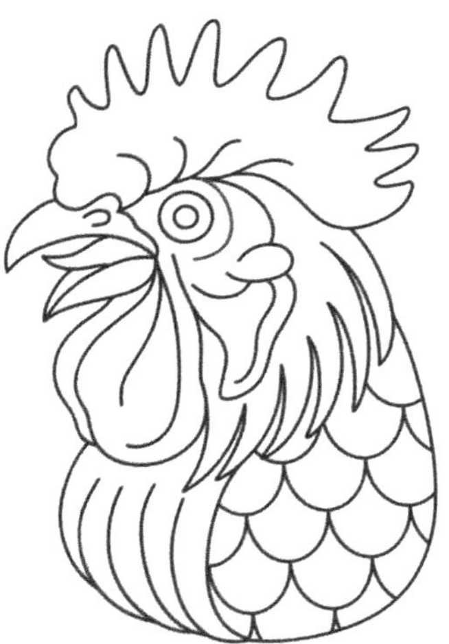

RAM

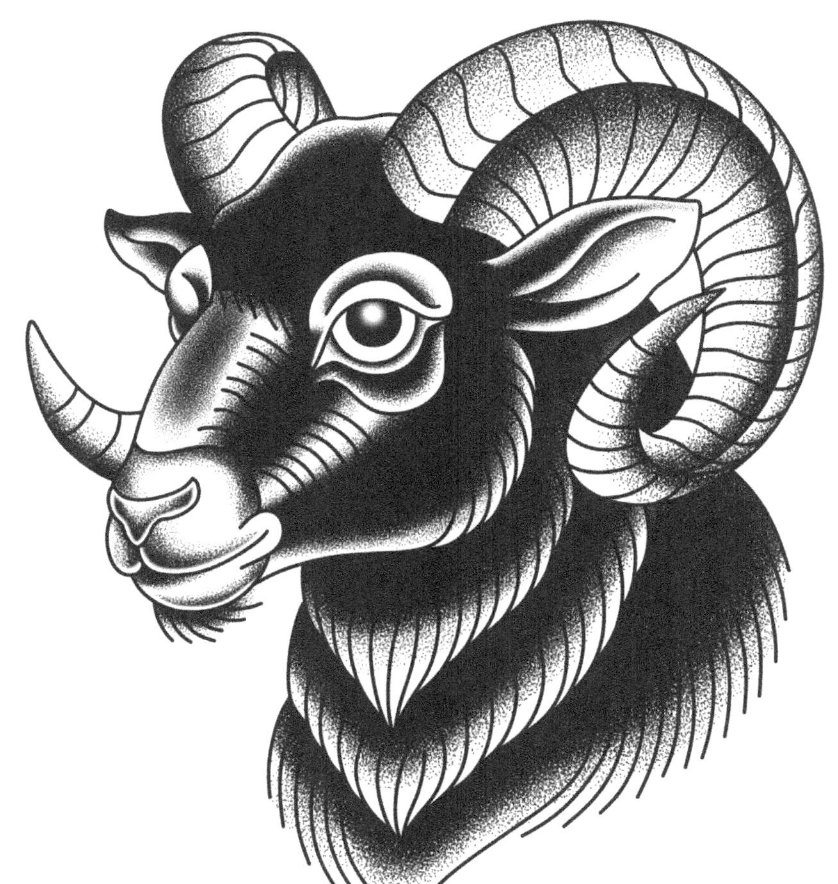

The ram tattoo symbolises determination, courage, and leadership. Known for charging forward, it represents bold action, resilience, and willpower.

01

02

03

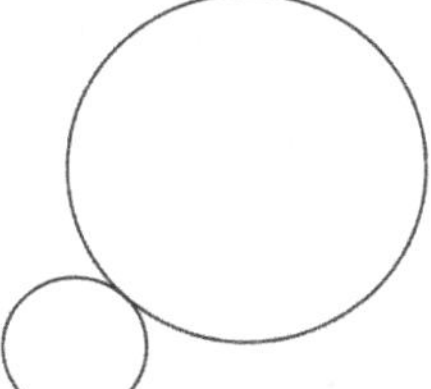

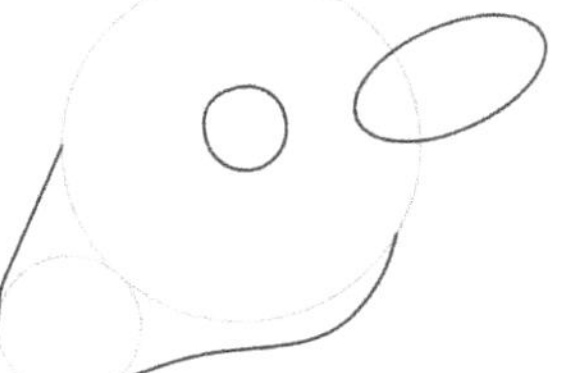

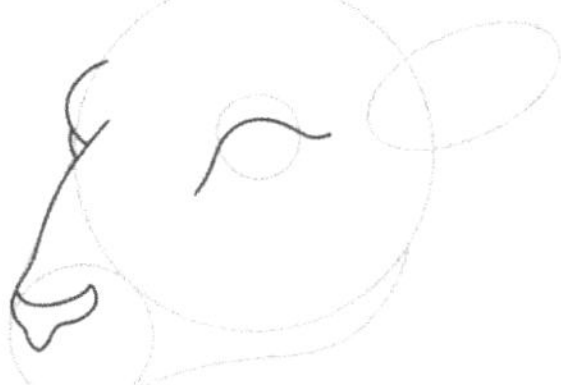

04

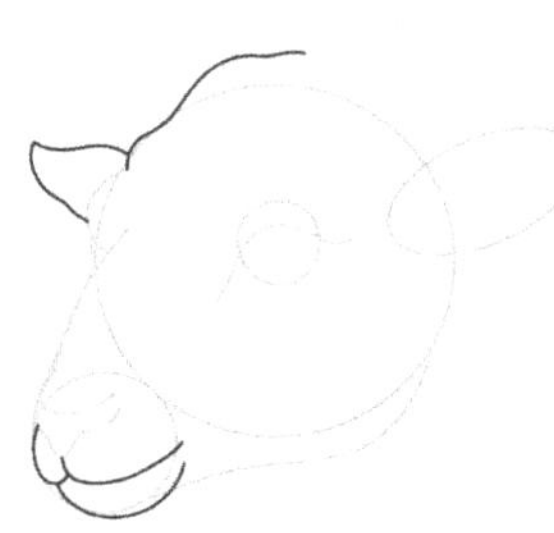

05

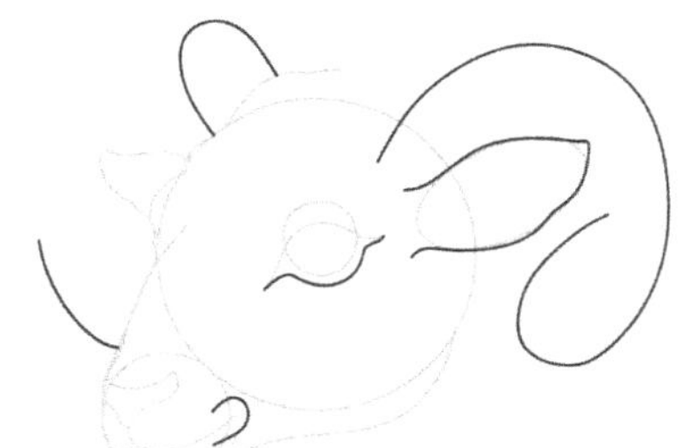

06

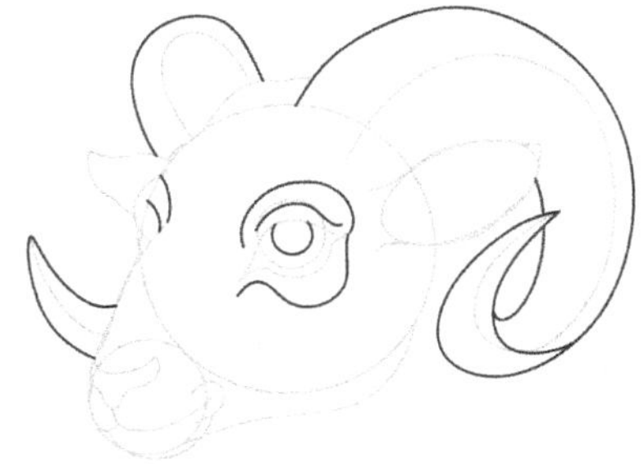

07

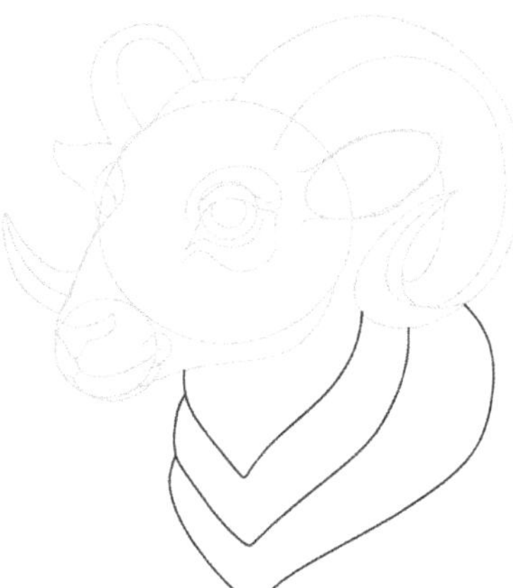

08

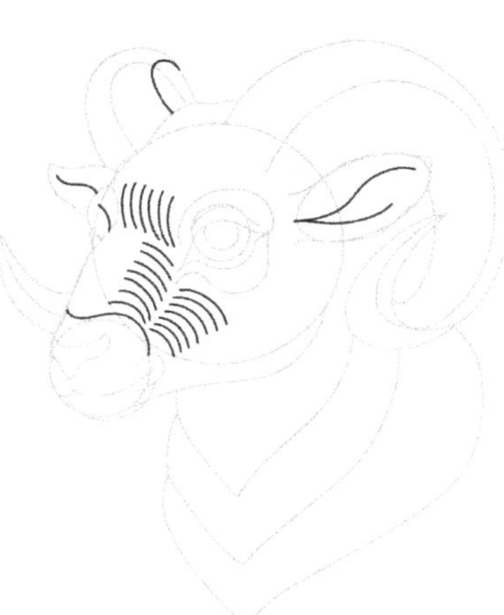

09

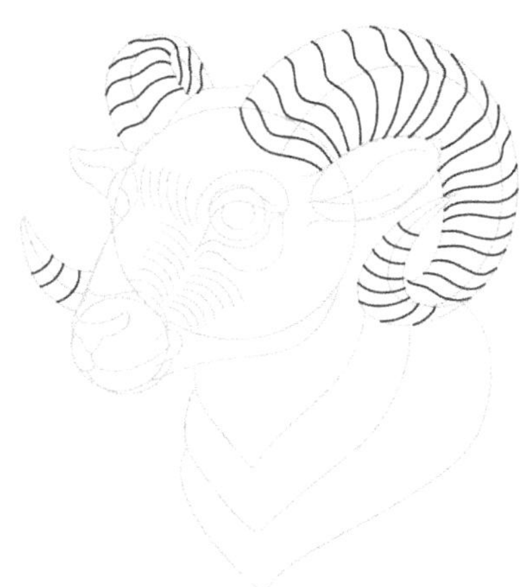

10

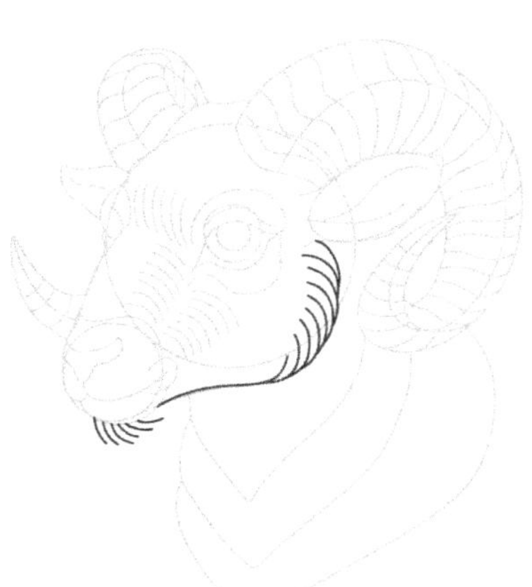

11

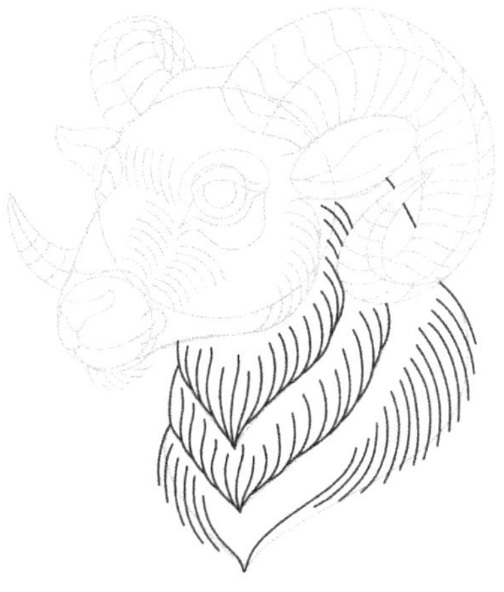

12

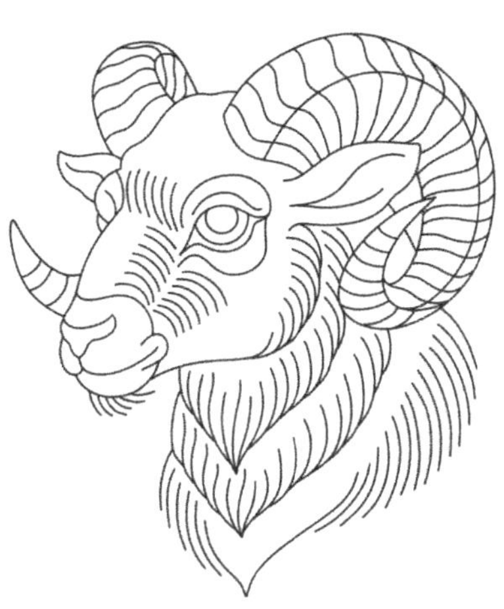

DEATH'S-HEAD MOTH

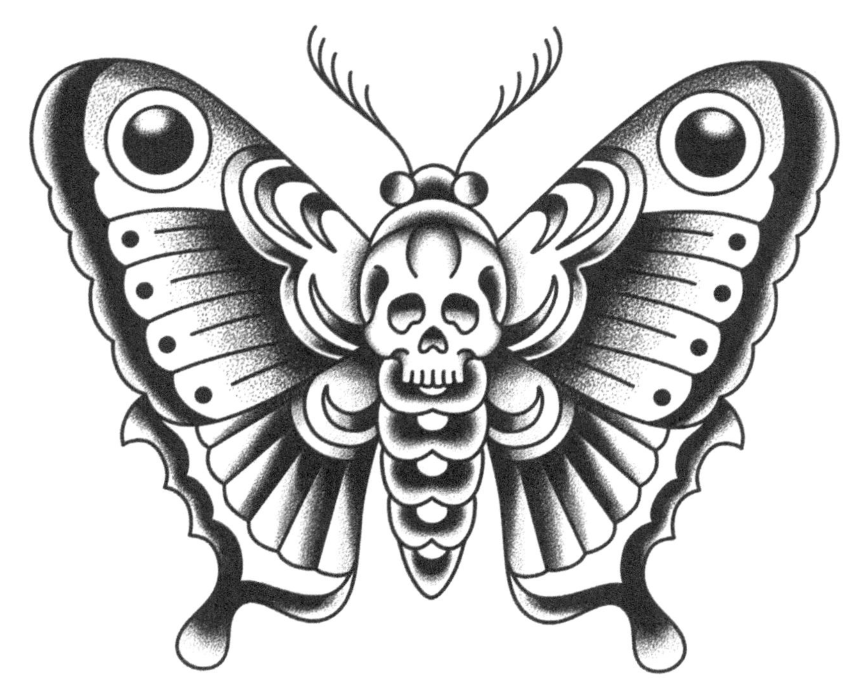

The death moth tattoo symbolises transformation, mortality, and mystery. It represents the delicate balance between life and death.

01

02

03

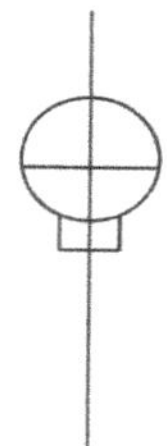

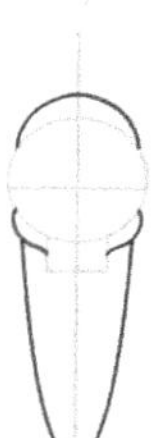

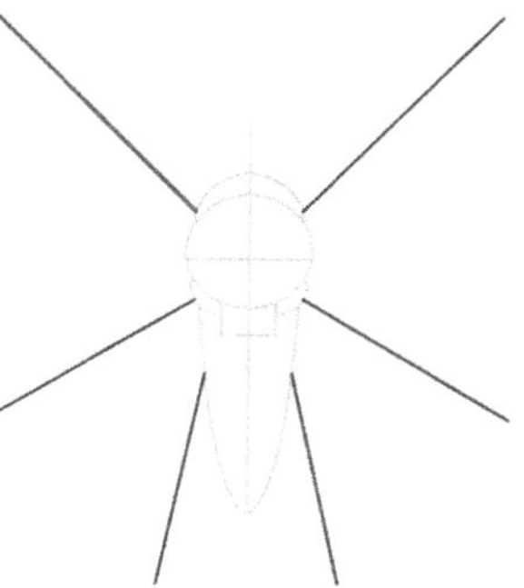

04

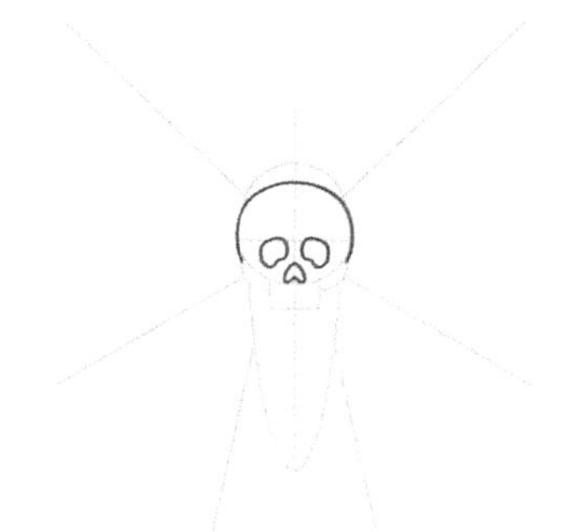

05

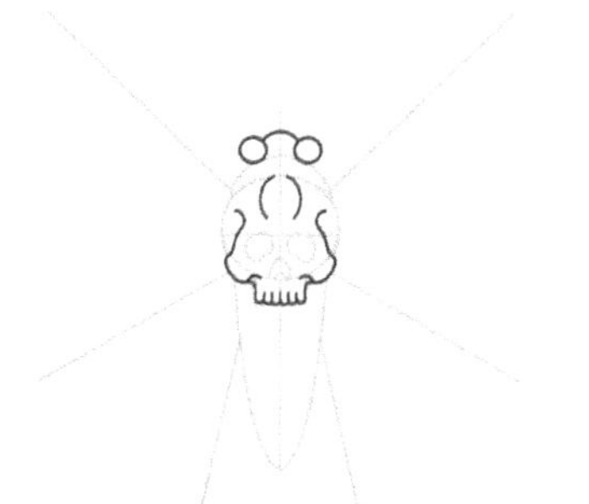

06

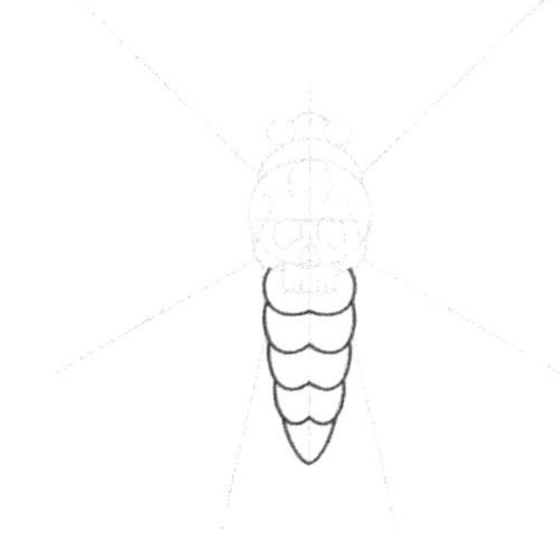

07

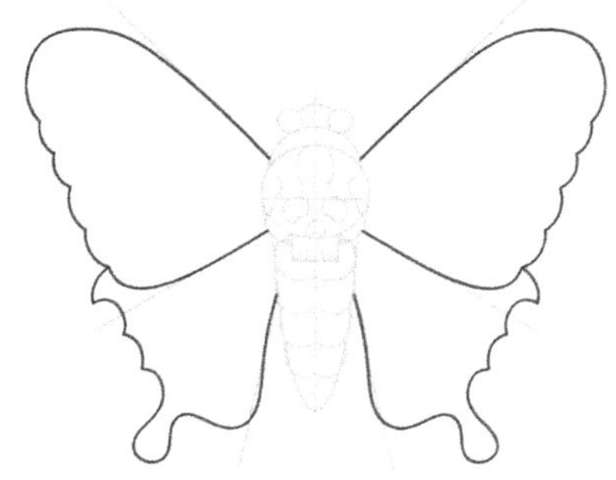

08

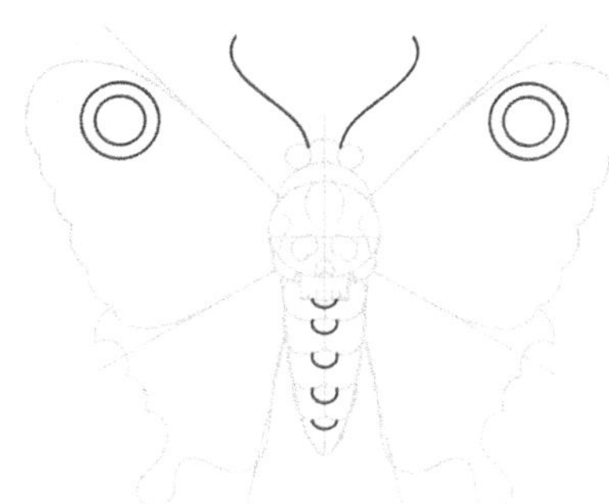

09

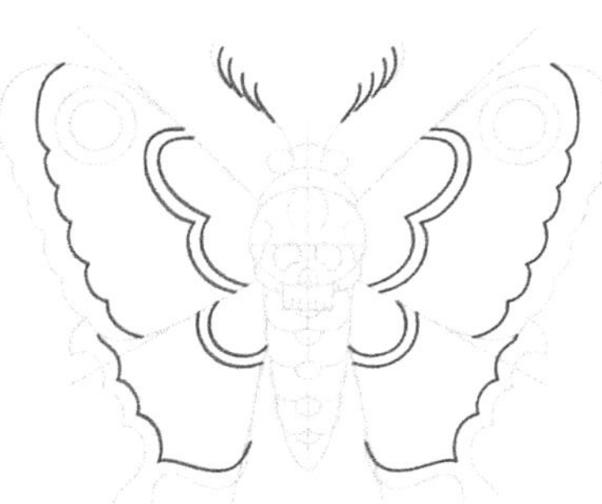

10

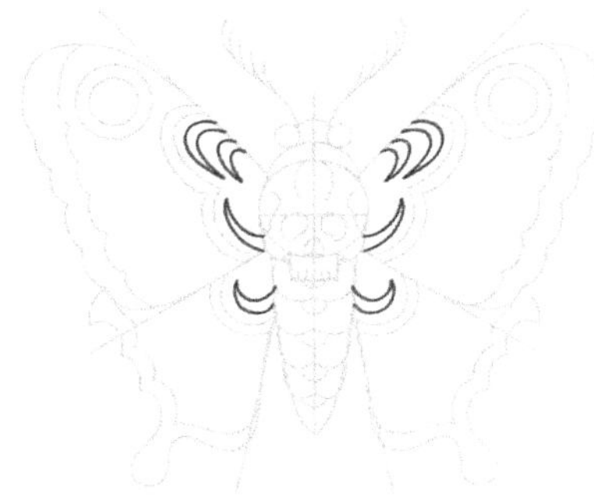

11

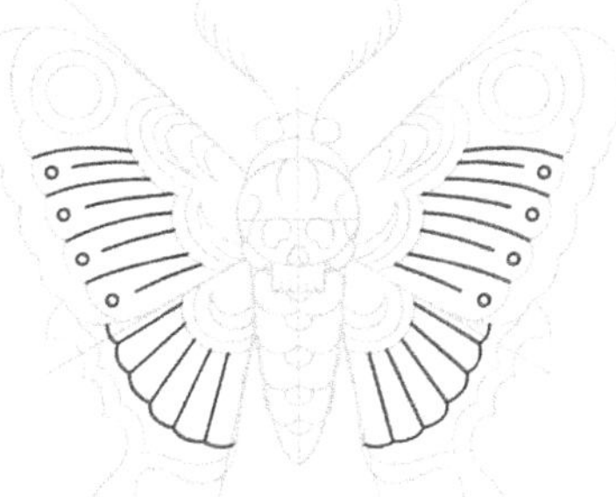

12

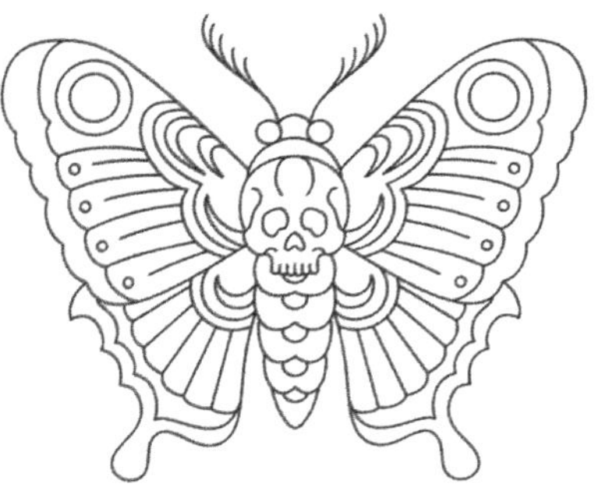

ANIMAL TATTOOS

BUTTERFLY

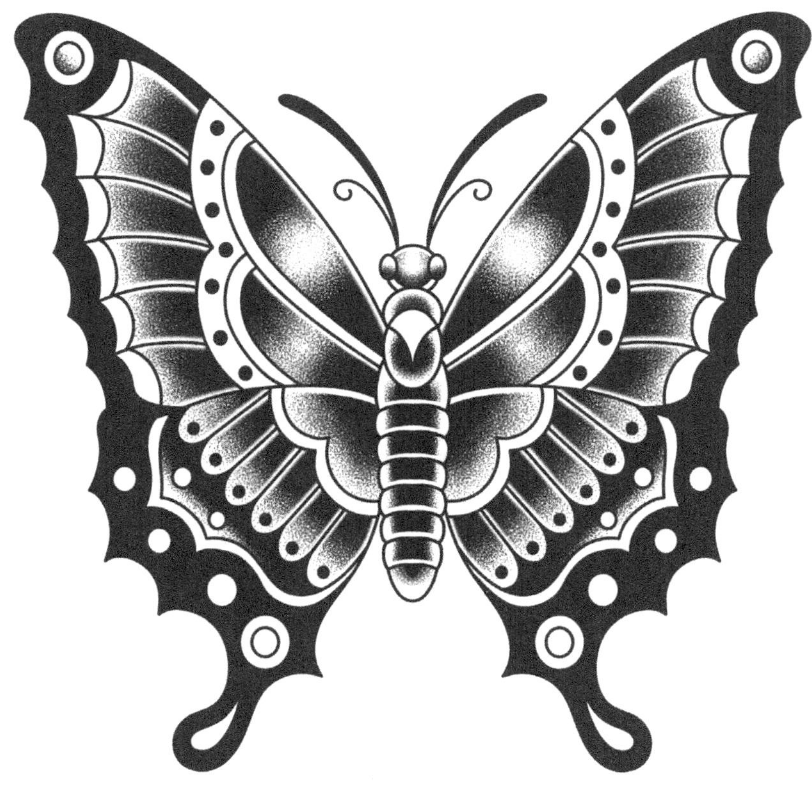

The butterfly tattoo symbolises transformation, freedom, and the soul. It represents personal growth, fleeting beauty, and the journey through change and renewal.

01   02   03

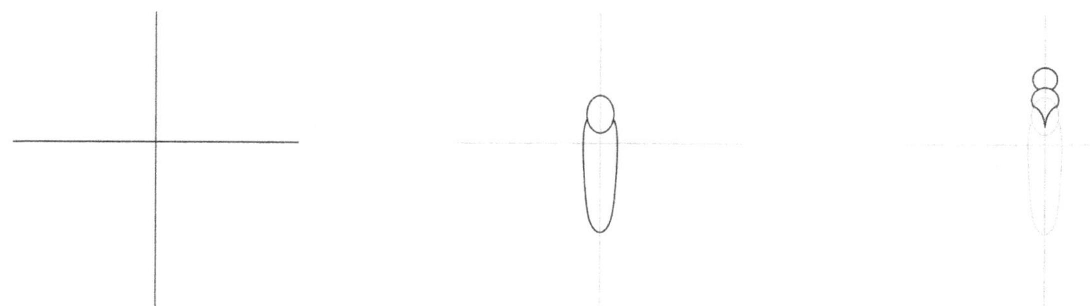

04

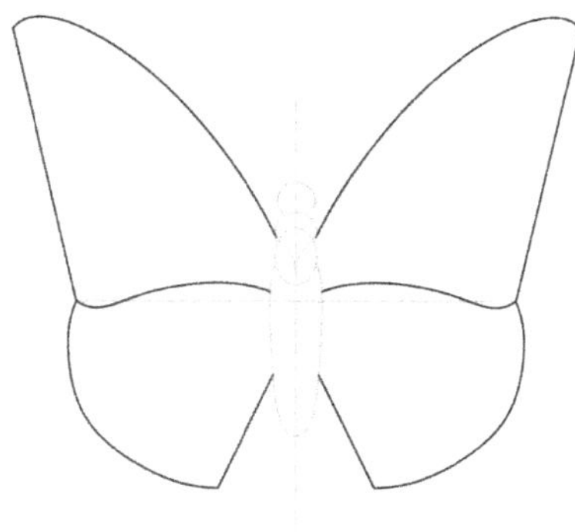

05

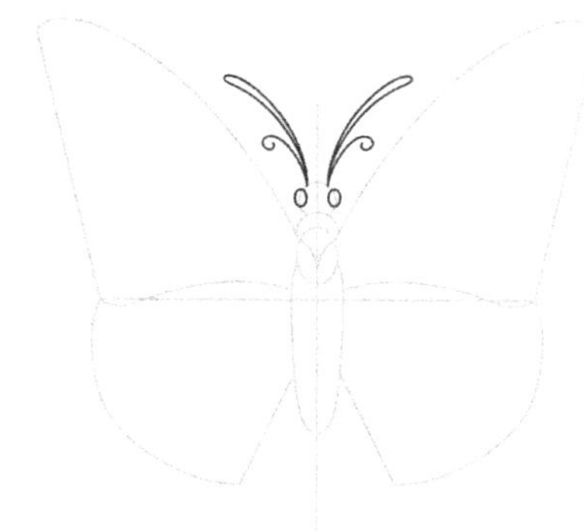

06

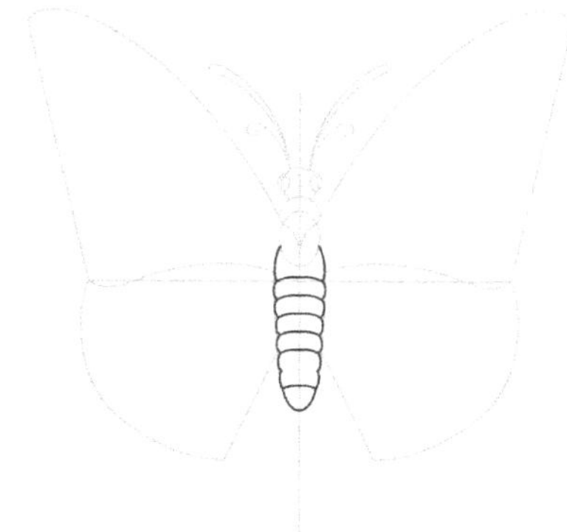

07

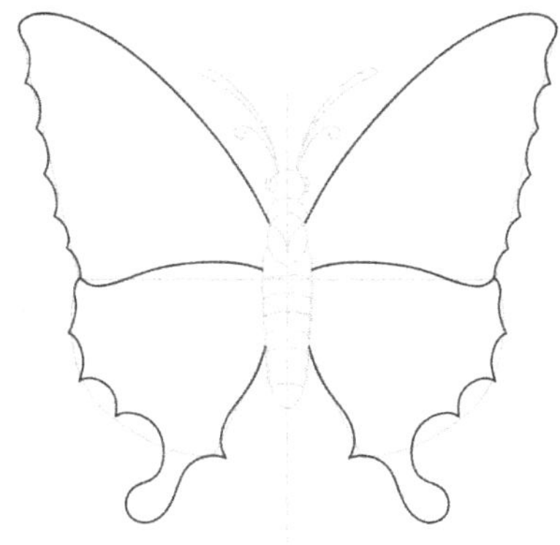

08

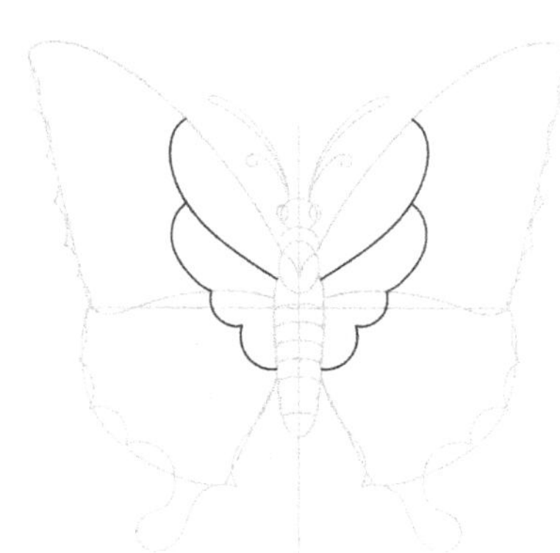

09

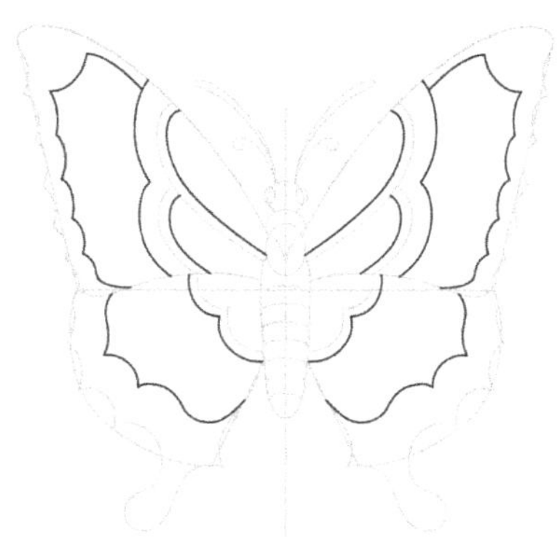

10

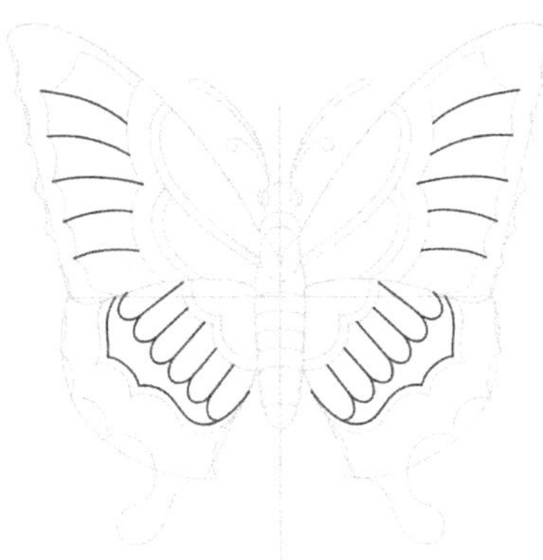

11

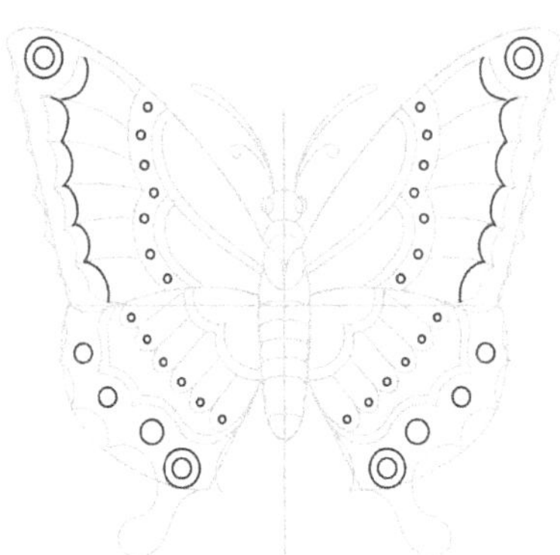

12

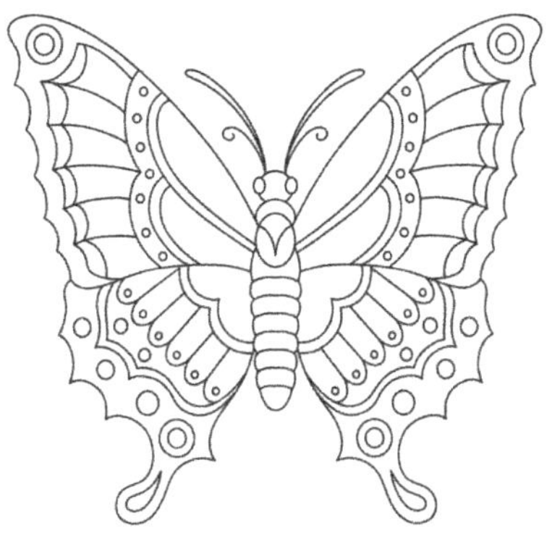

KOI FISH

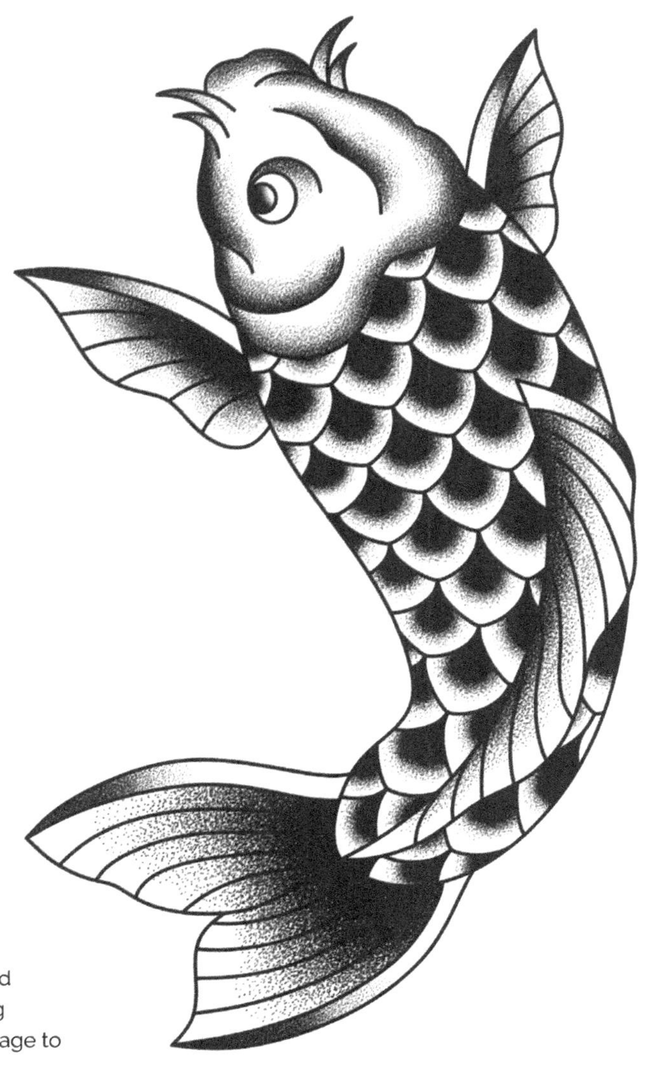

The koi fish tattoo symbolises perseverance, strength, and good fortune. It represents overcoming adversity, ambition, and the courage to swim against the current.

01

02

03

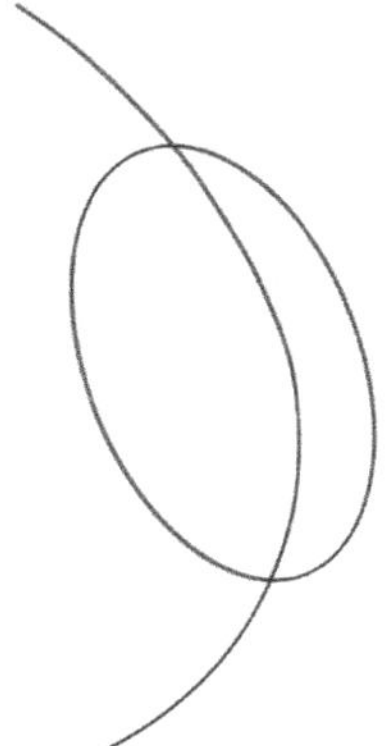

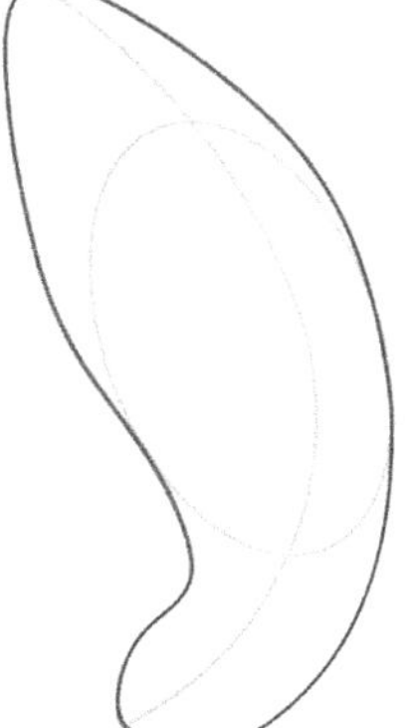

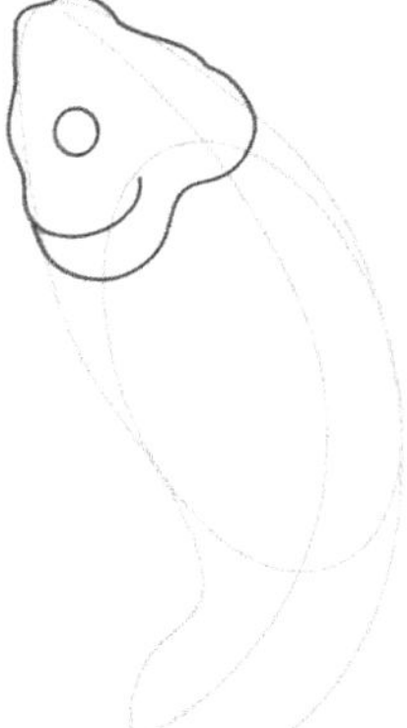

04

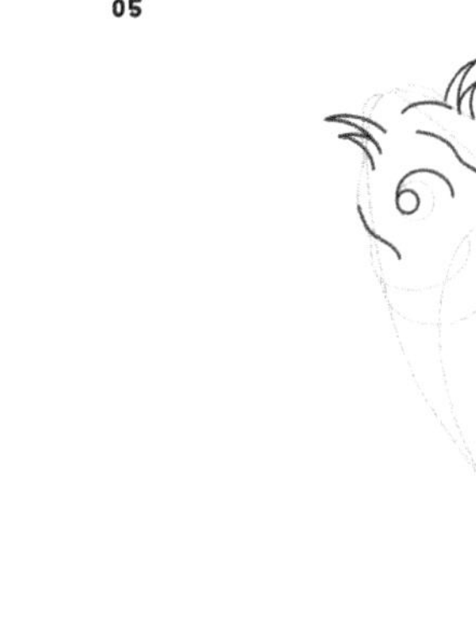

05

06

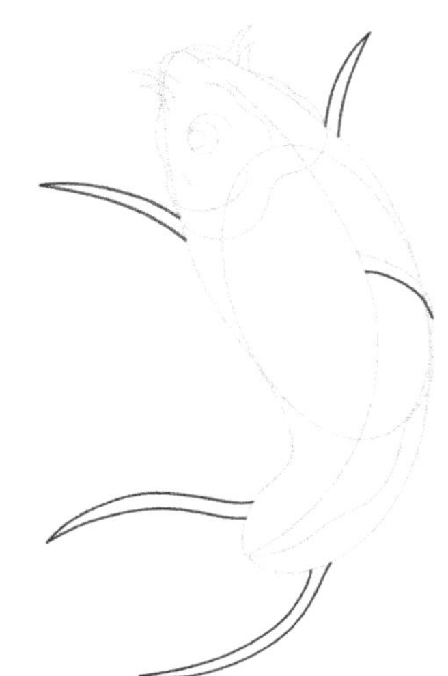

07

08

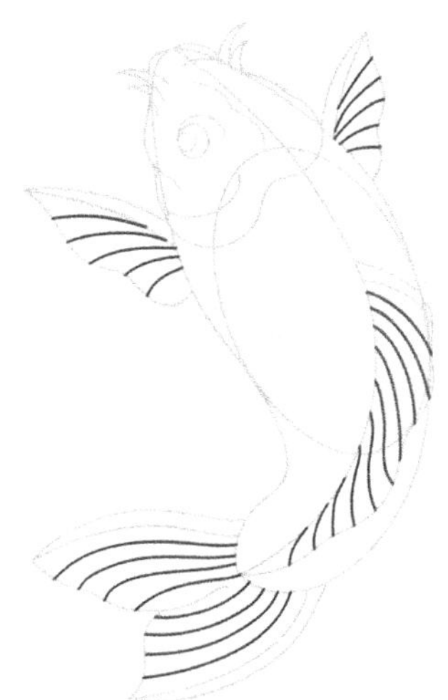

09

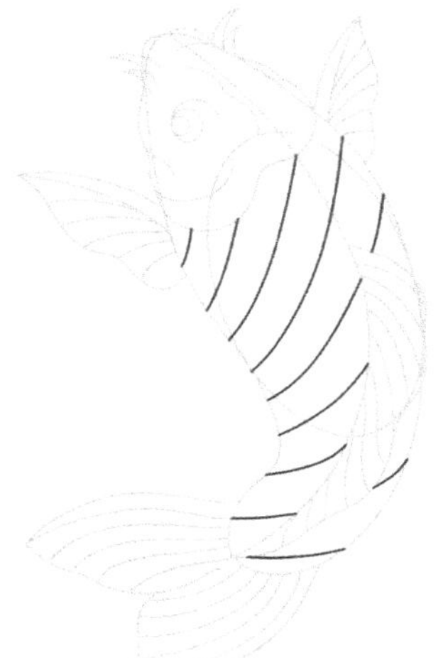

ANIMAL TATTOOS

10

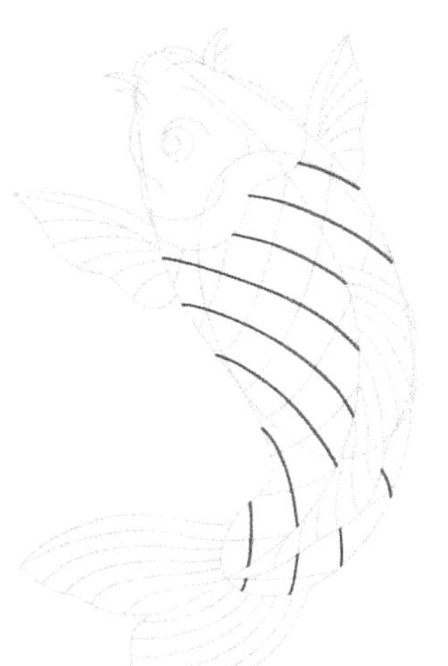

11

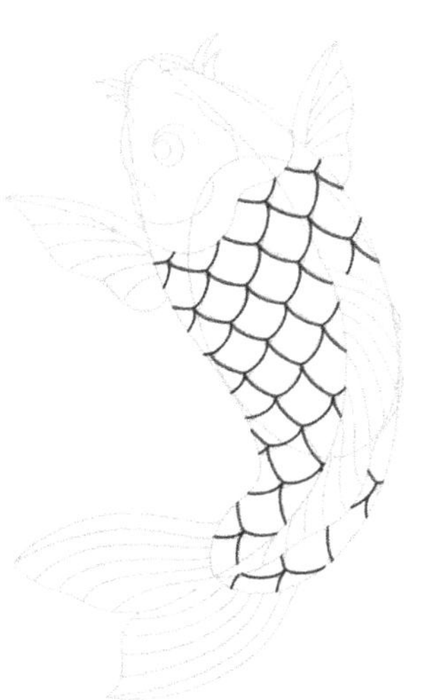

12

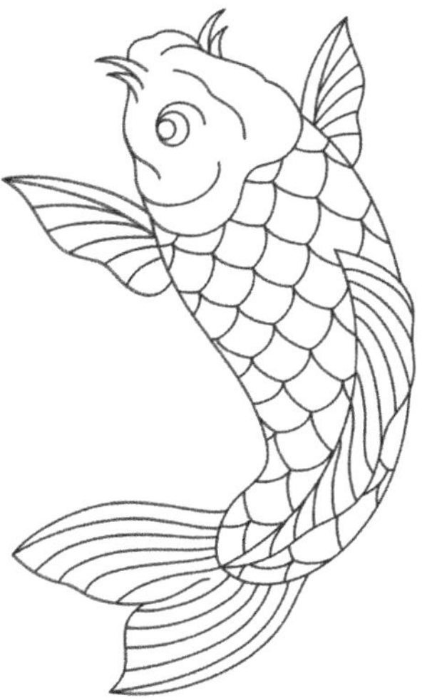

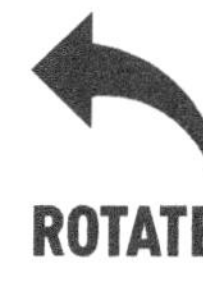

ALLIGARTOR

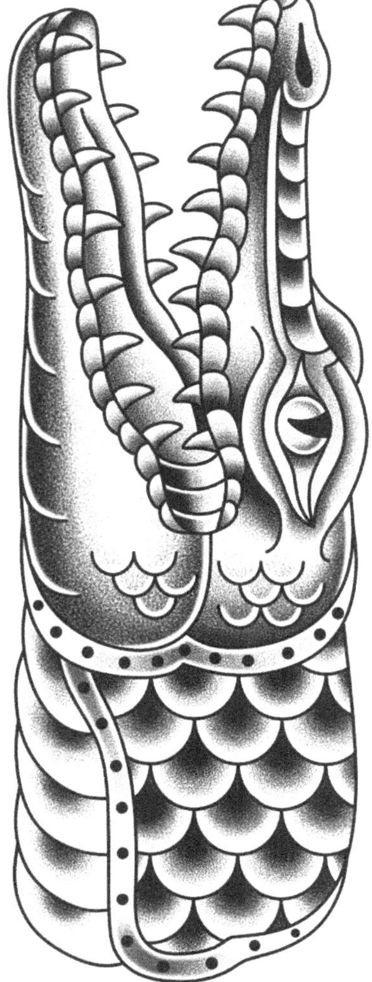

The alligator tattoo symbolises primal power, patience, and survival. It represents ancient wisdom, stealth, and the ability to strike with precision when the moment is right.

01

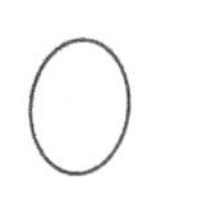

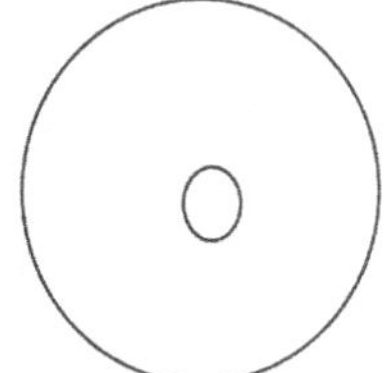

02

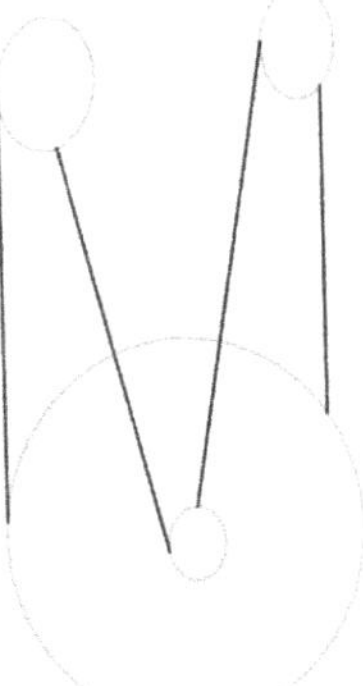

03

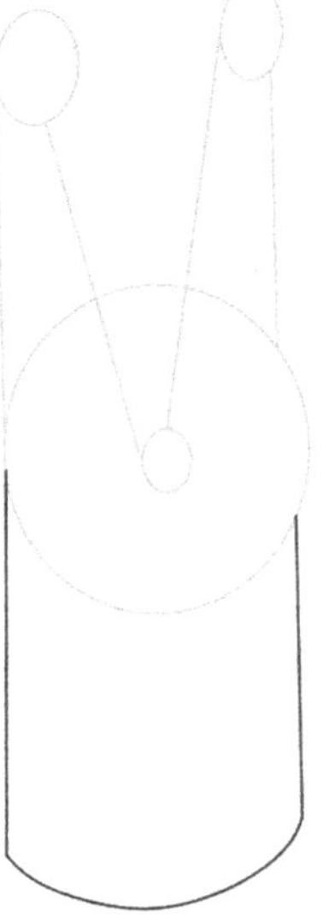

04

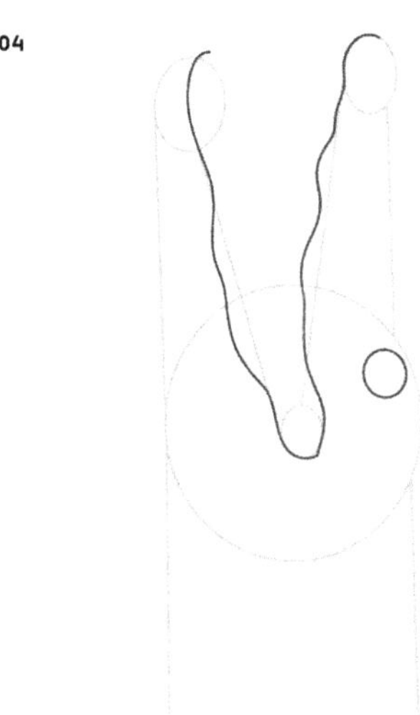

05

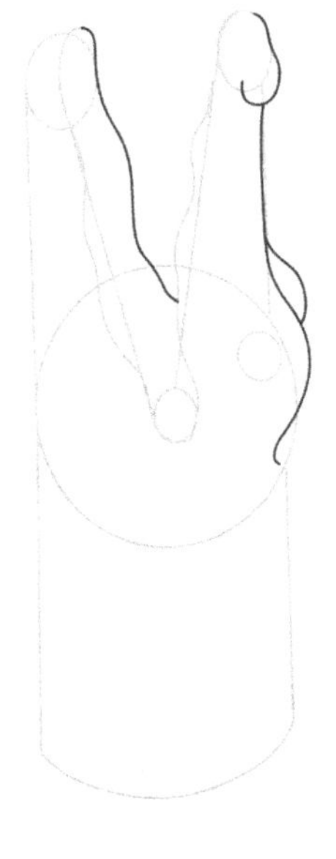

06

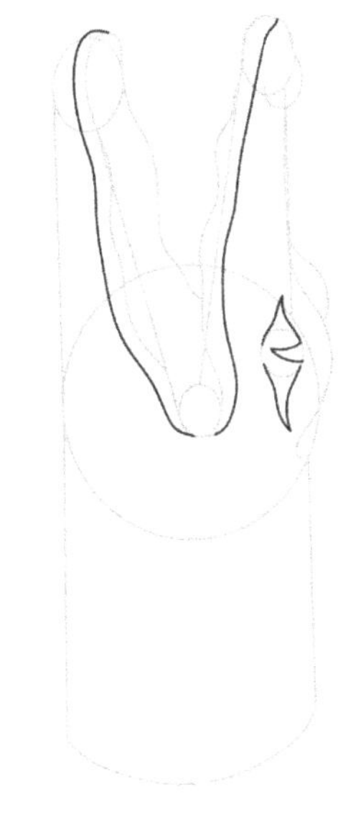

07

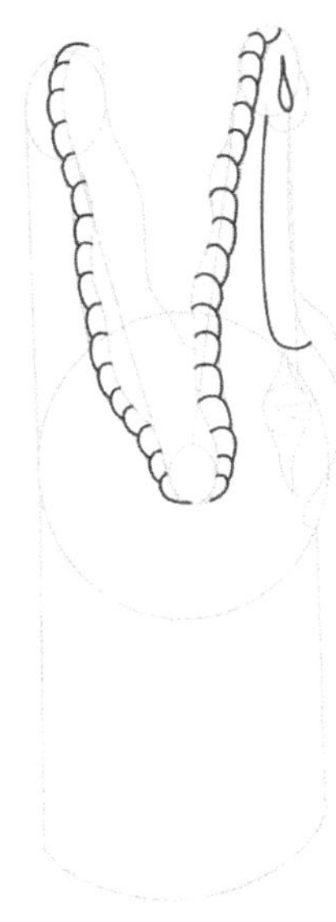

08

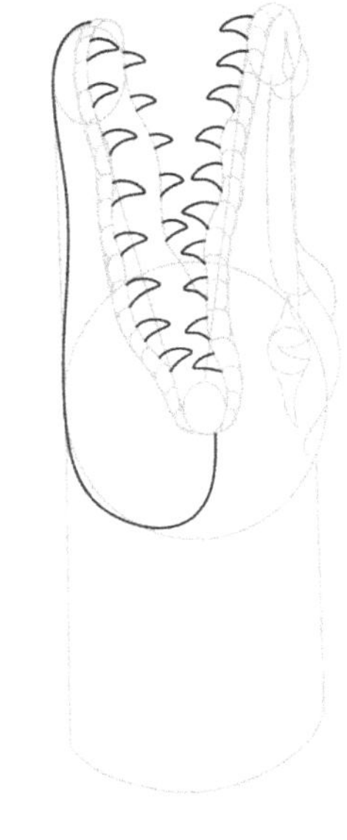

09

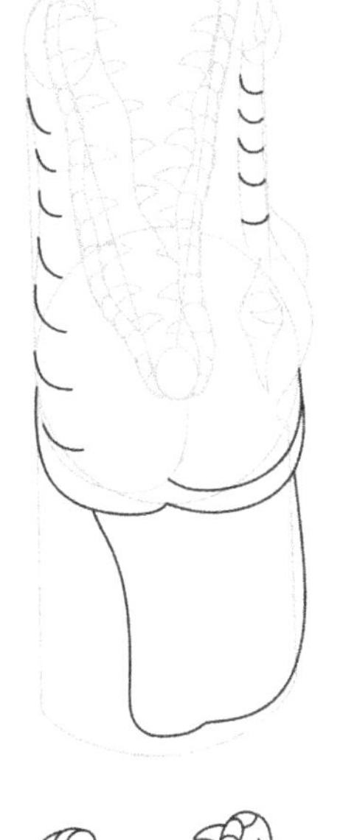

10

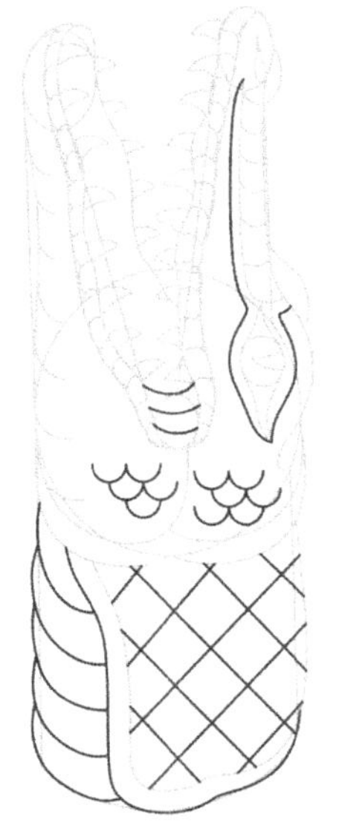

11

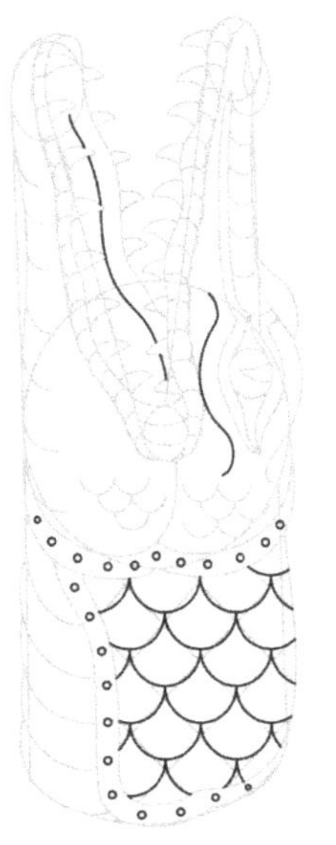

12

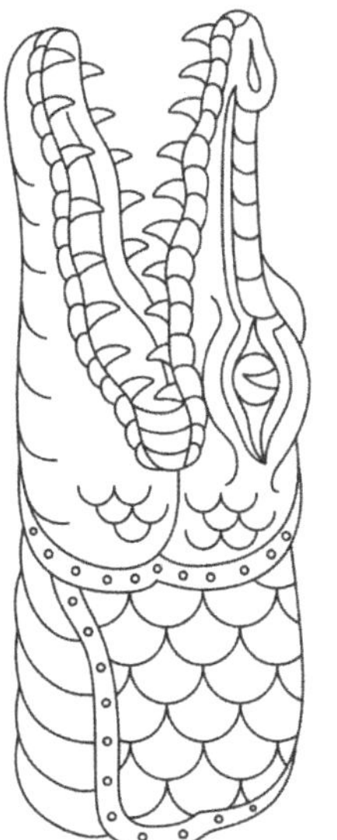

ANIMAL TATTOOS

BOAR

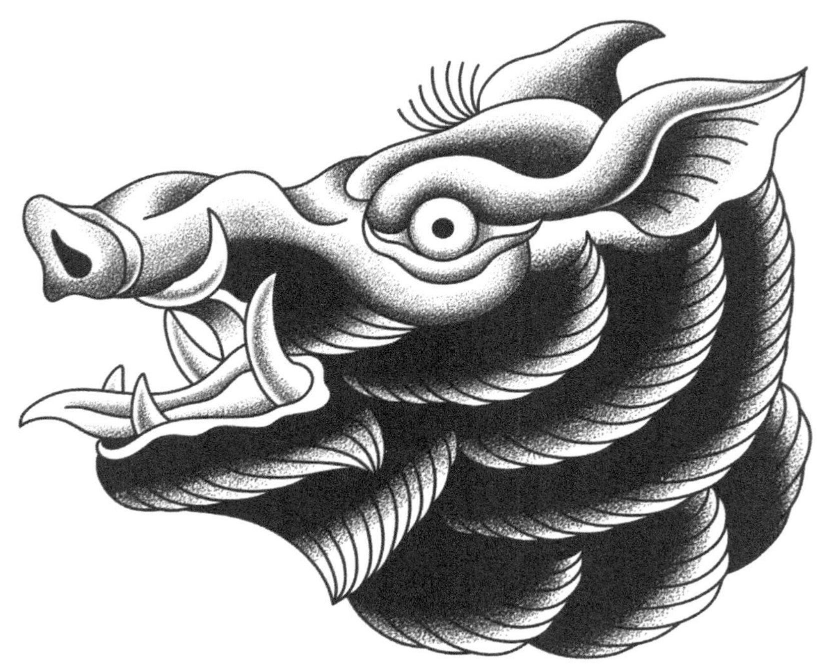

The boar tattoo symbolises ferocity, courage, and unyielding determination. It represents a warrior spirit, fearlessness in battle, and a refusal to back down.

01

02

03

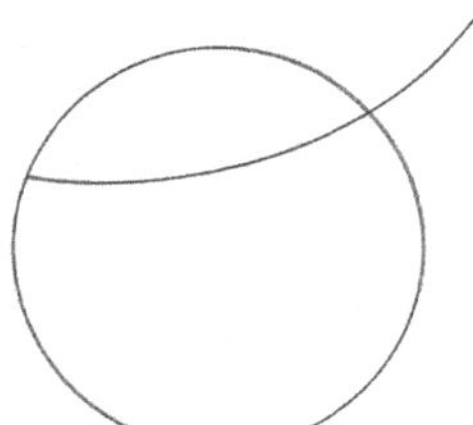

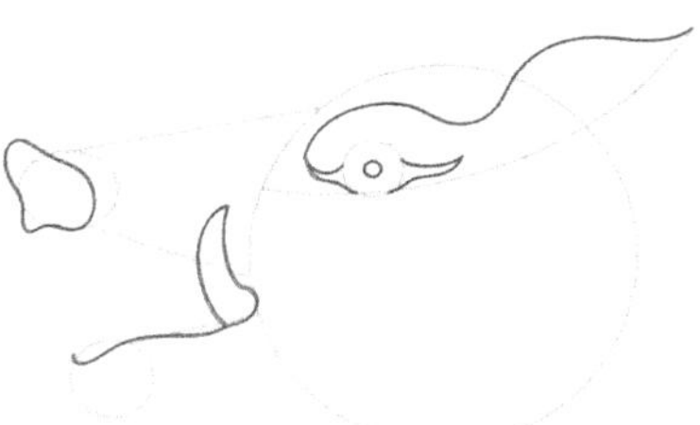

04

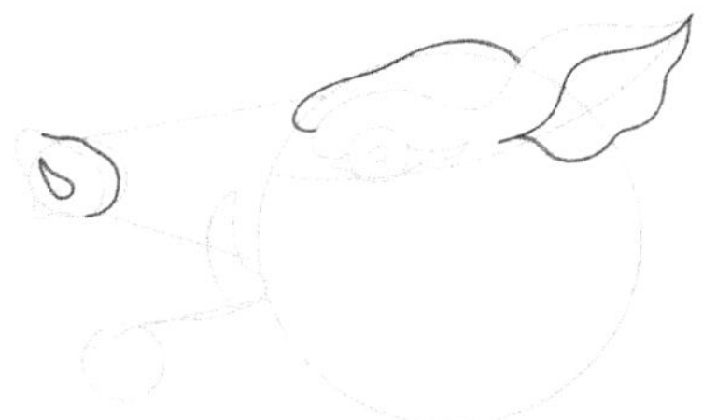

05

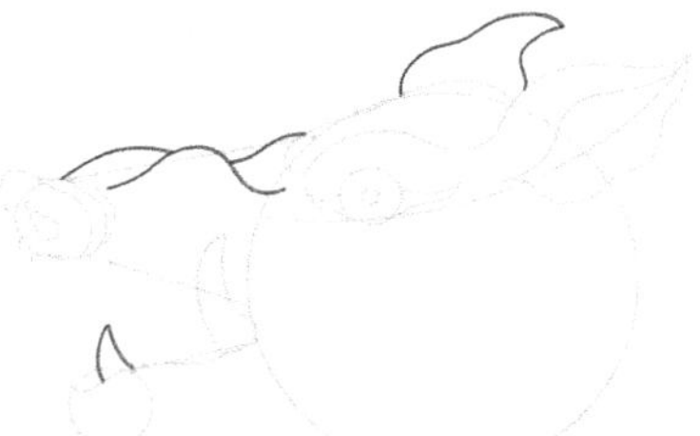

06

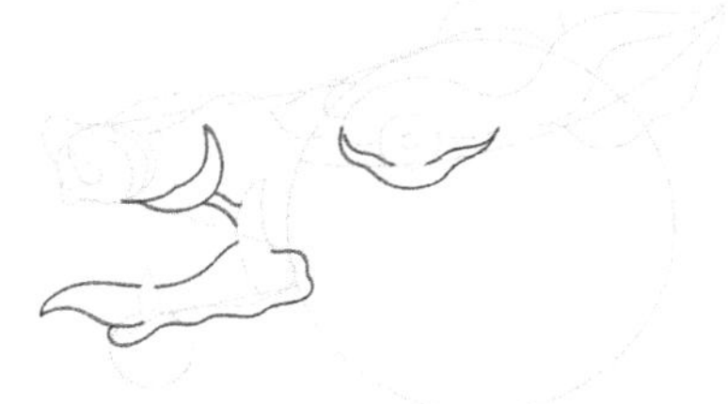

07

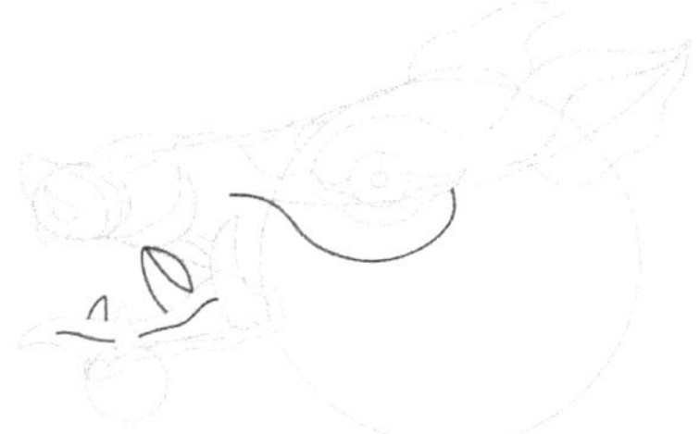

08

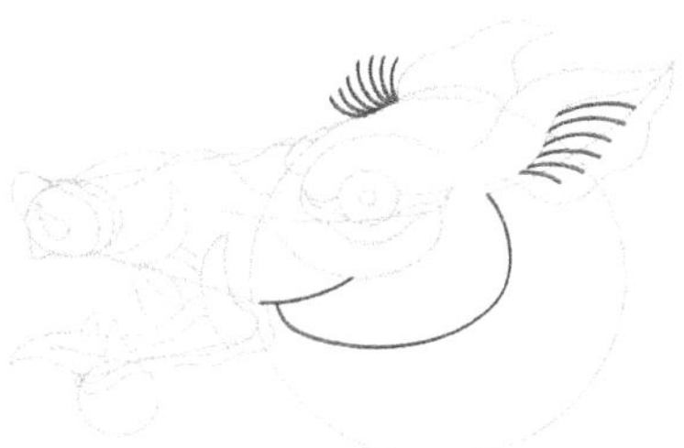

09

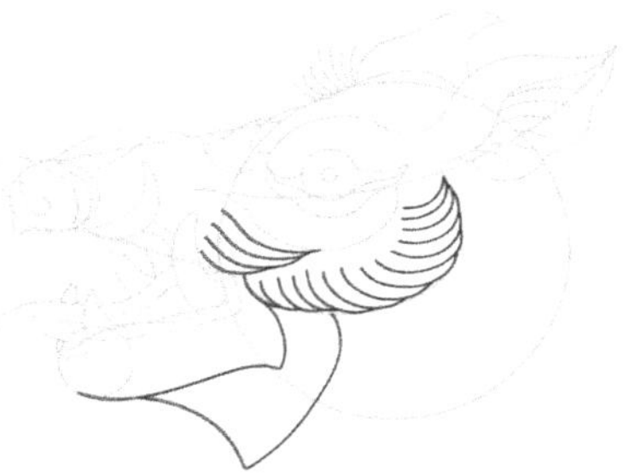

10

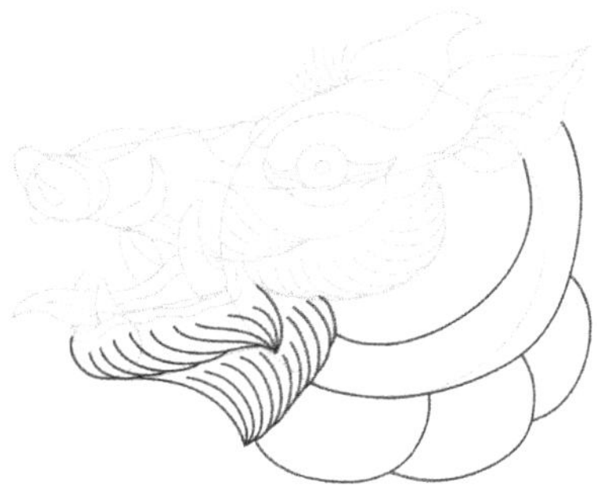

11

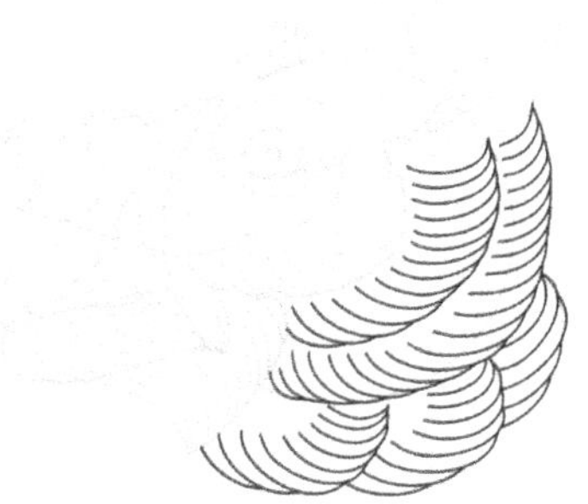

12

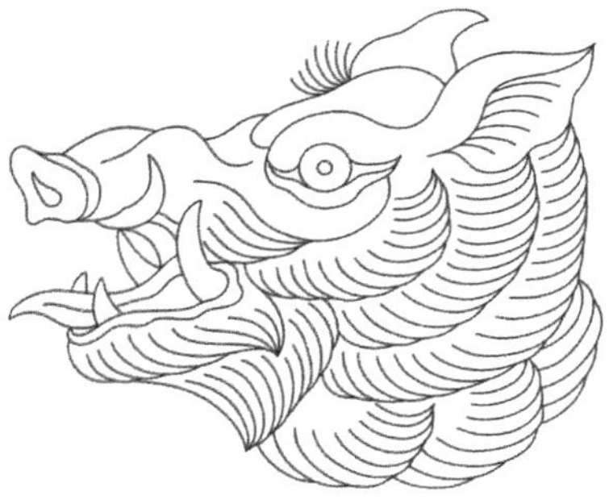

ANIMAL TATTOOS

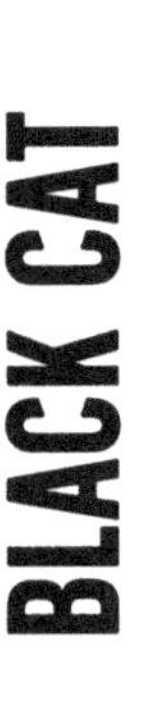

BLACK CAT

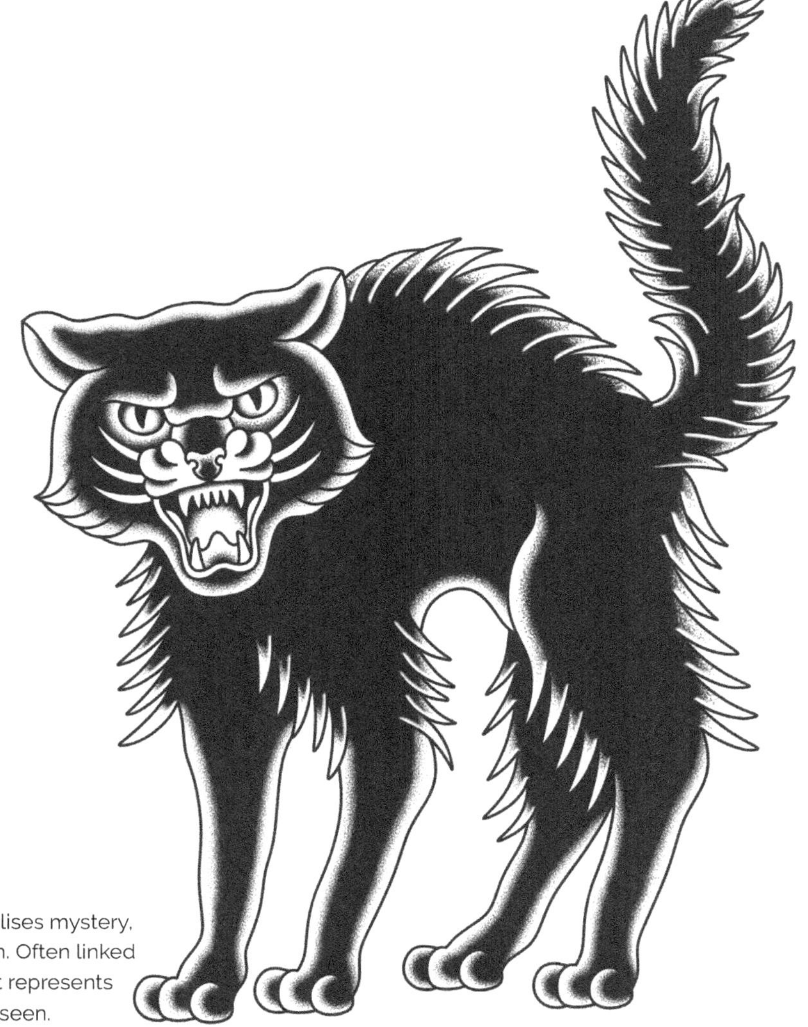

The black cat tattoo symbolises mystery, independence, and intuition. Often linked to magic and superstition, it represents protection, luck, and the unseen.

01

02

03

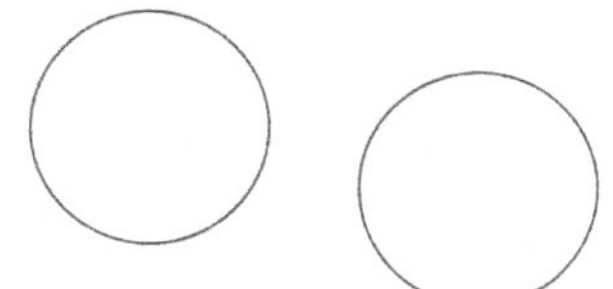

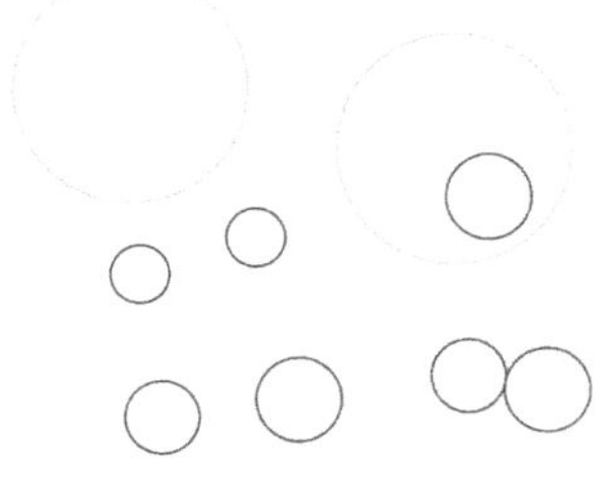

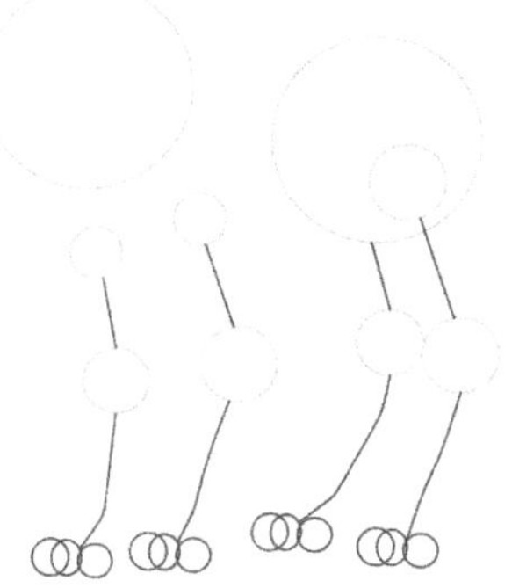

04

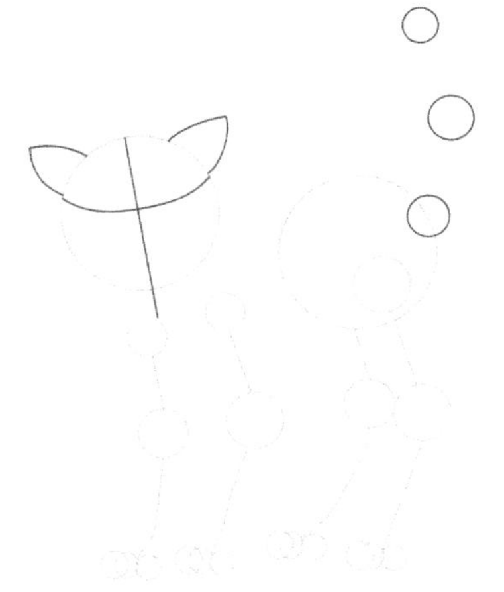

05

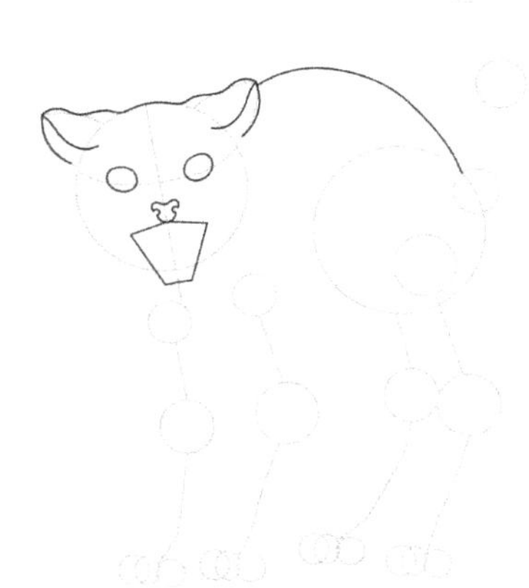

06

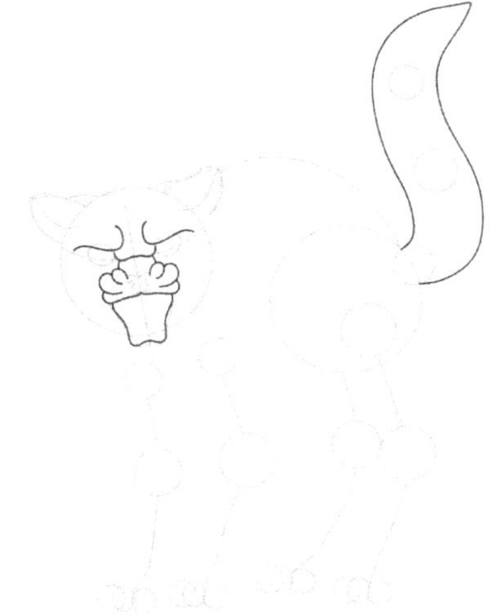

07

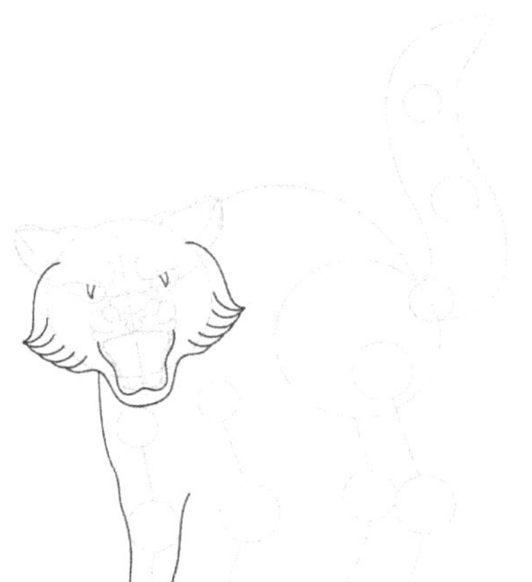

08

09

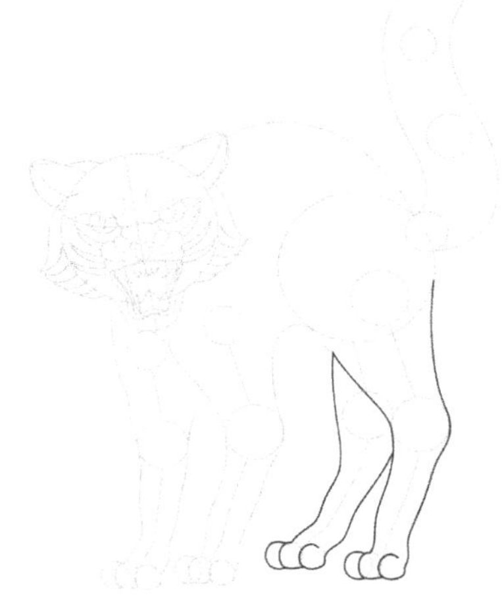

10

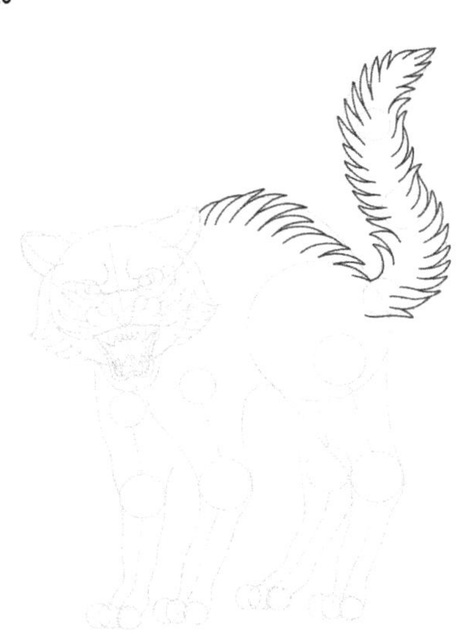

11

12

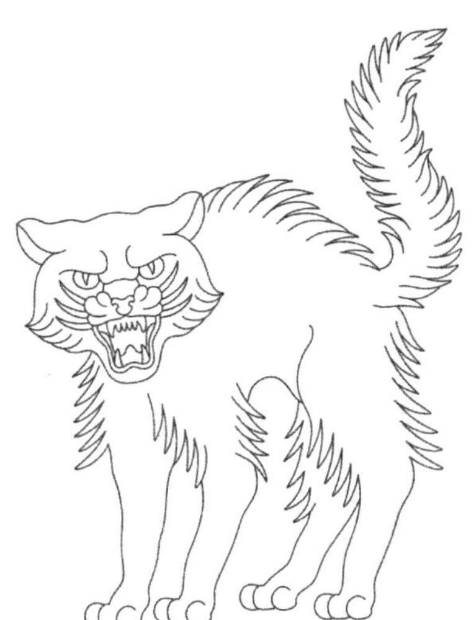

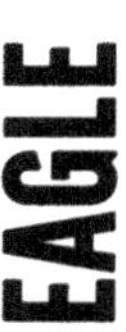

EAGLE

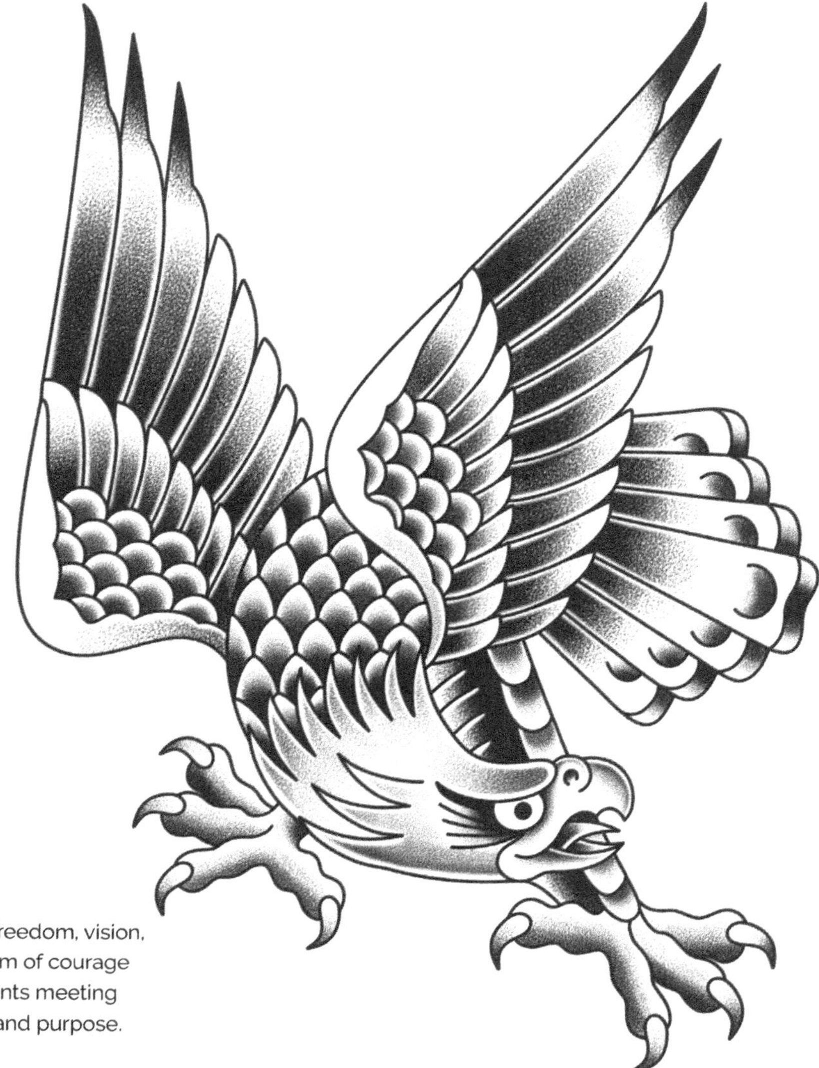

The eagle symbolises freedom, vision, and strength. An emblem of courage and authority, it represents meeting challenges with clarity and purpose.

01 **02** **03**

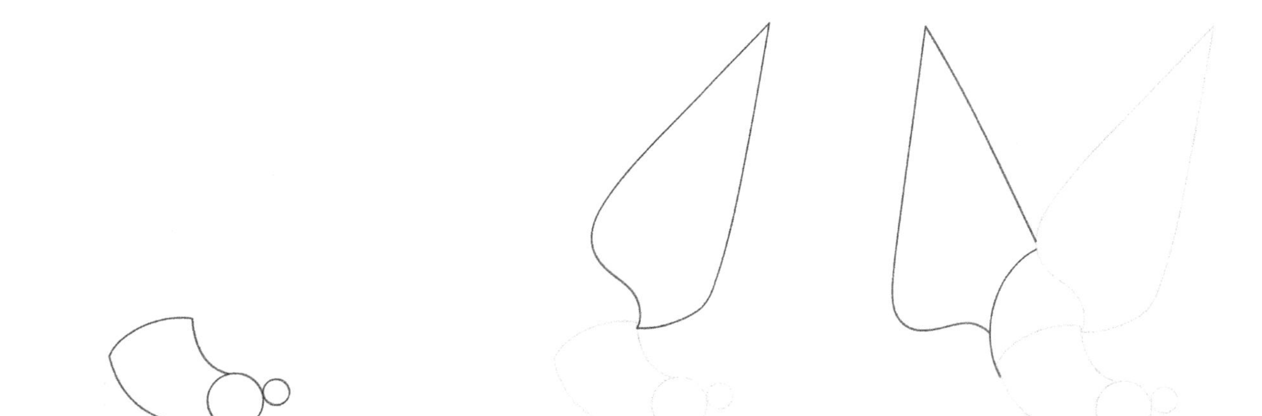

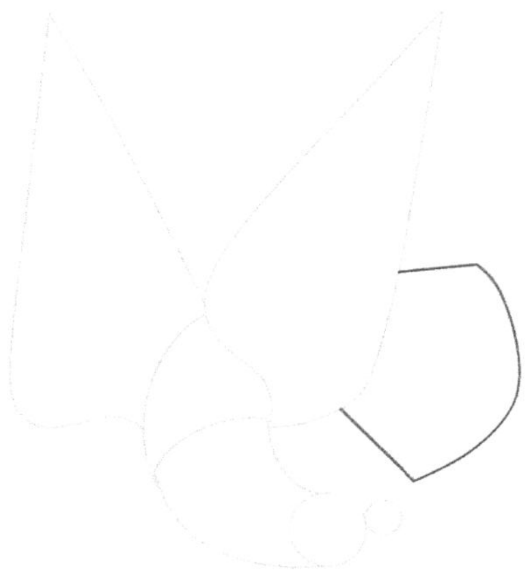

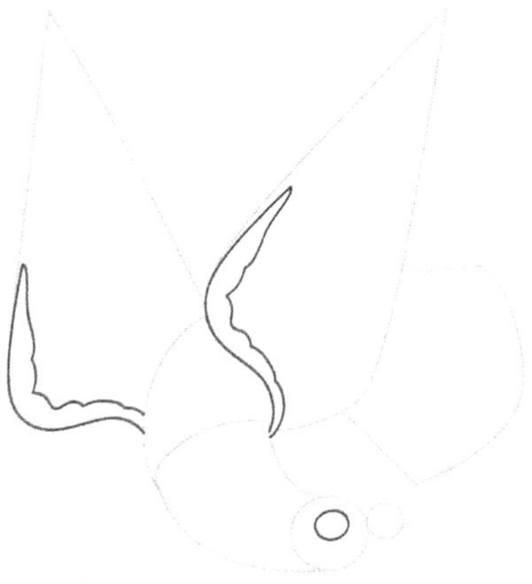

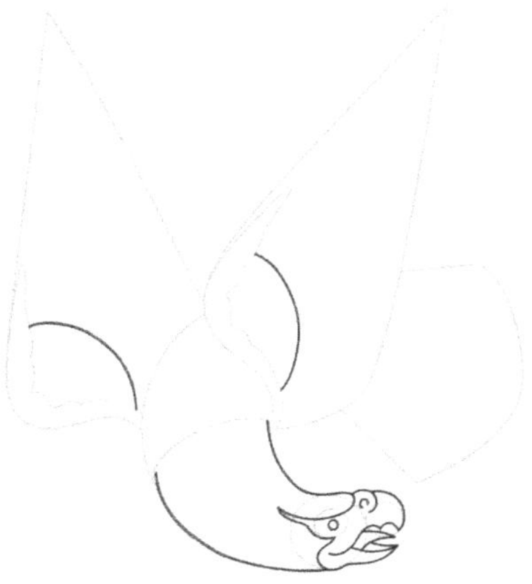

07

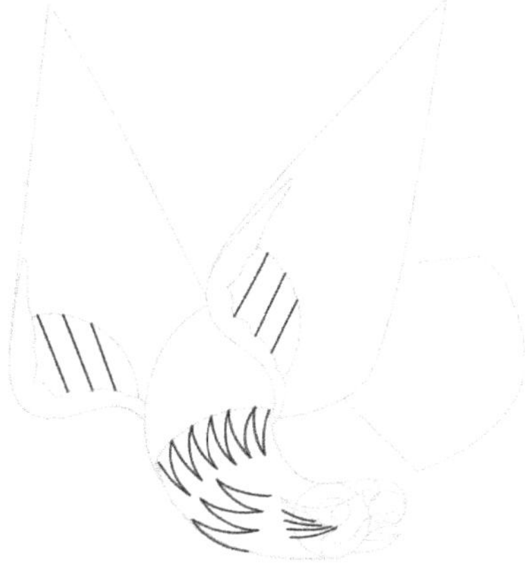

08

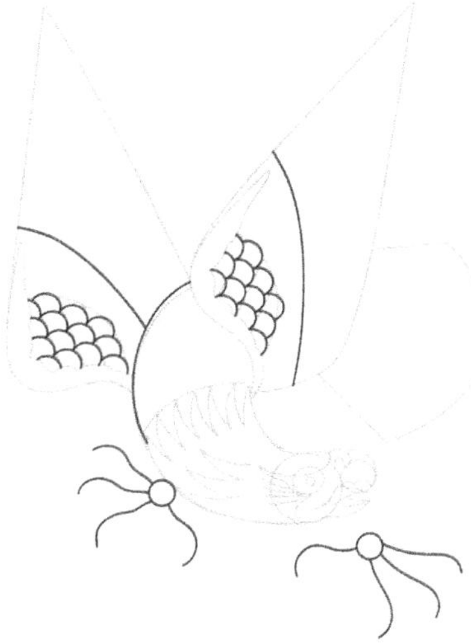

09

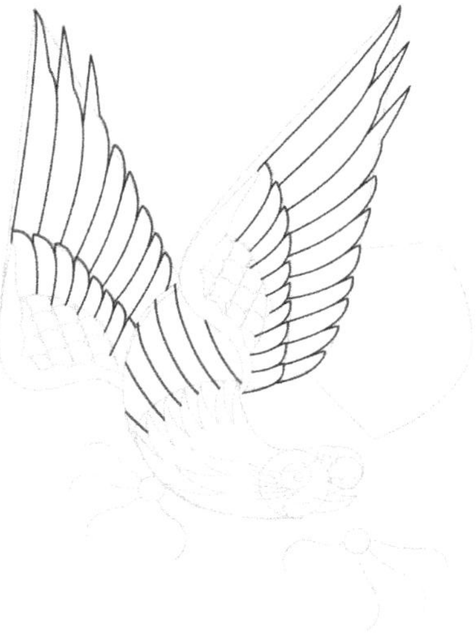

10

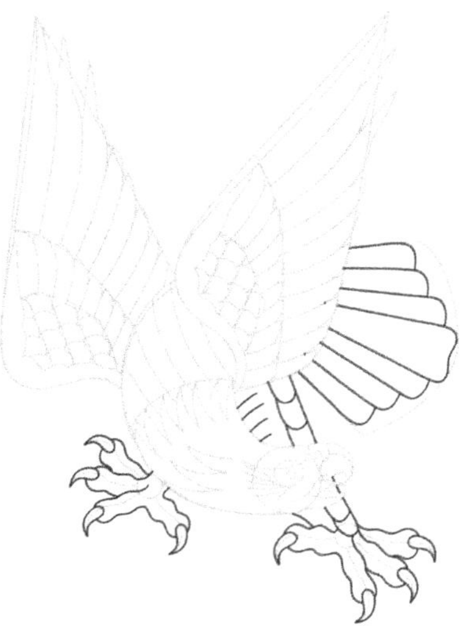

11

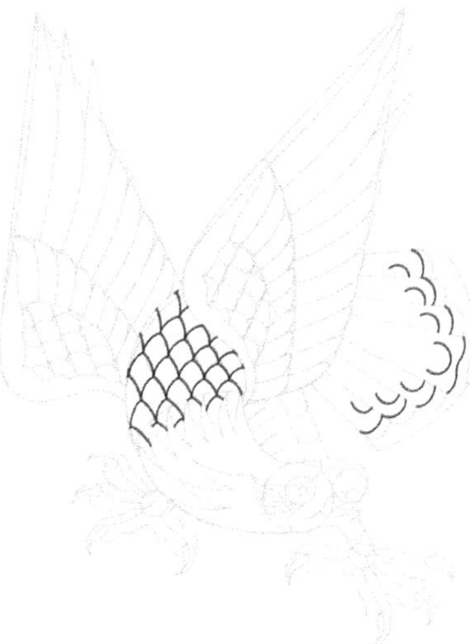

12

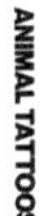

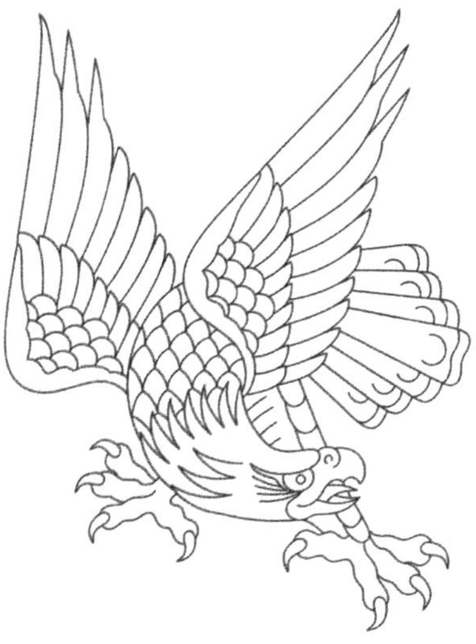

EAGLE VS SNAKE

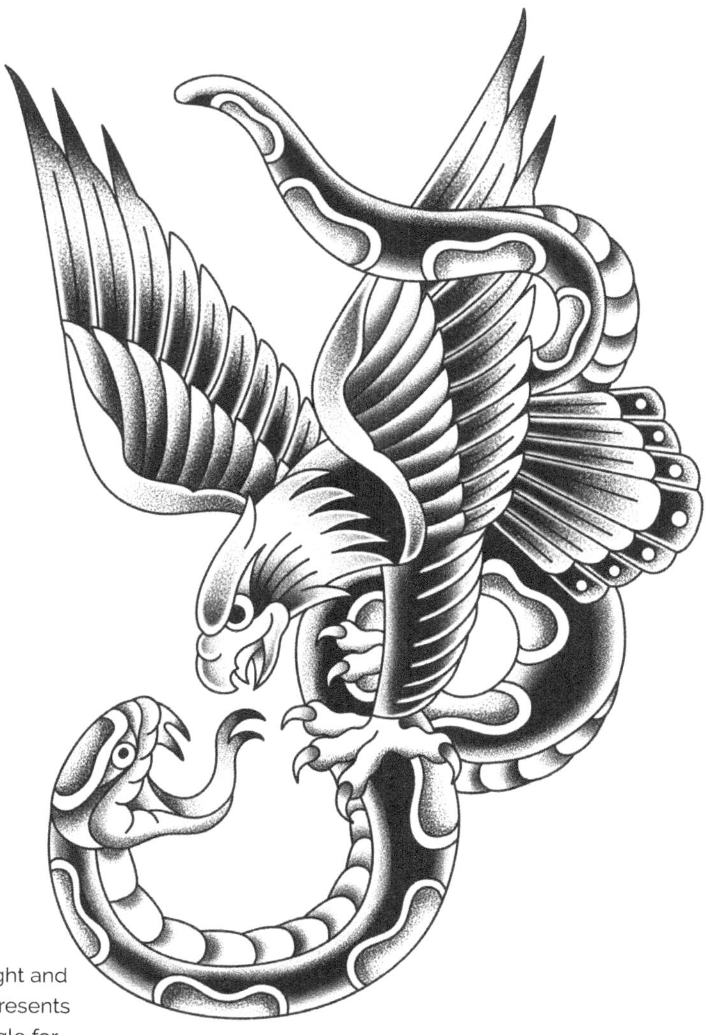

The eagle fighting a snake tattoo symbolises the battle between light and darkness, spirit and instinct. It represents triumph, resilience, and the struggle for higher truth.

01

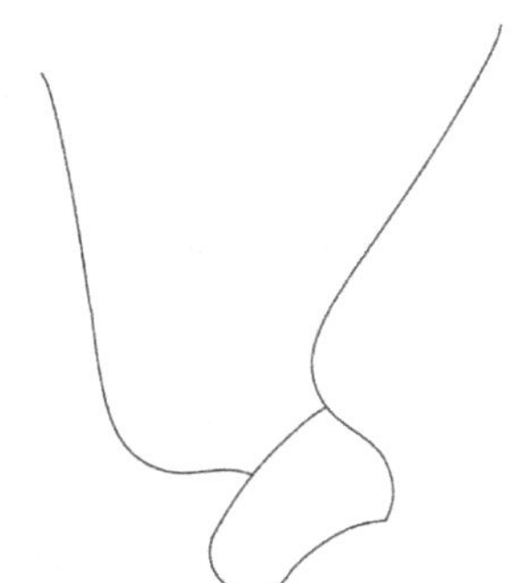

02

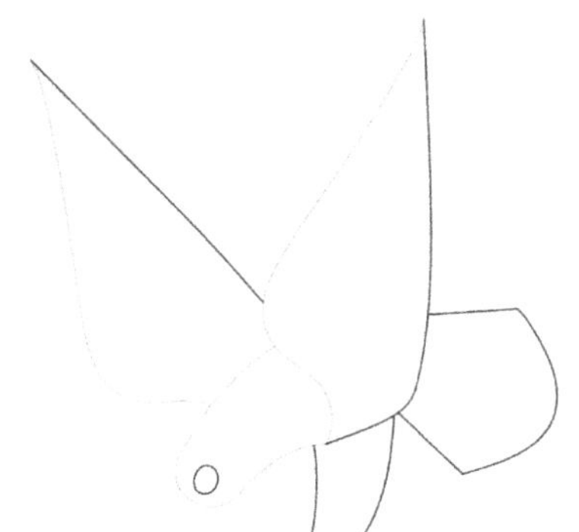

03

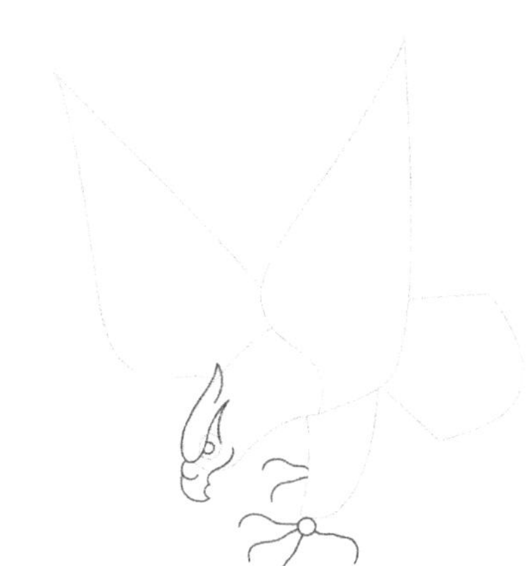

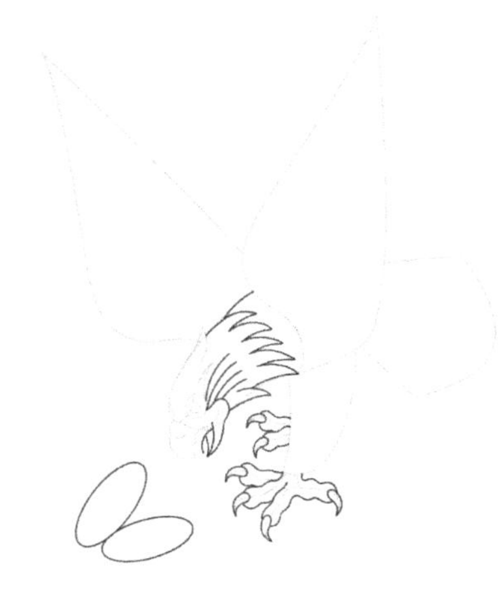

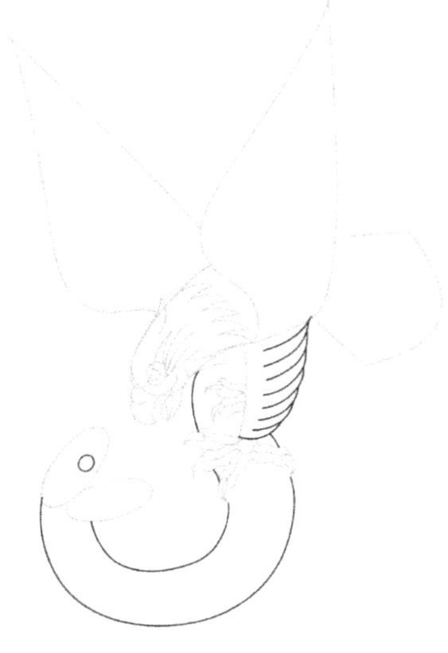

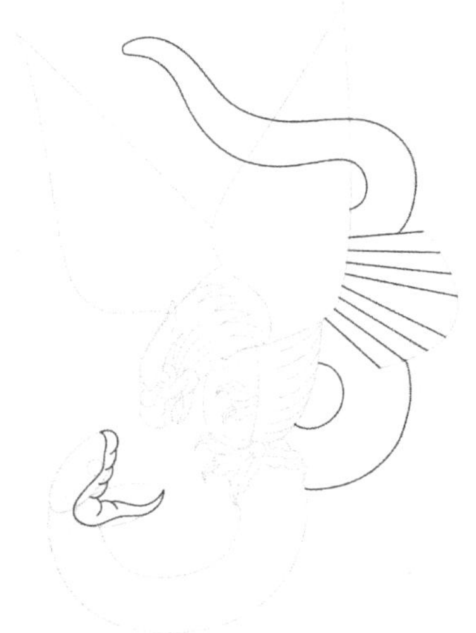

07

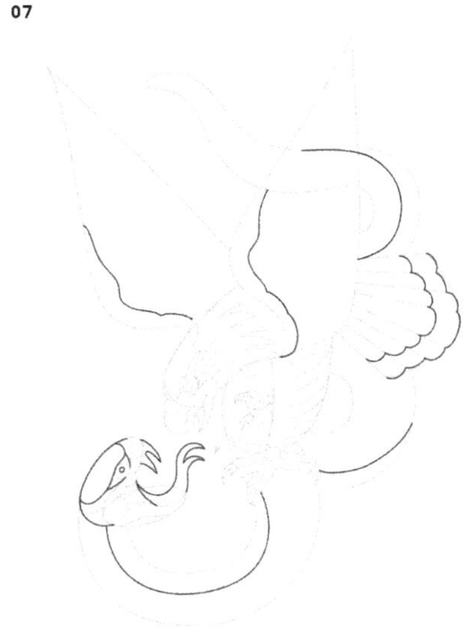

08

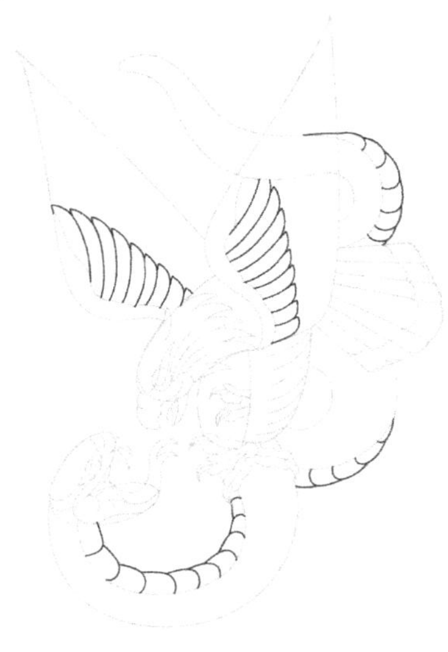

09

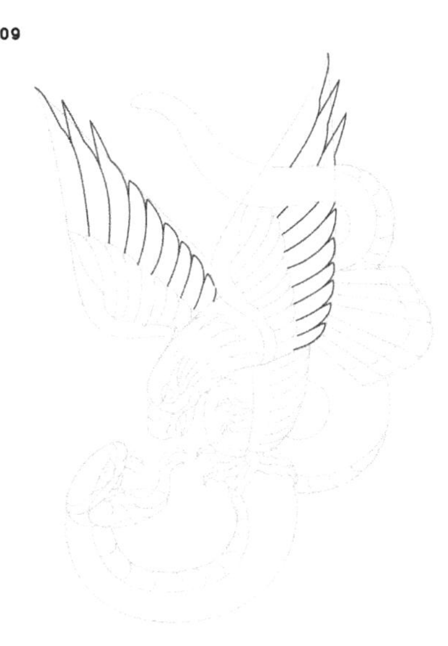

10

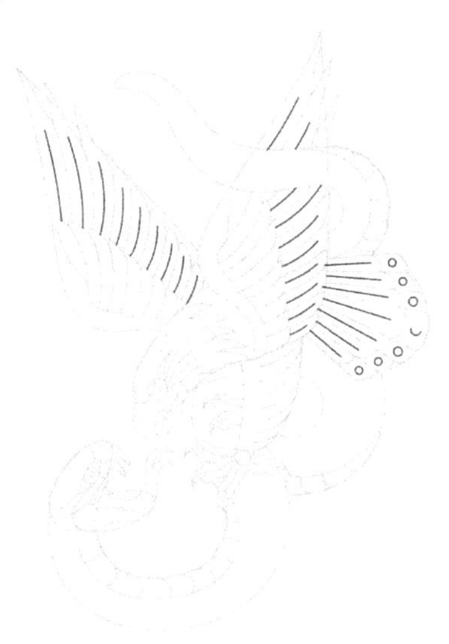

11

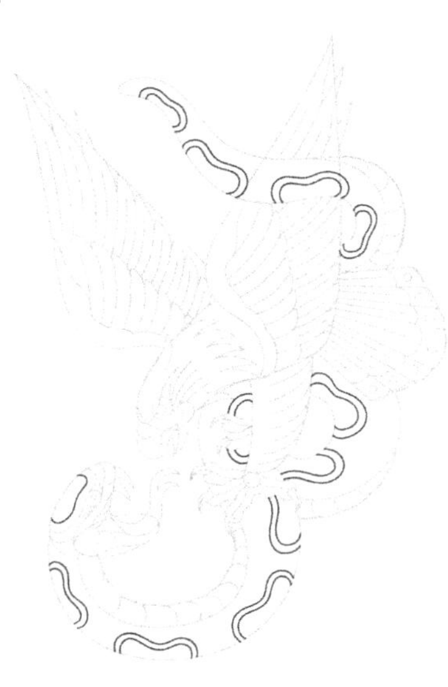

12

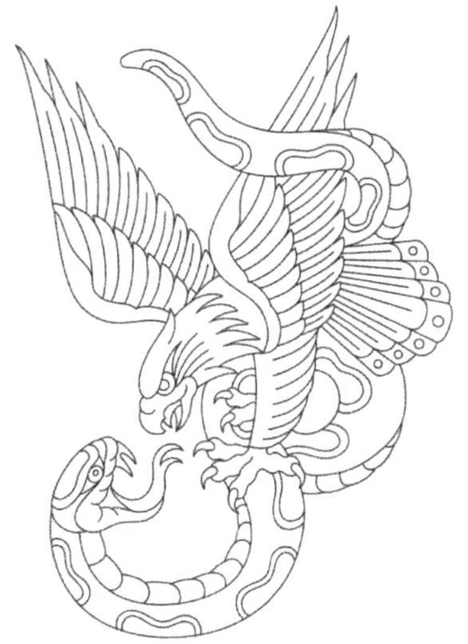

ELEPHANT

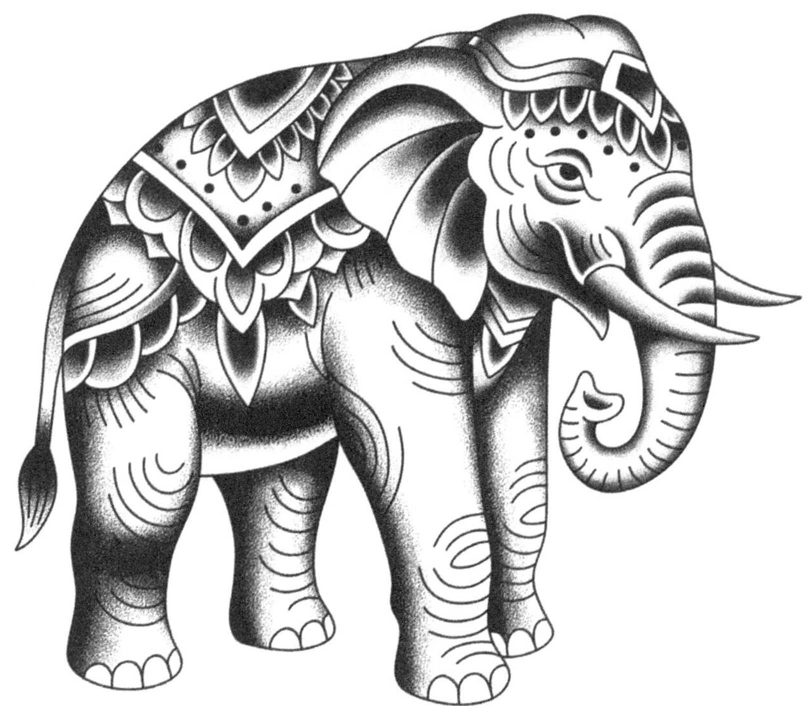

The elephant tattoo symbolises wisdom, strength, and loyalty. Revered for memory and patience, it represents protection, family, and spiritual power.

01

02

03

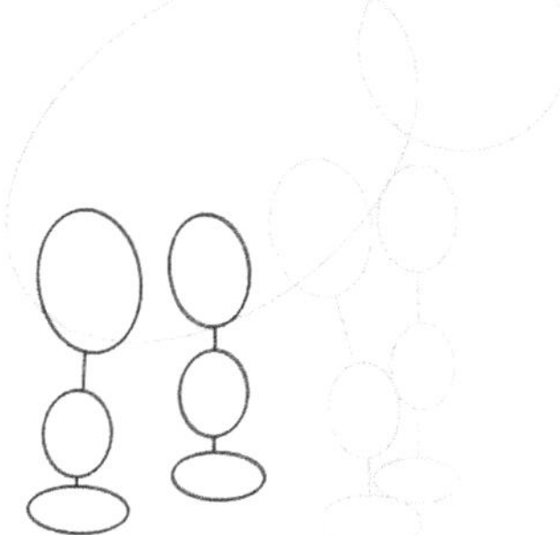

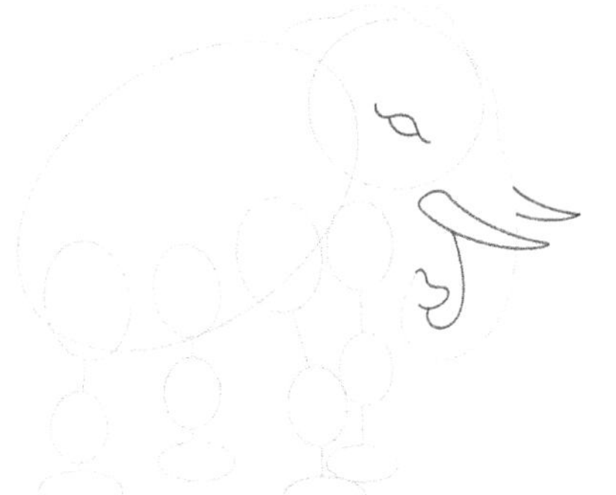

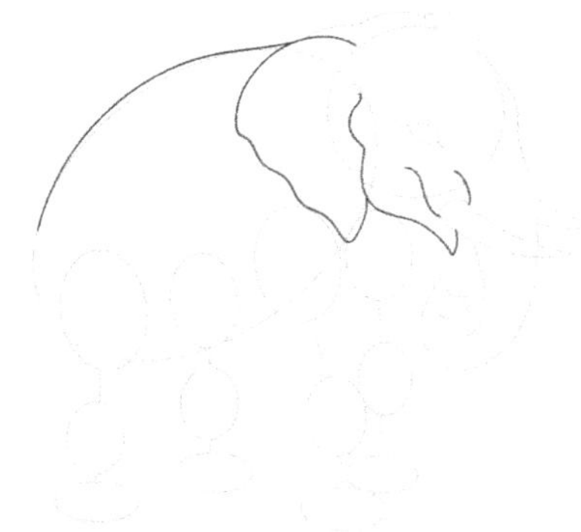

07

08

09

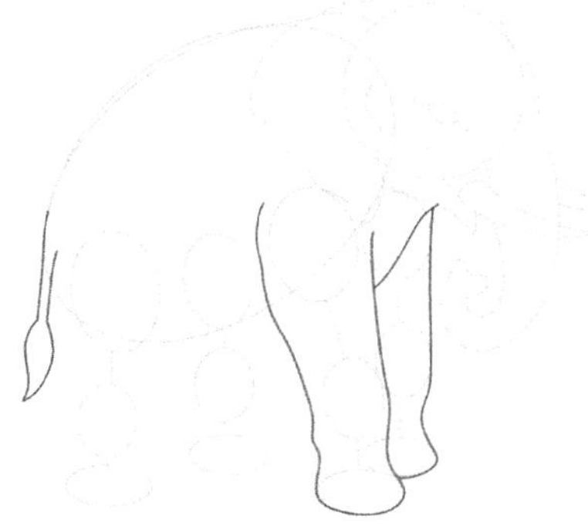

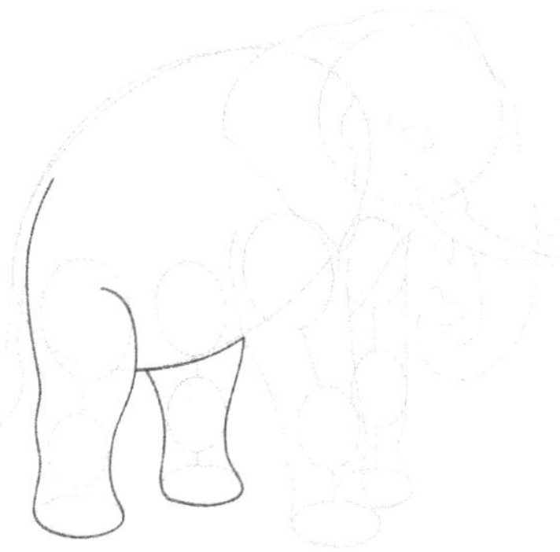

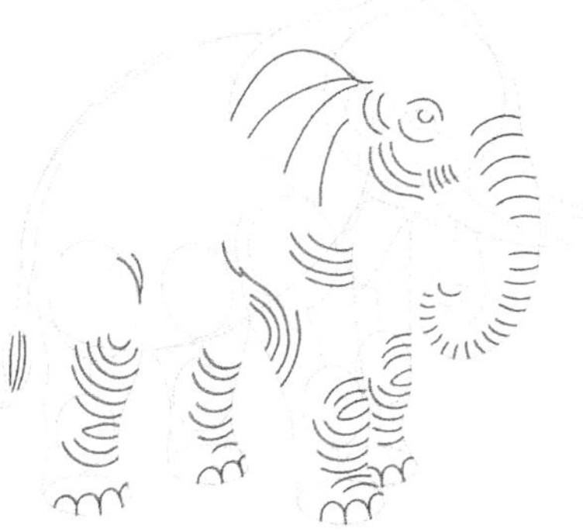

10

11

12

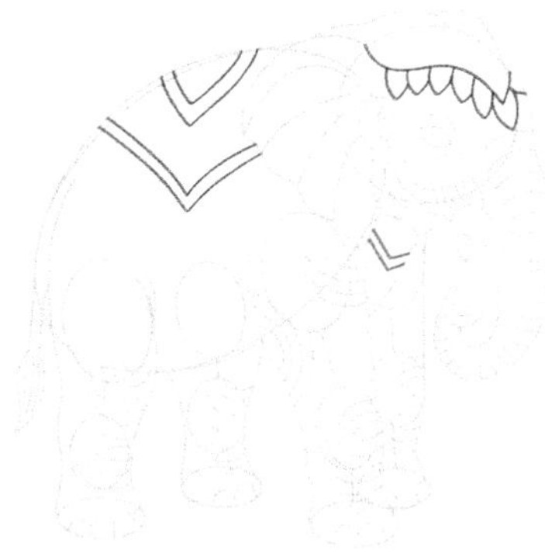

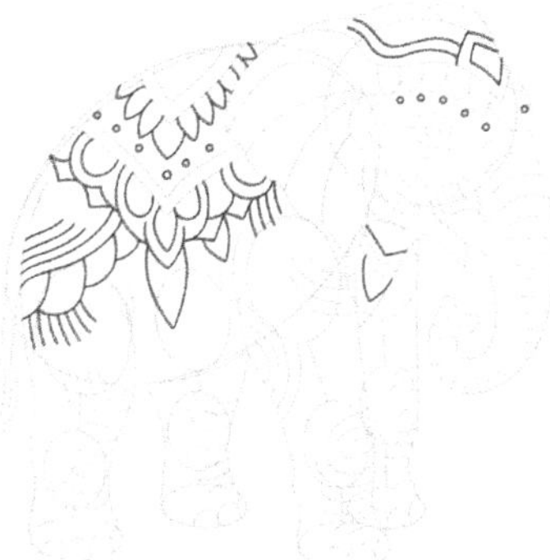

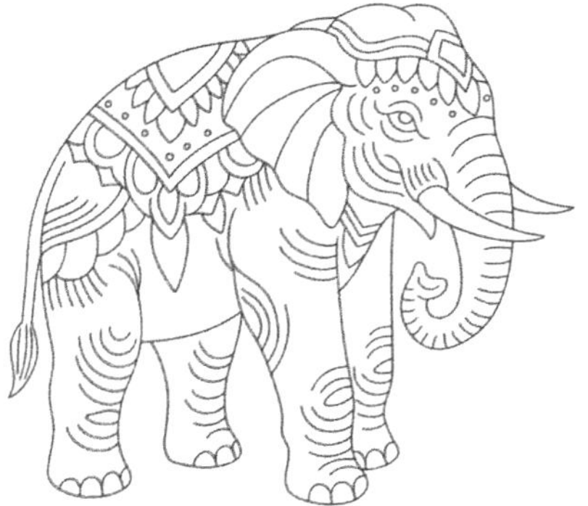

FOX

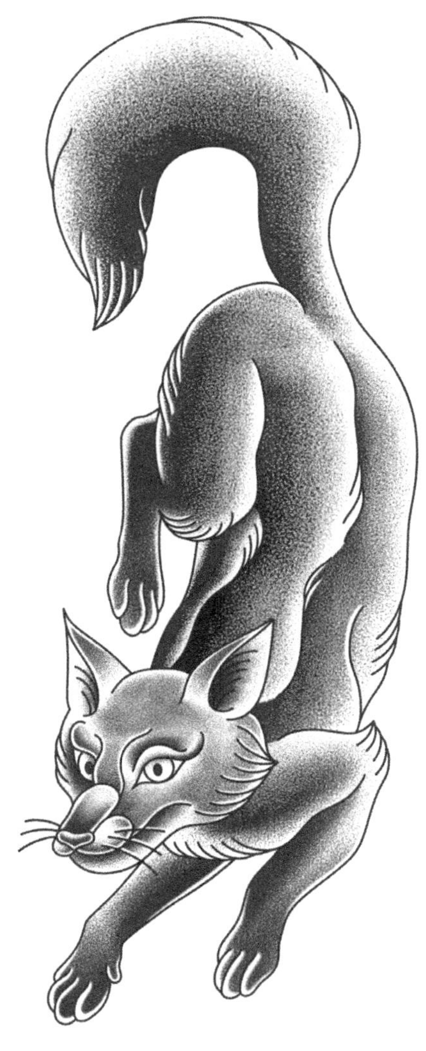

The fox tattoo symbolises cunning,
adaptability, and intelligence.
It represents quick thinking,
resourcefulness, and the ability to
navigate life's challenges with wit.

01   **02**   **03**

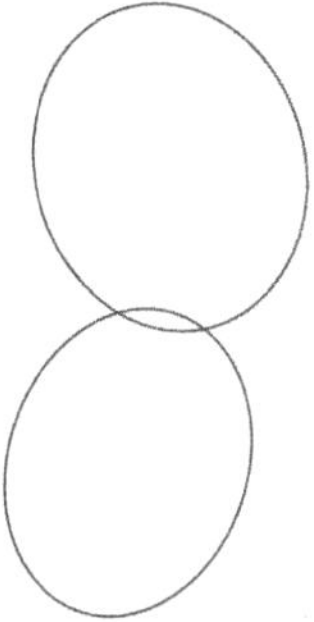

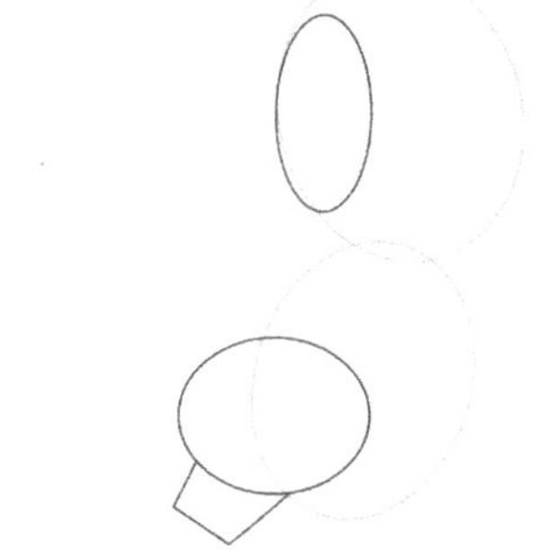

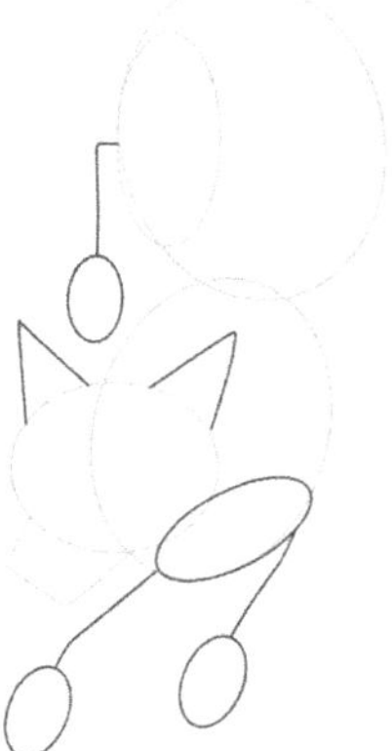

04

05

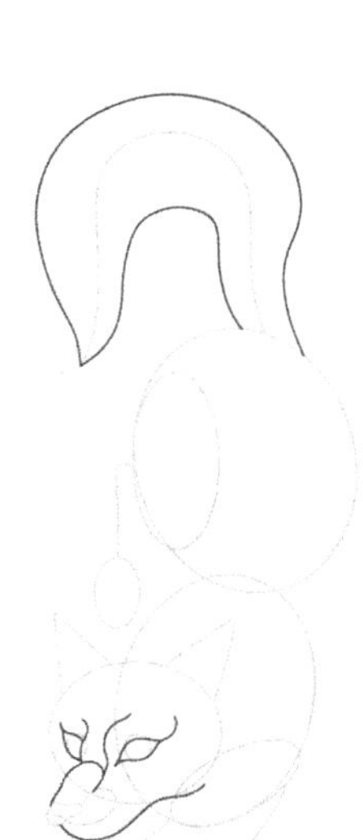

06

07

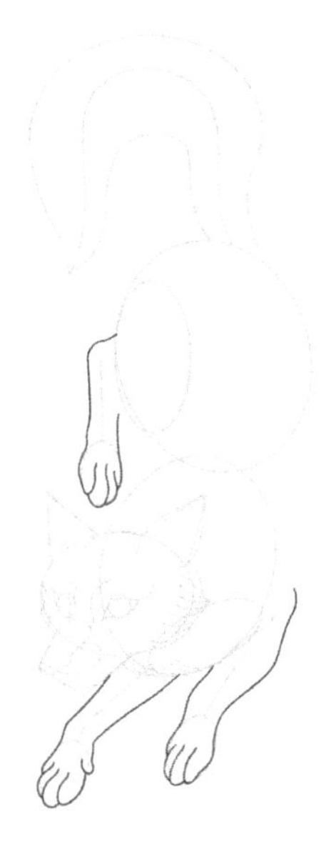

08

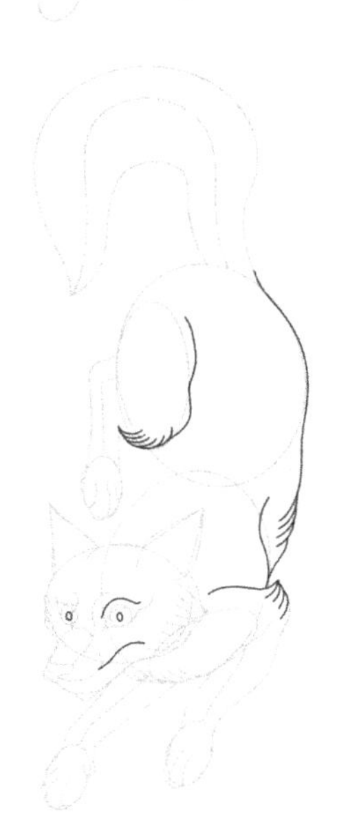

09

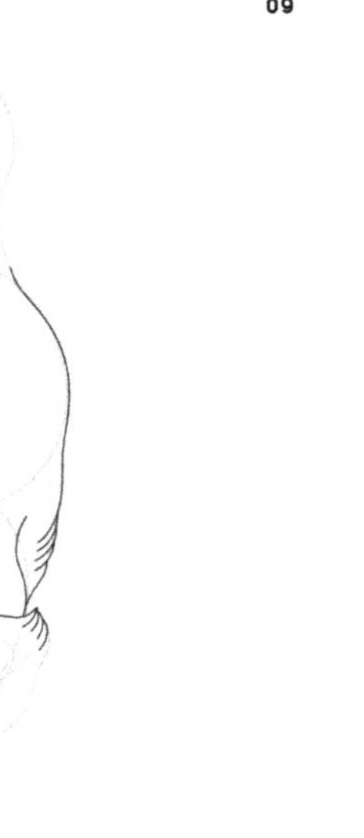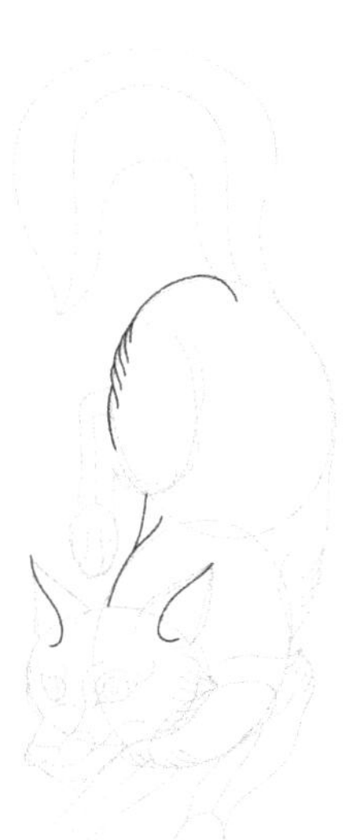

10

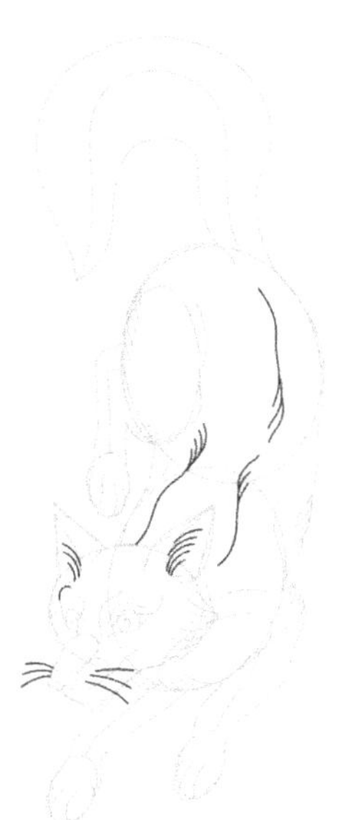

11

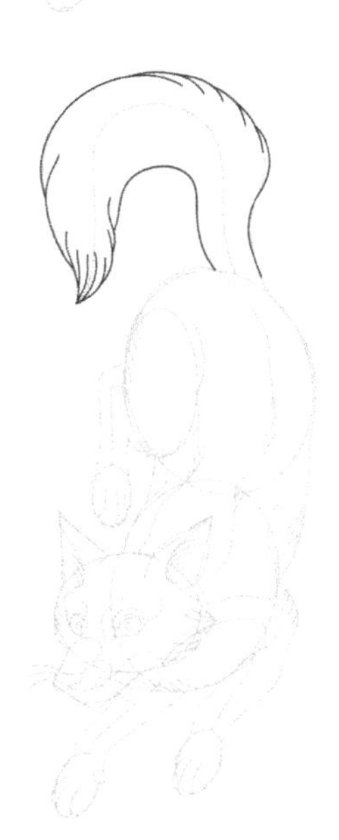

12

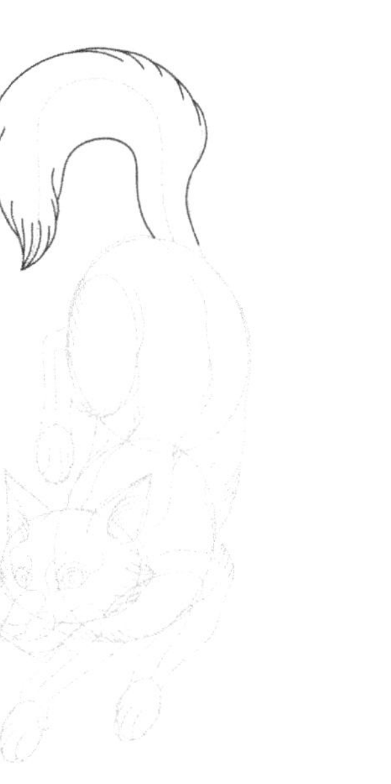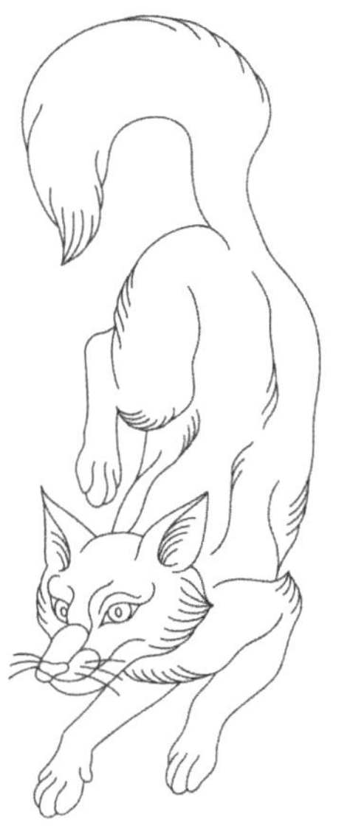

GOAT

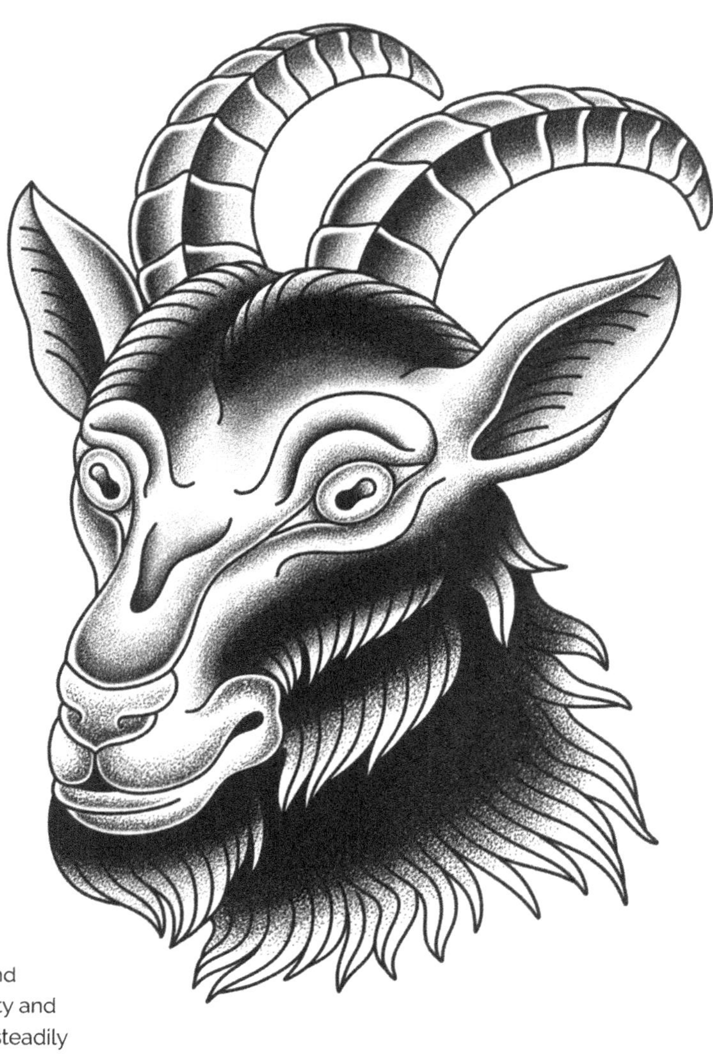

The goat tattoo symbolises independence, determination, and resilience. Often linked to curiosity and ambition, it represents climbing steadily toward one's goals.

01

02

03

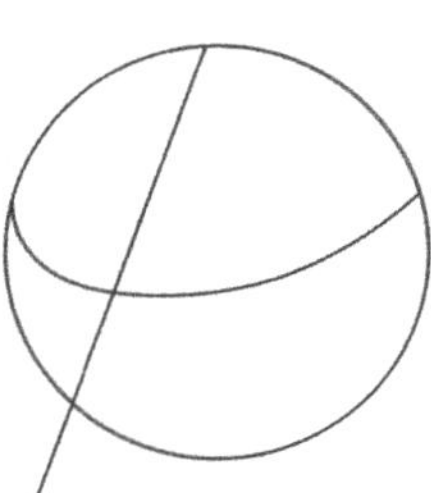

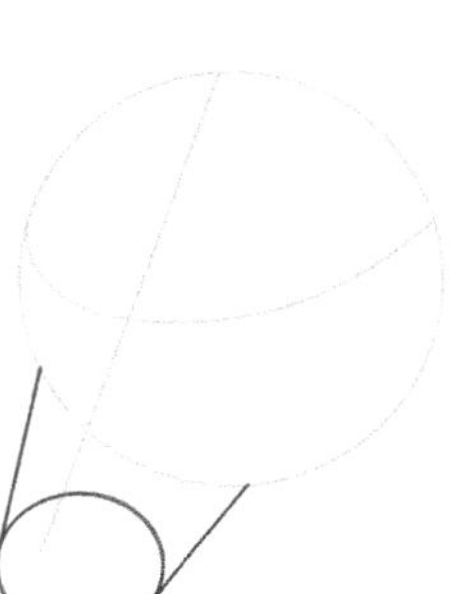

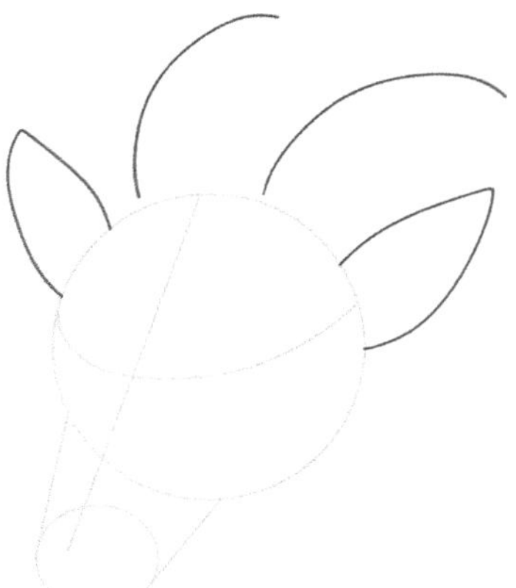

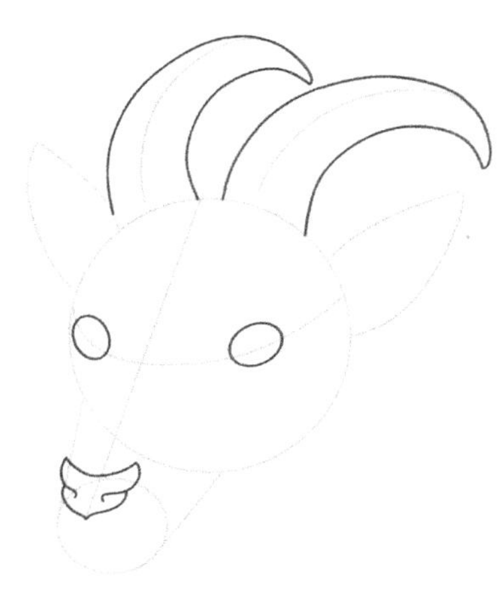
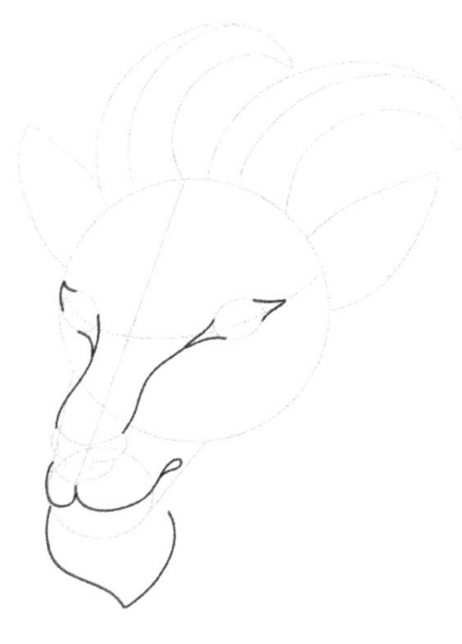
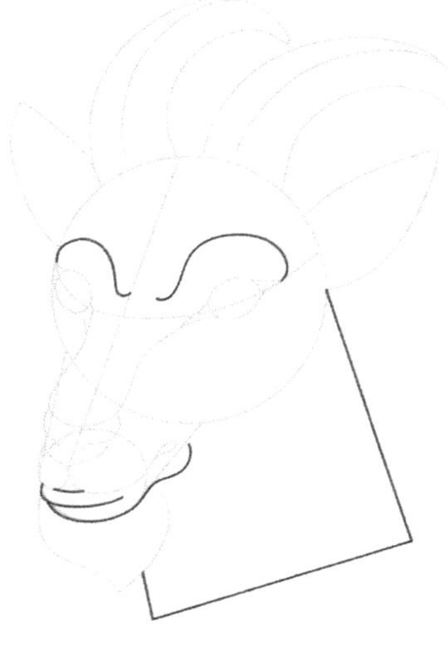

07

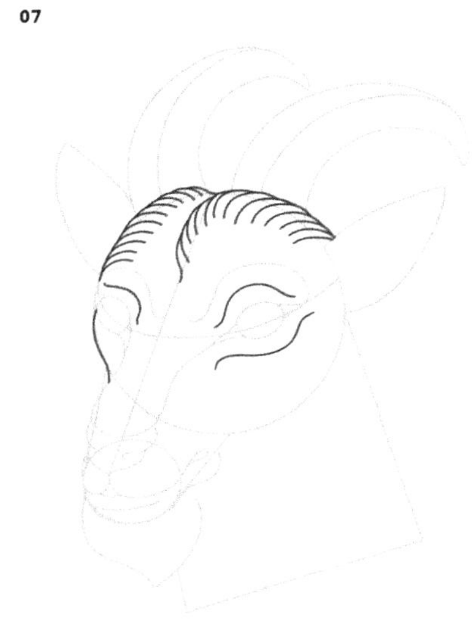

08

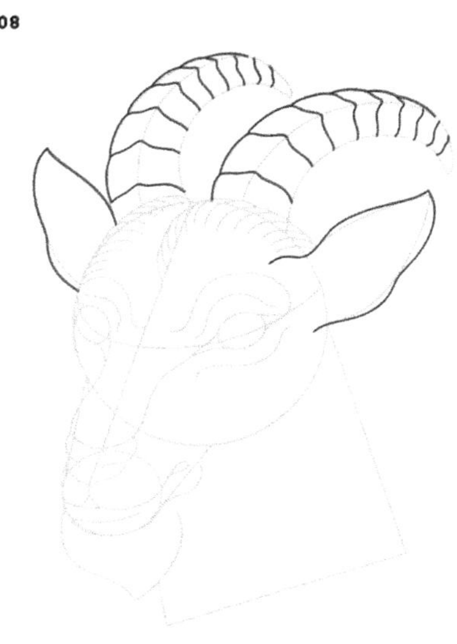

09

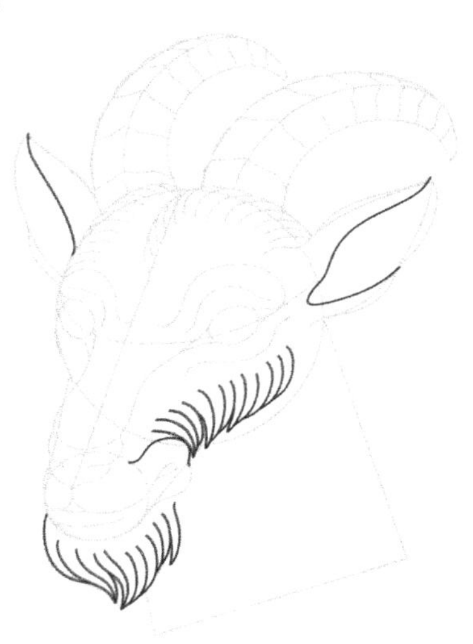

10

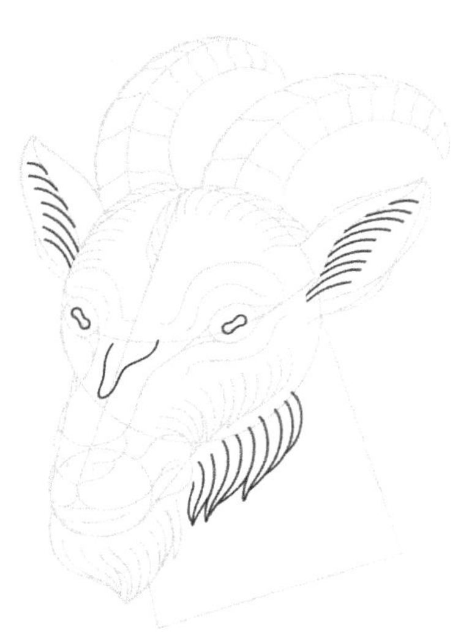

11

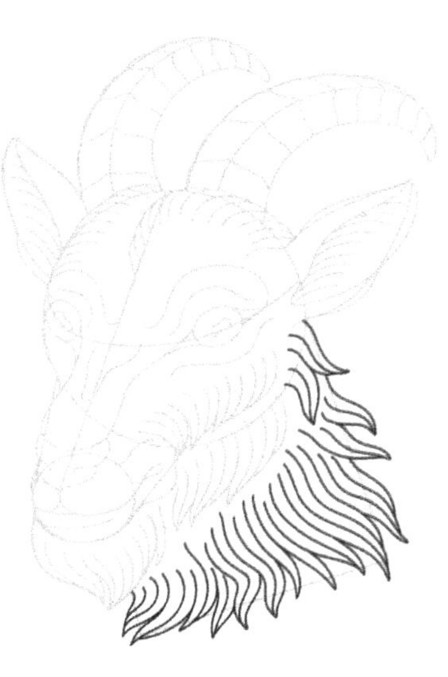

12

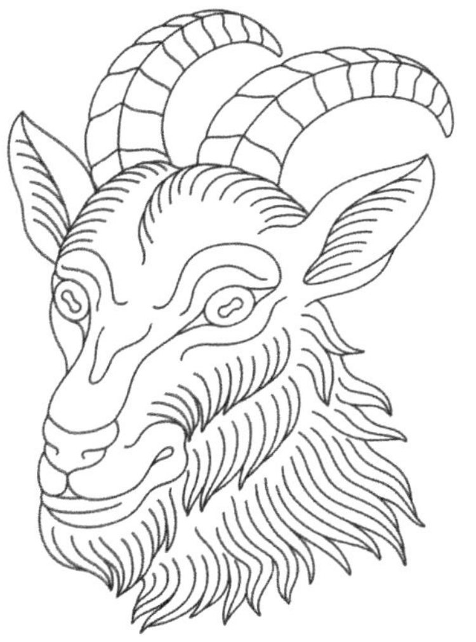

TOAD PLAYING THE LUTE

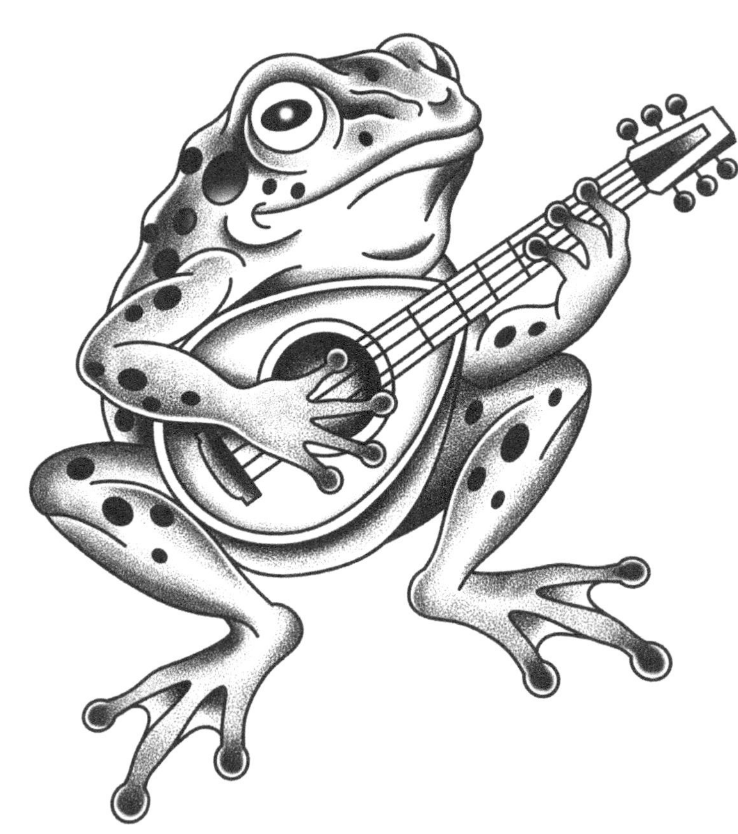

The toad playing the lute tattoo symbolises whimsy, transformation, and hidden wisdom. It blends folklore and humour, representing joy, creativity, and the unexpected.

01

02

03

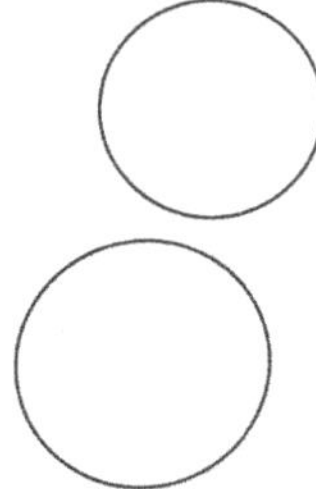

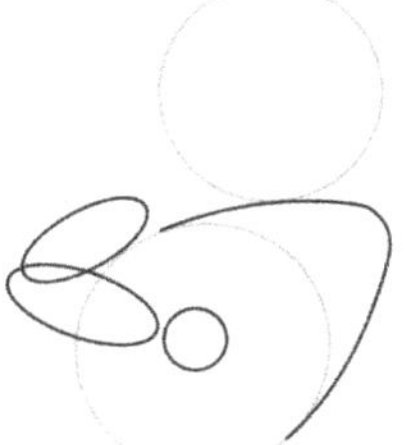

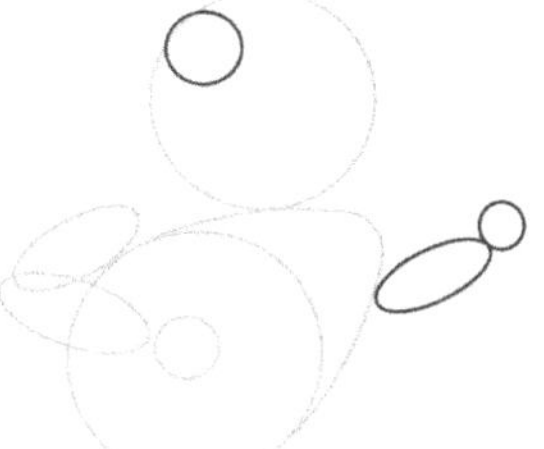

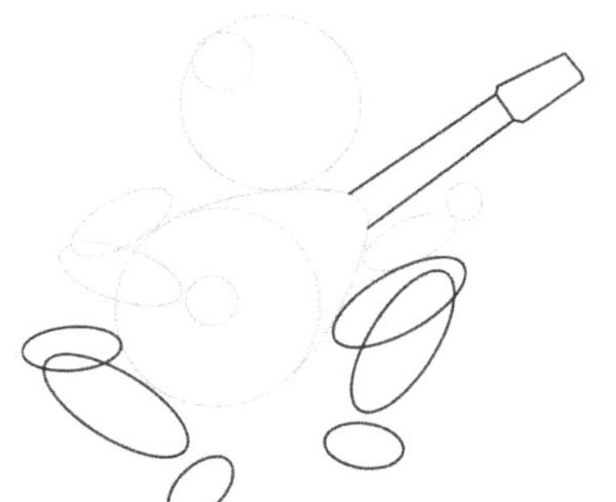

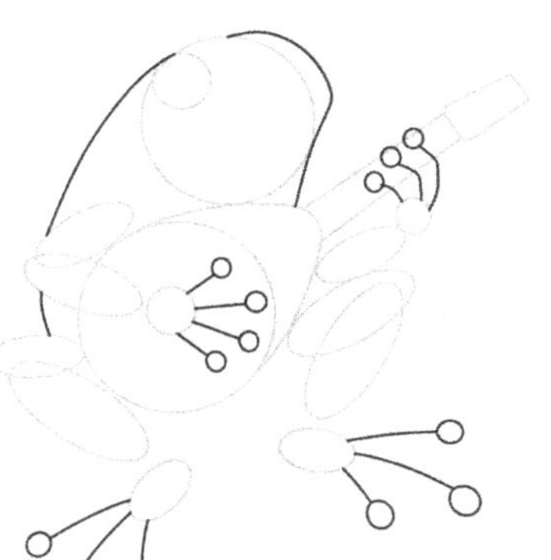

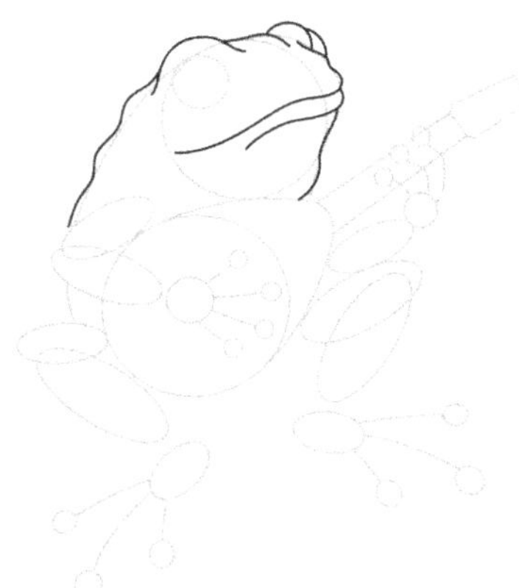

07

08

09

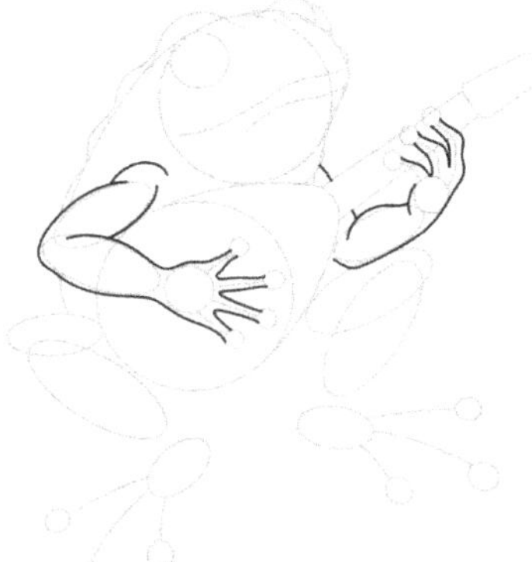

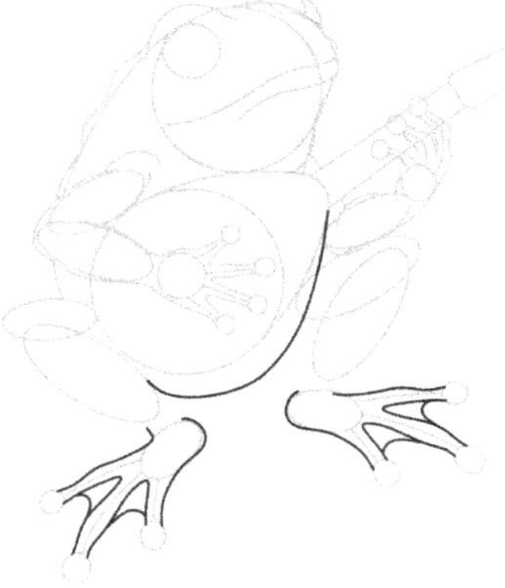

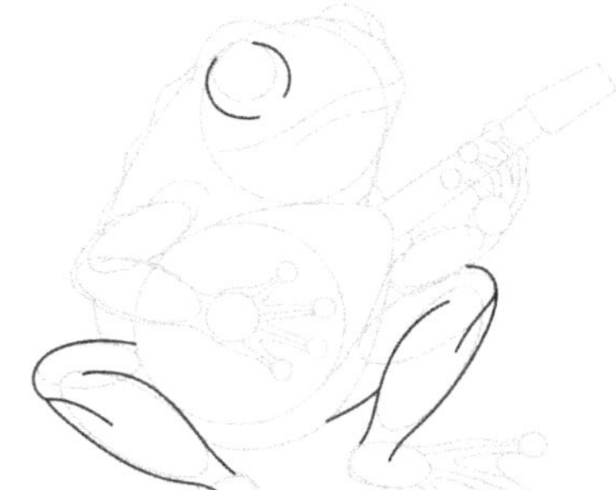

10

11

12

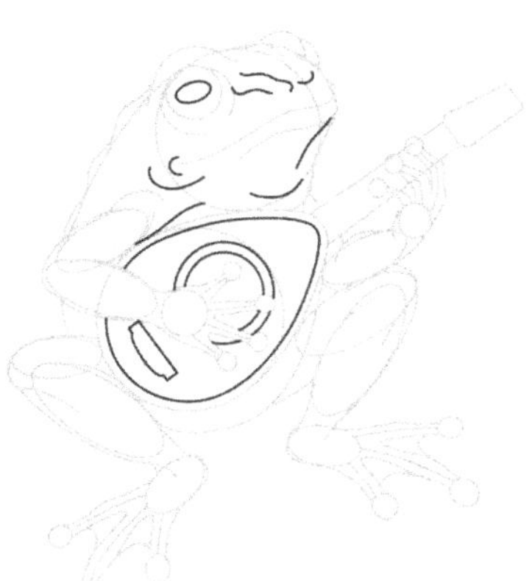

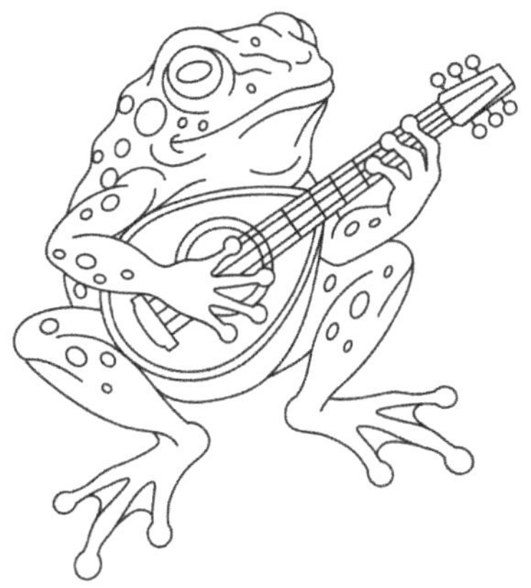

OWL

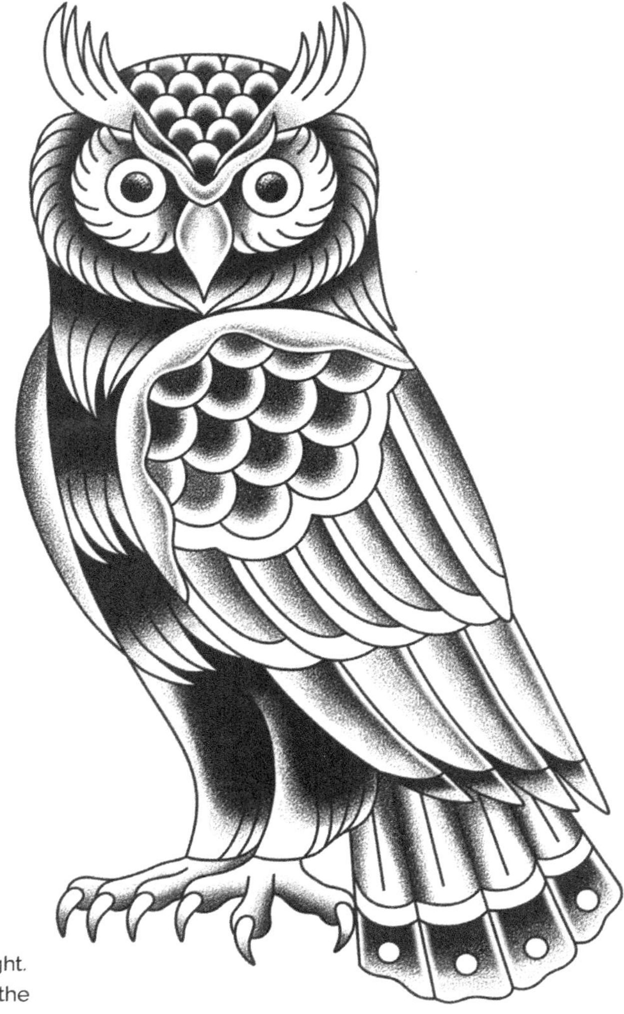

The owl tattoo symbolises wisdom, intuition, and the mysteries of the night. It represents insight, protection, and the ability to see what others cannot.

01

02

03

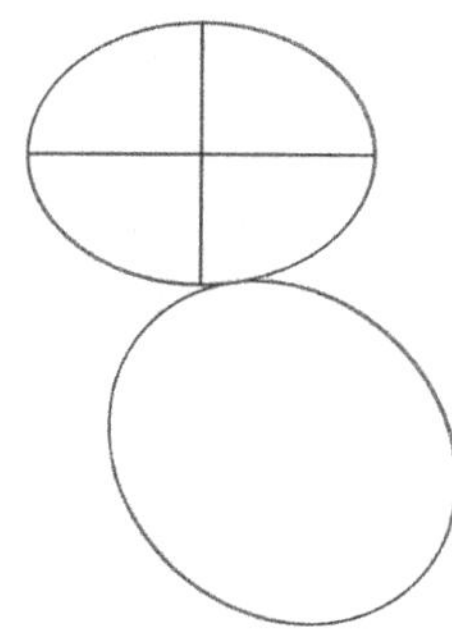

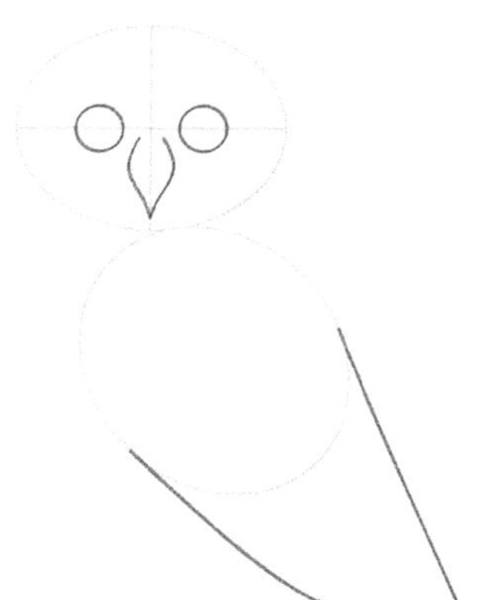

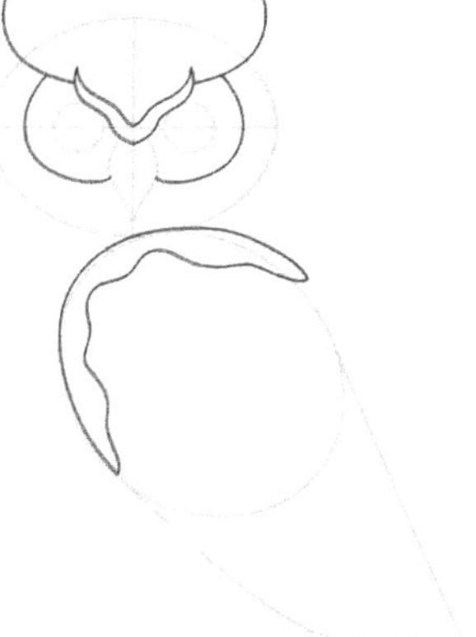

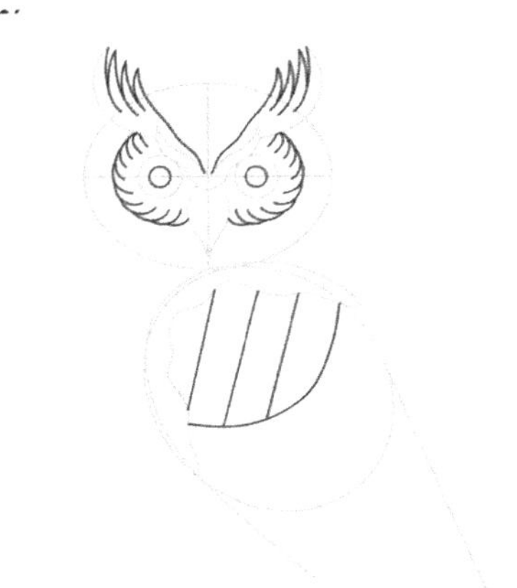

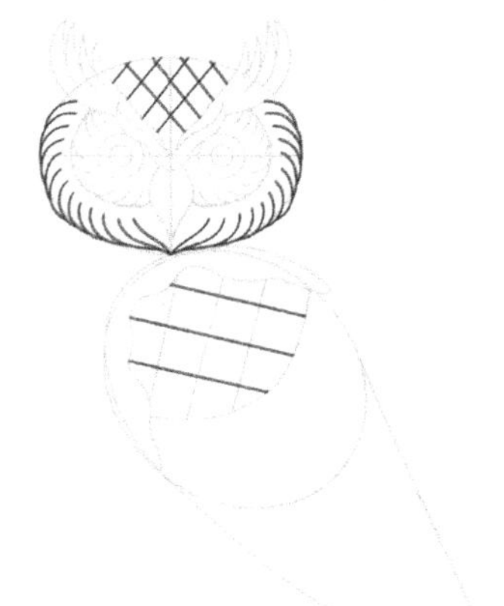

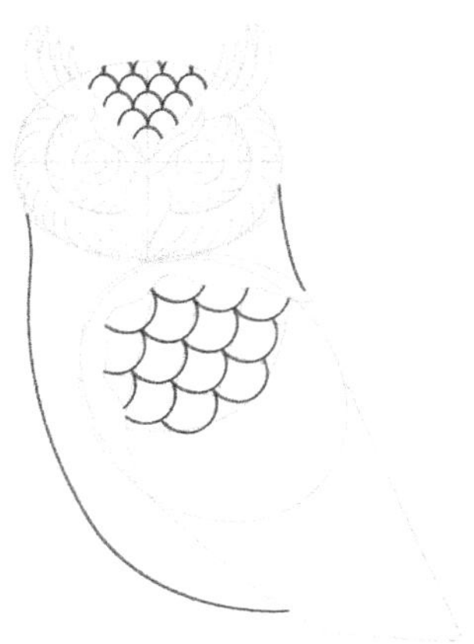

07

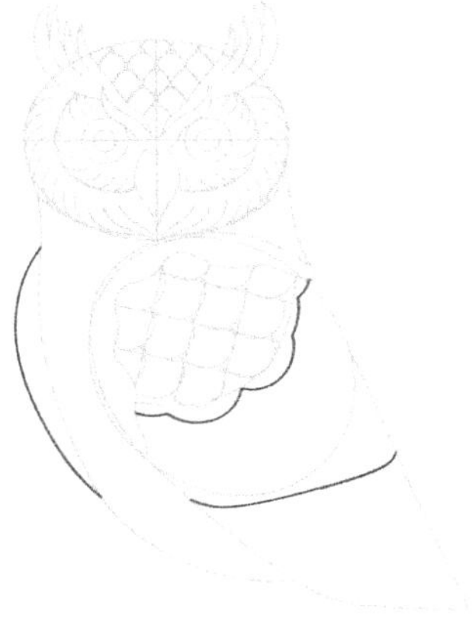

08

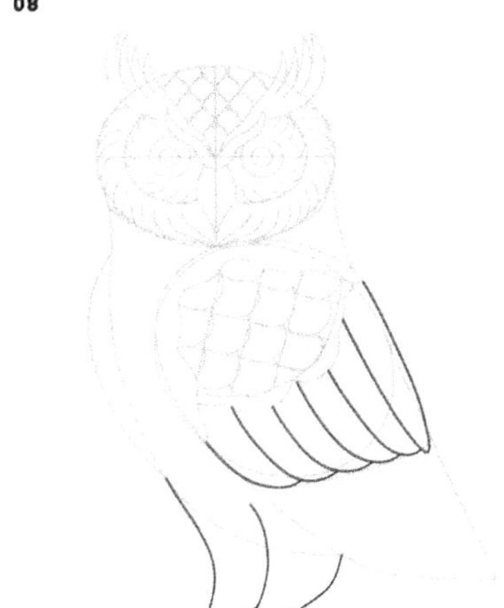

09

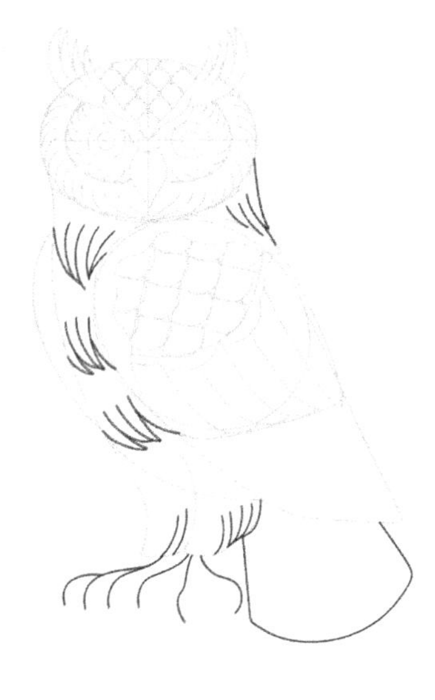

10

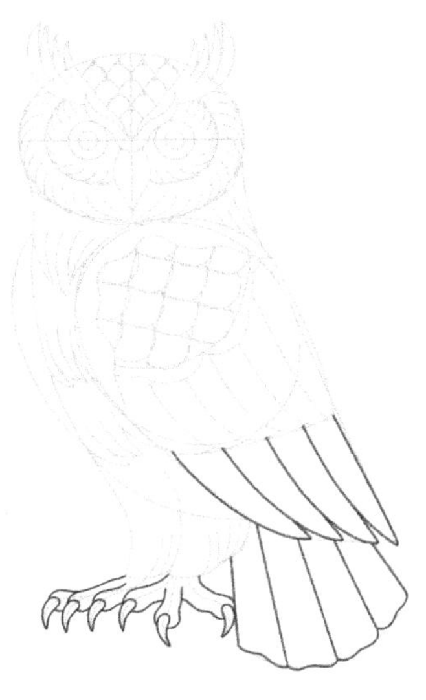

11

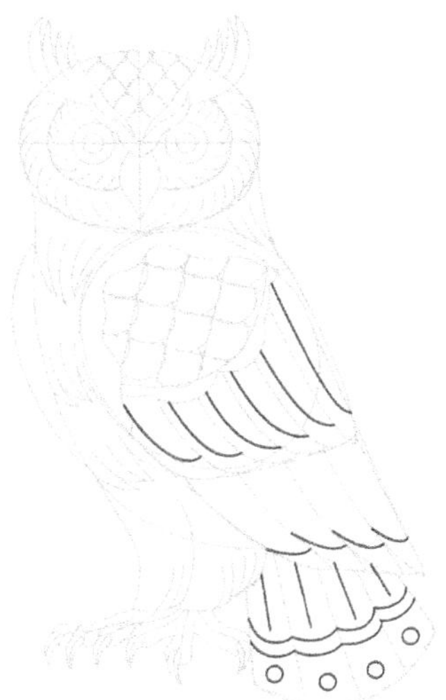

12

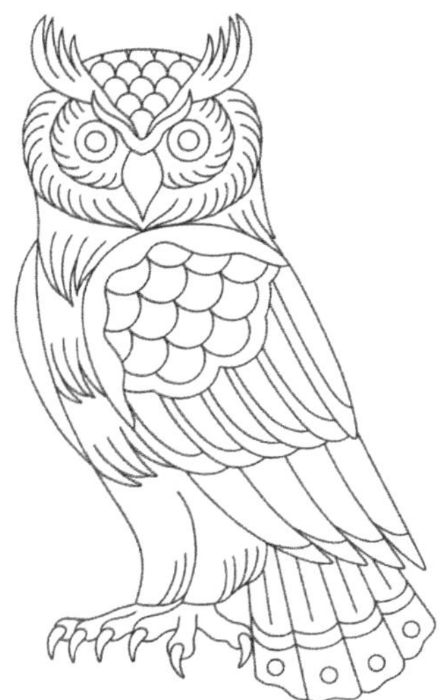

HORSE

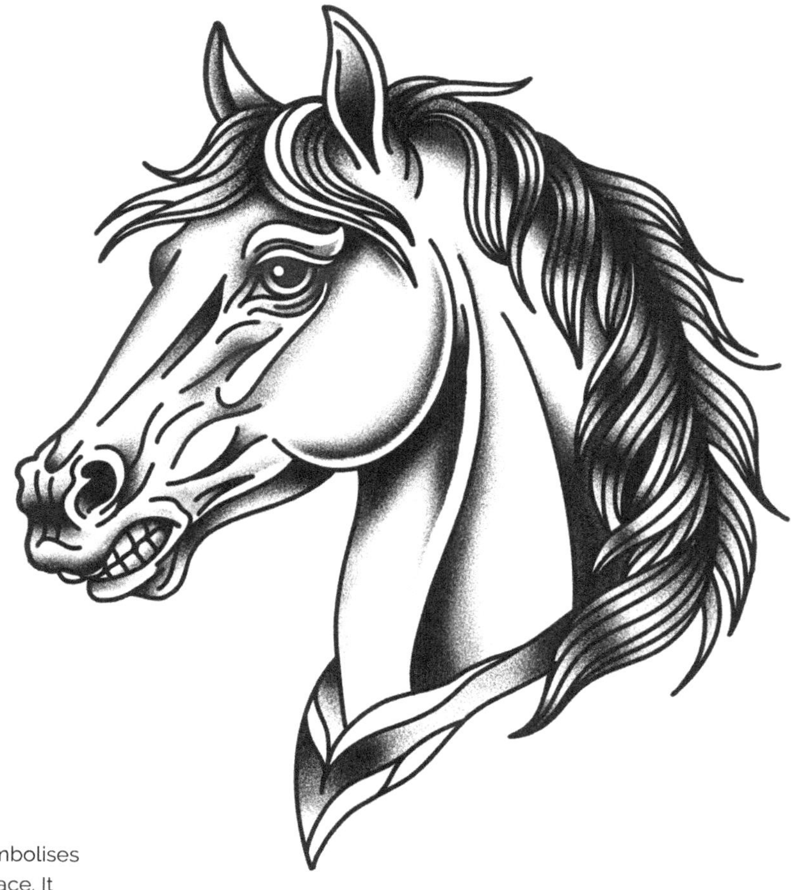

The horse head tattoo symbolises freedom, strength, and grace. It represents loyalty, endurance, and a powerful, untamed spirit driven by instinct and will.

01

02

03

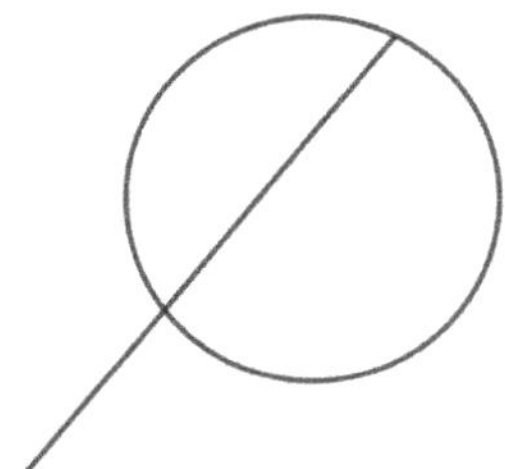

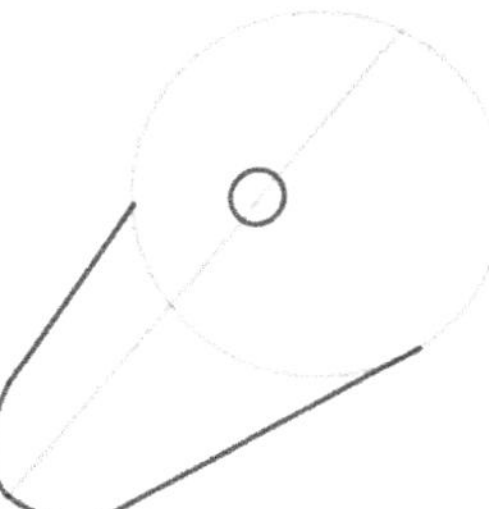

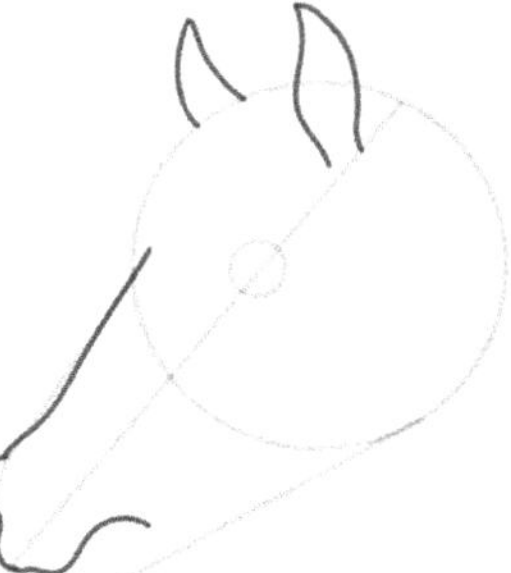

04

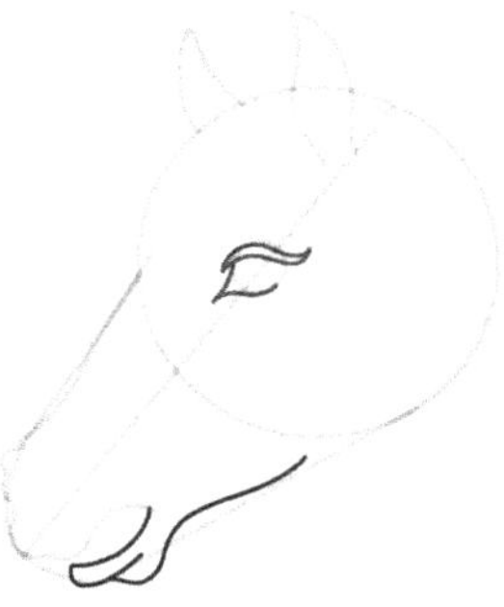

05

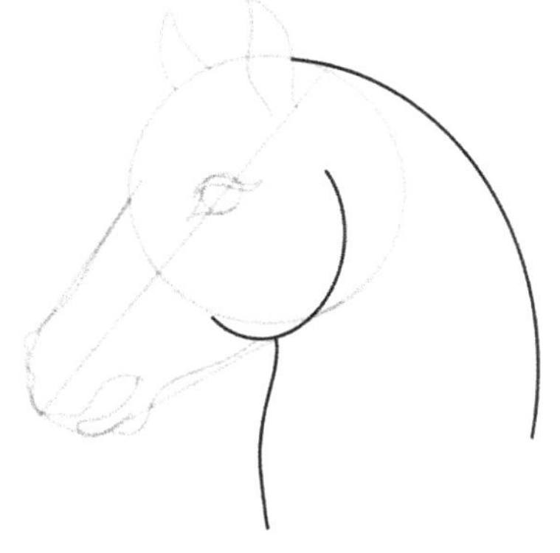

06

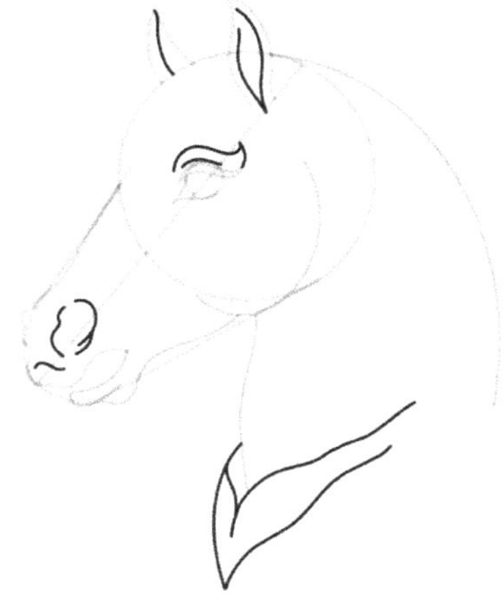

07

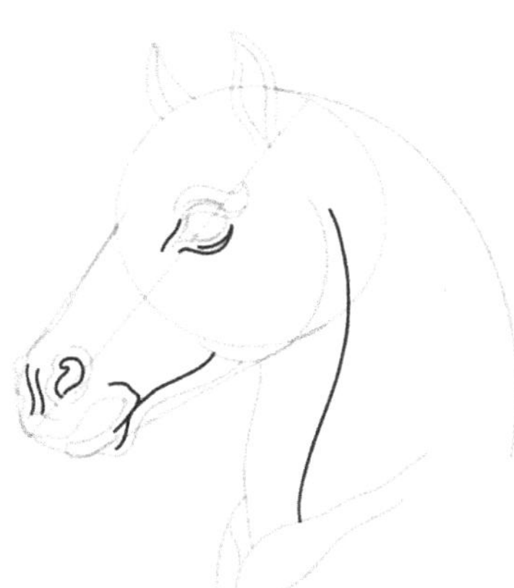

08

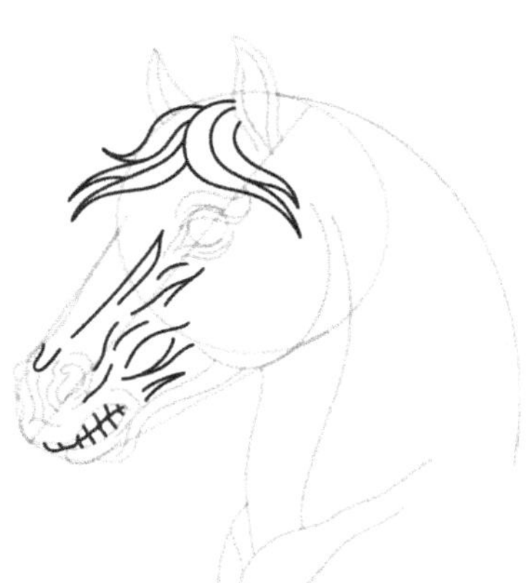

09

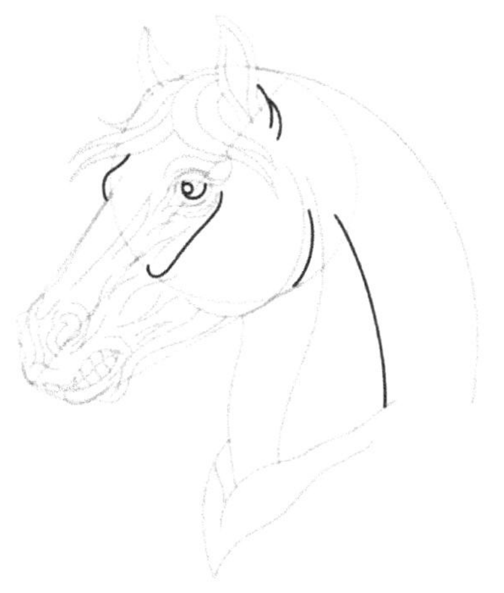

ANIMAL TATTOOS

10

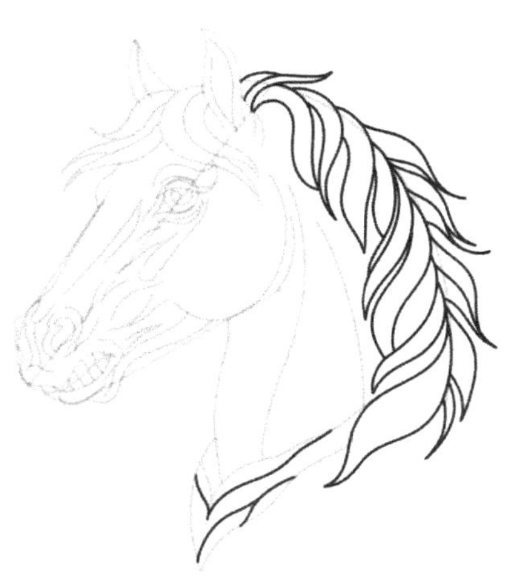

11

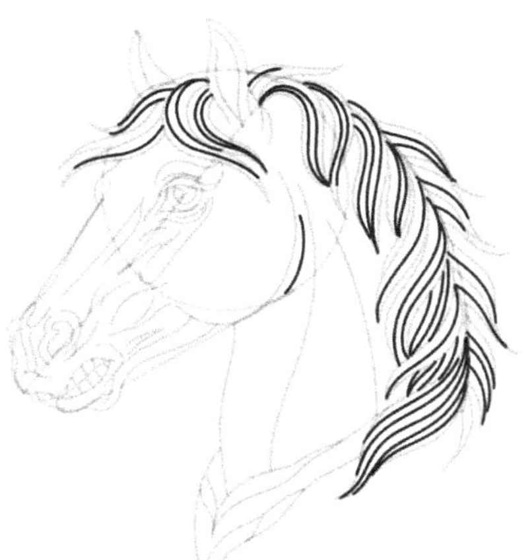

12

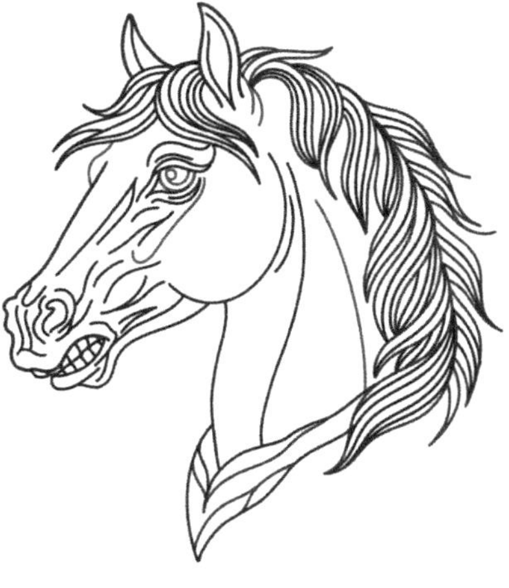

PANTHER

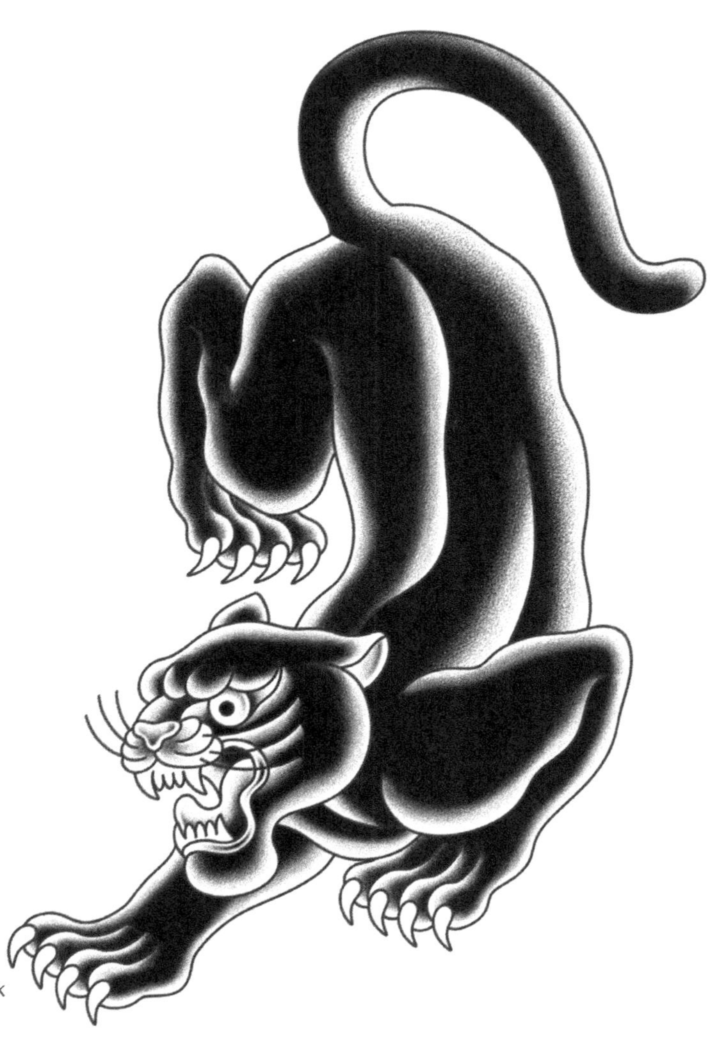

The panther symbolises power, protection, and fearless courage. Sleek and stealthy, it embodies a fierce guardian spirit and primal energy.

01

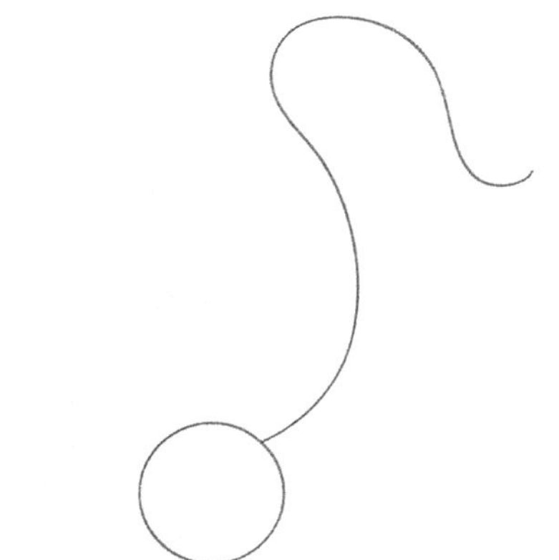

02

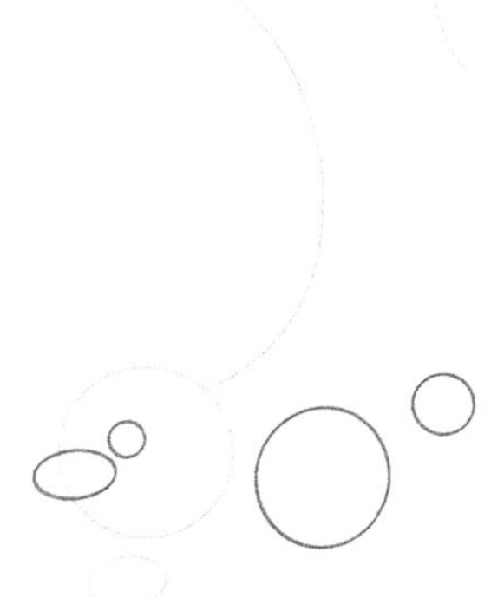

03

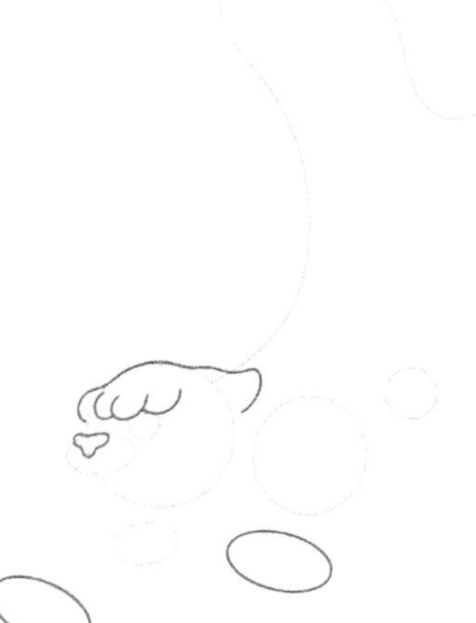

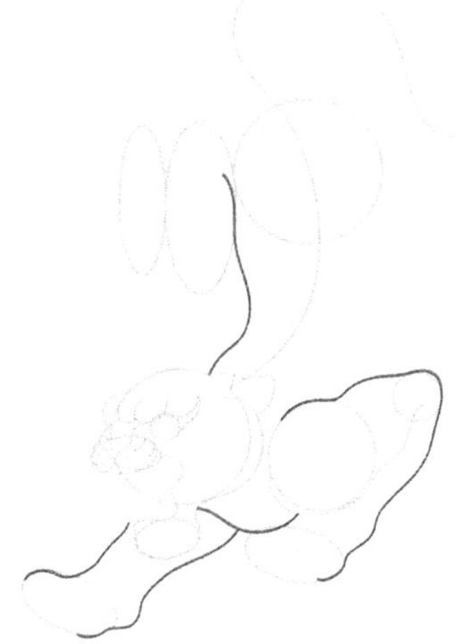

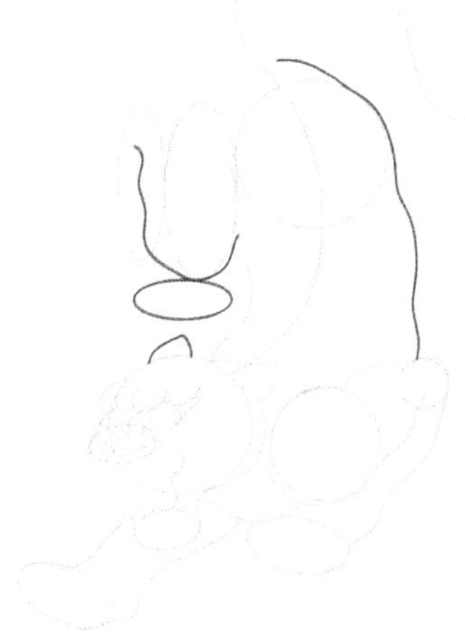

07

08

09

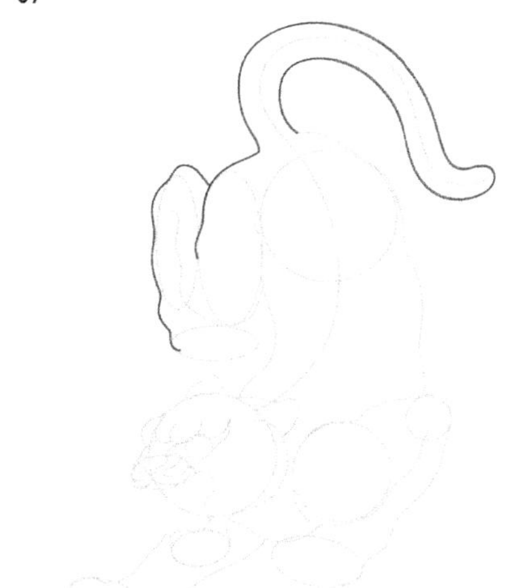

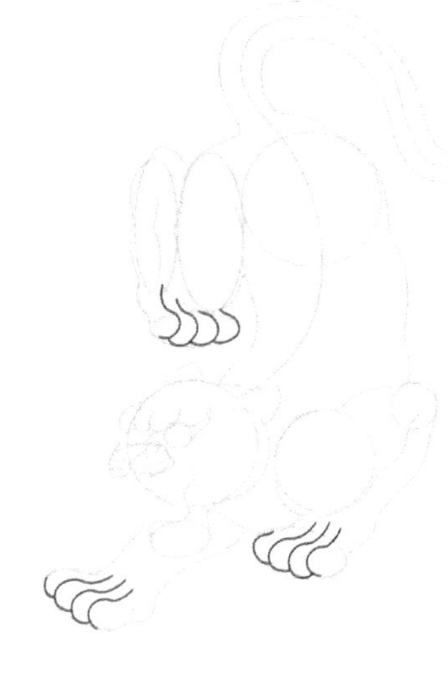

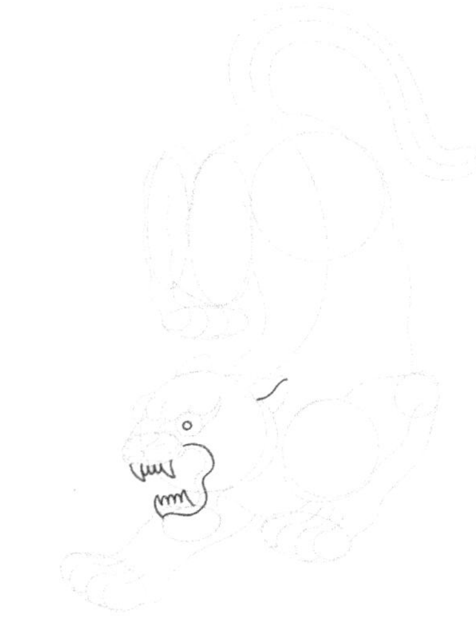

10

11

12

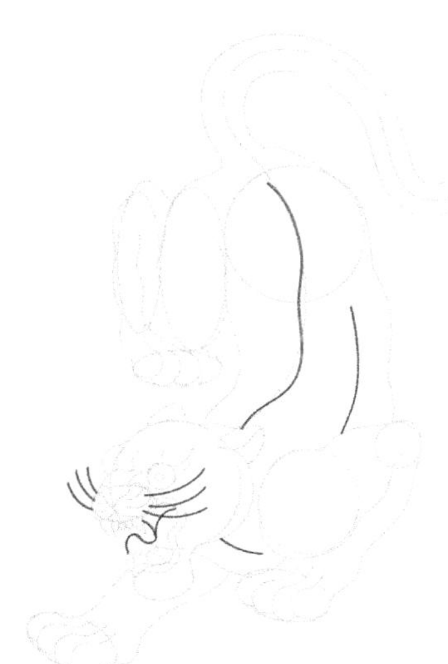

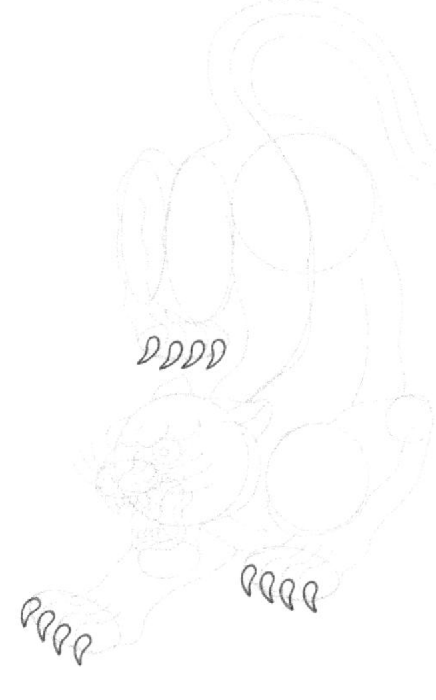

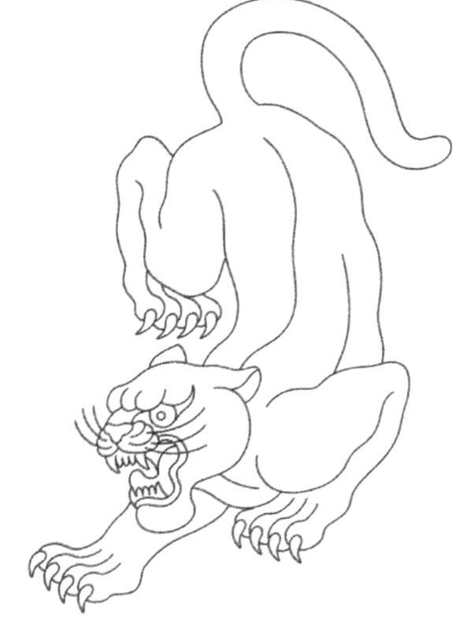

PEACOCK

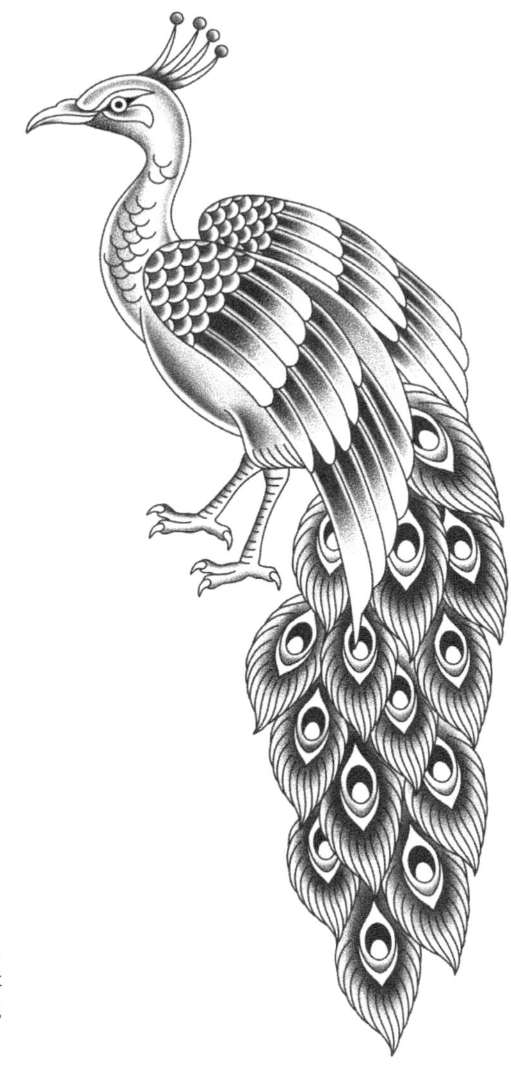

The peacock symbolises beauty, pride, and renewal. With its radiant feathers, it represents self-expression, immortality, and the courage to stand out.

01

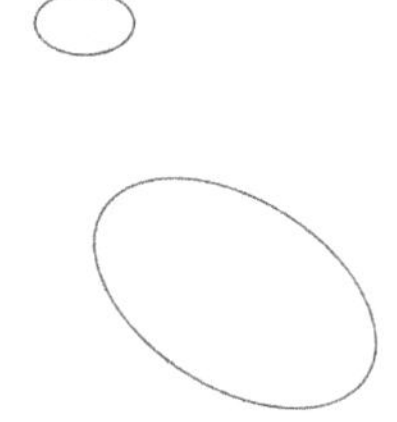

02

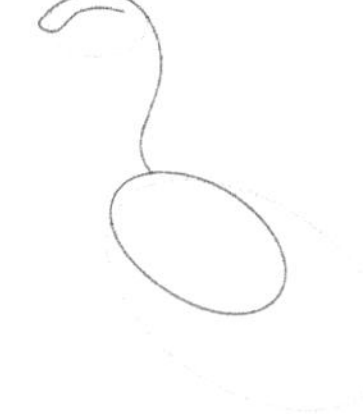

03

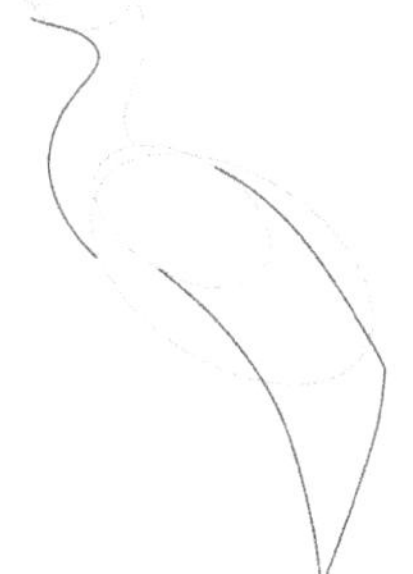

04

05

06

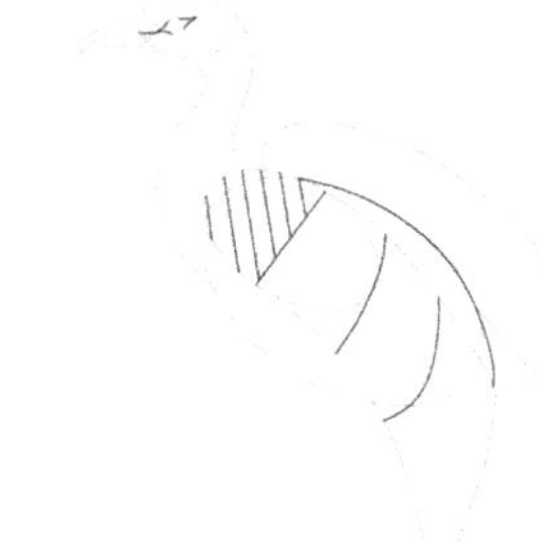

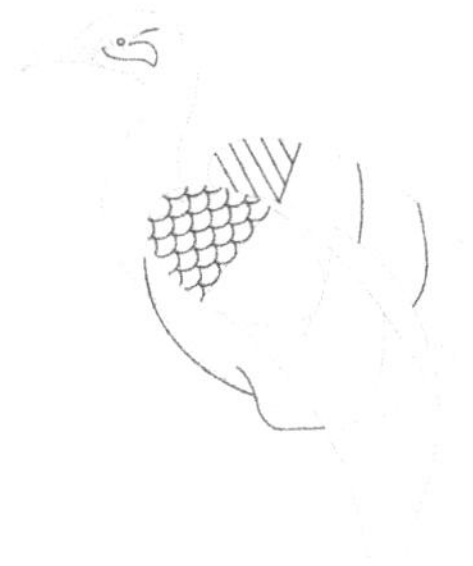

07

08

09

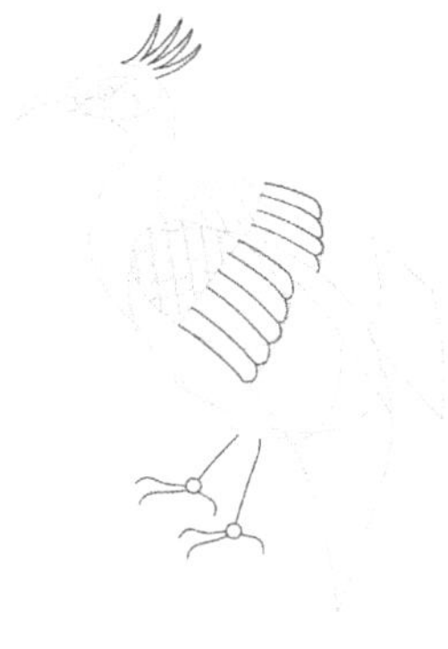

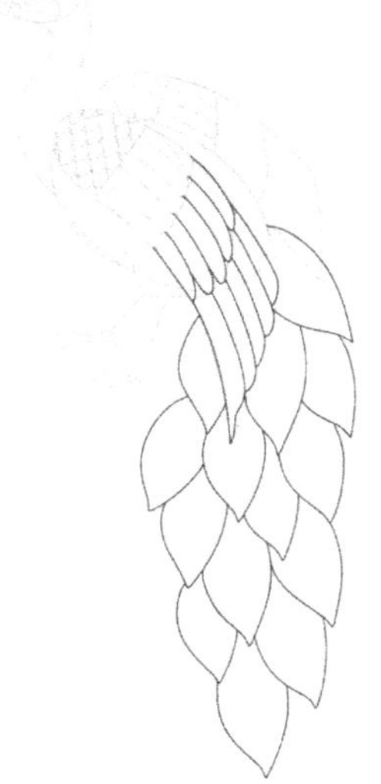

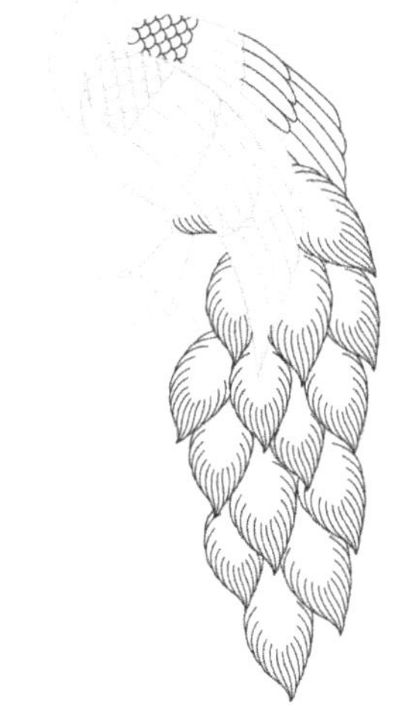

10

11

12

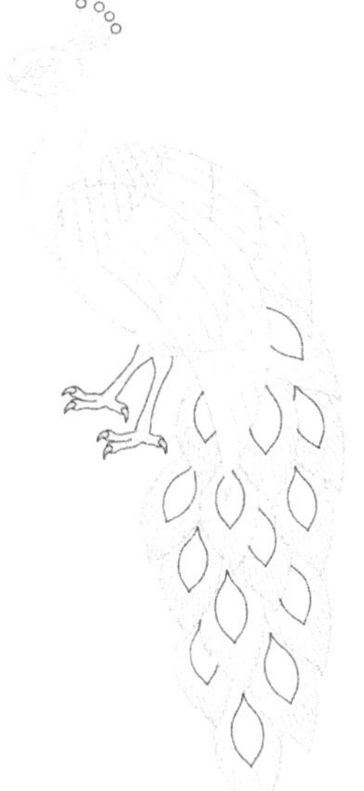

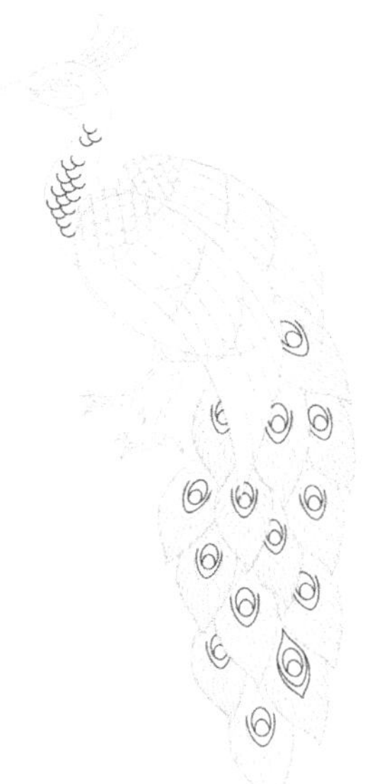

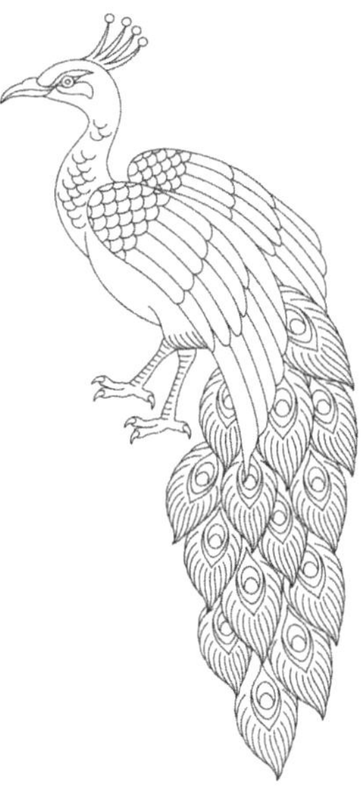

ANIMAL TATTOOS

RABBIT

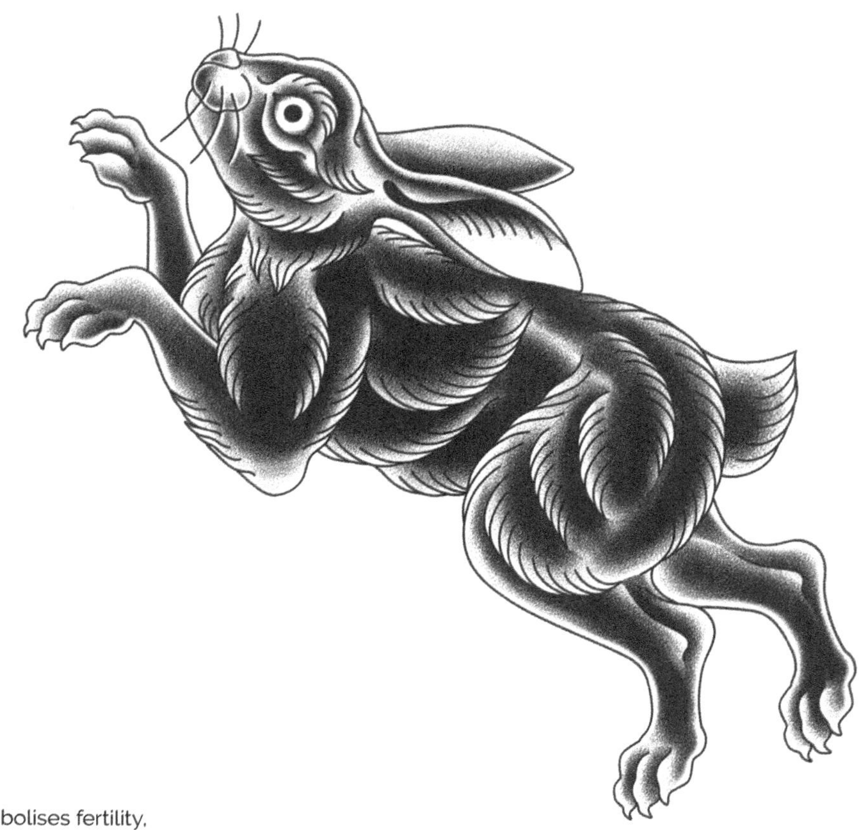

The rabbit tattoo symbolises fertility,
agility, and cleverness. It represents
renewal, intuition, and the ability to
navigate life with speed and subtlety.

01

02

03

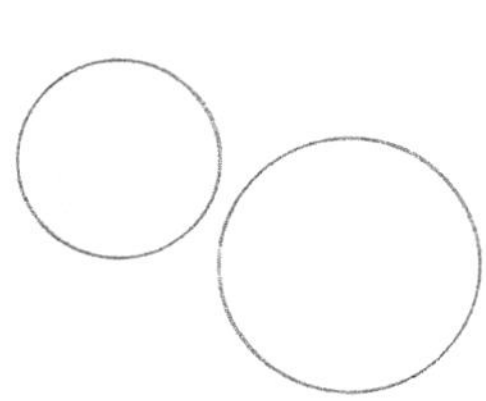

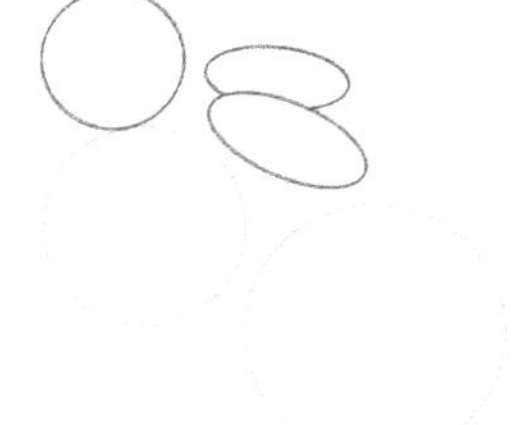

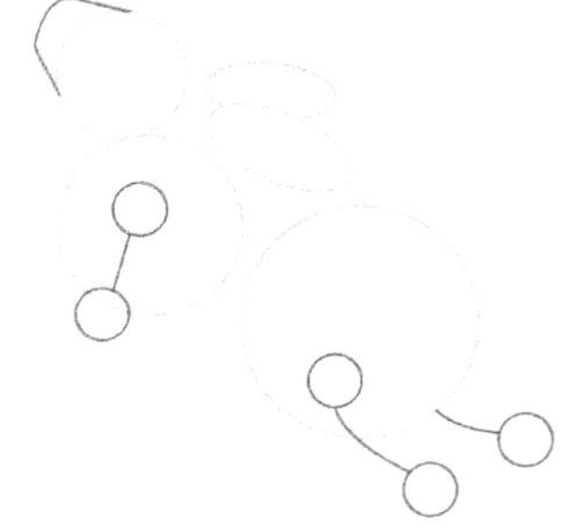

04

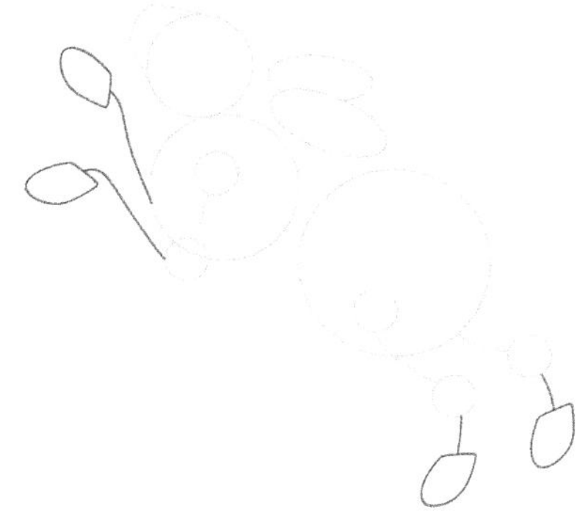

05

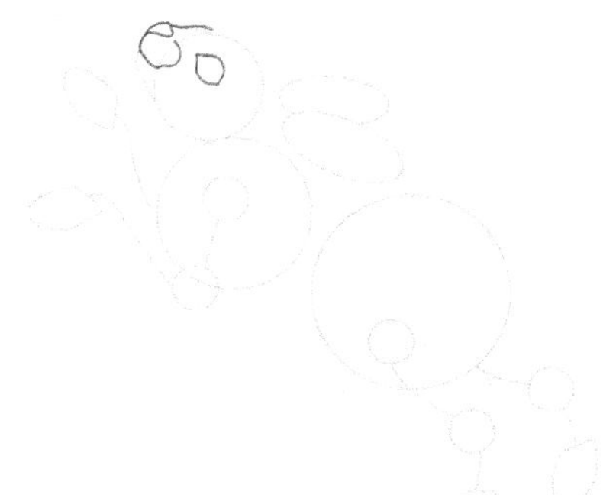

06

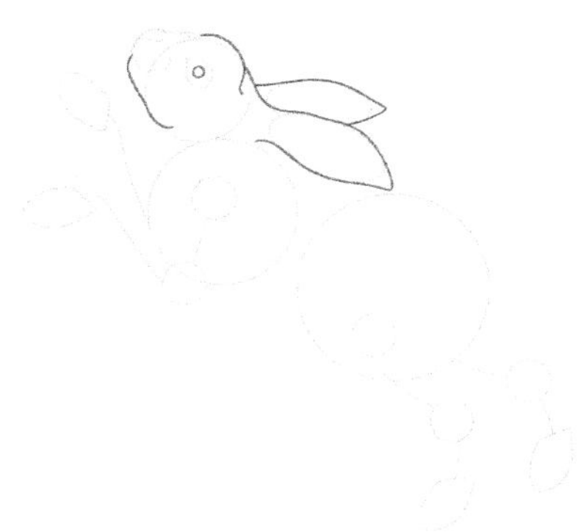

07

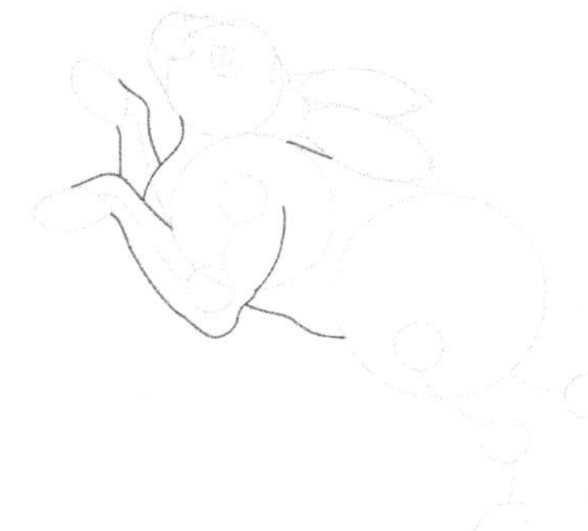

08

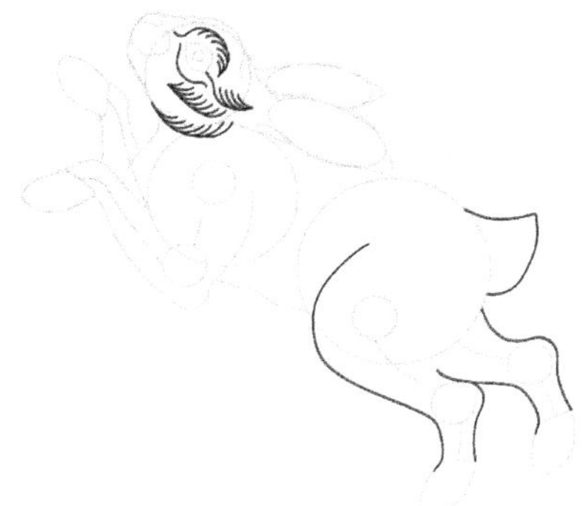

09

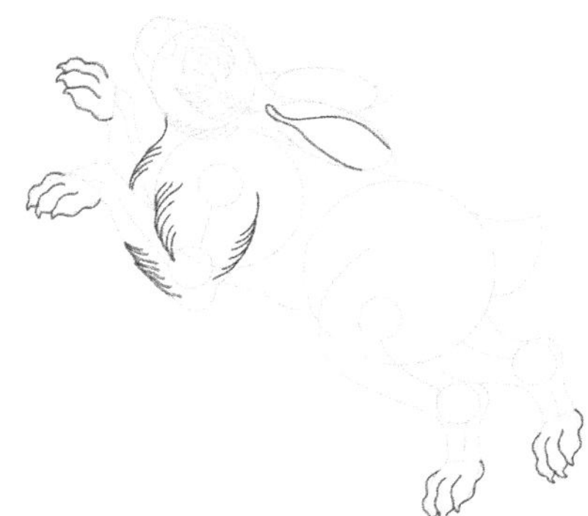

ANIMAL TATTOOS

10

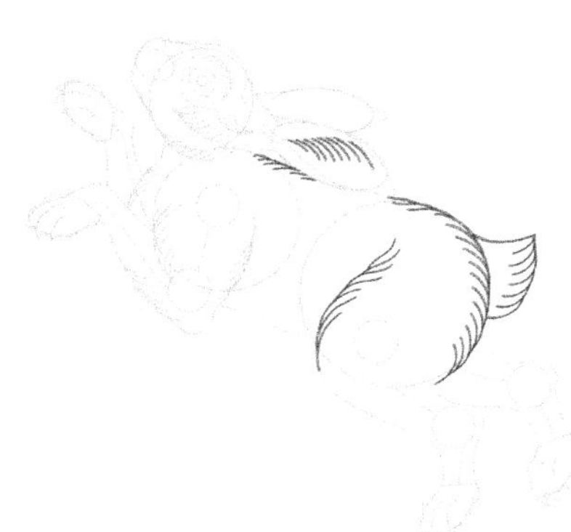

11

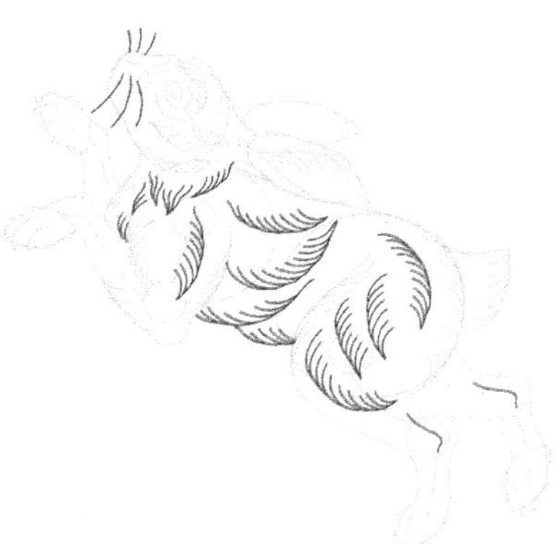

12

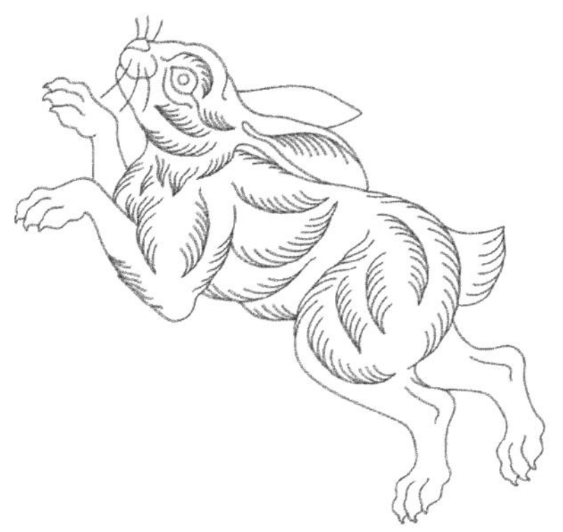

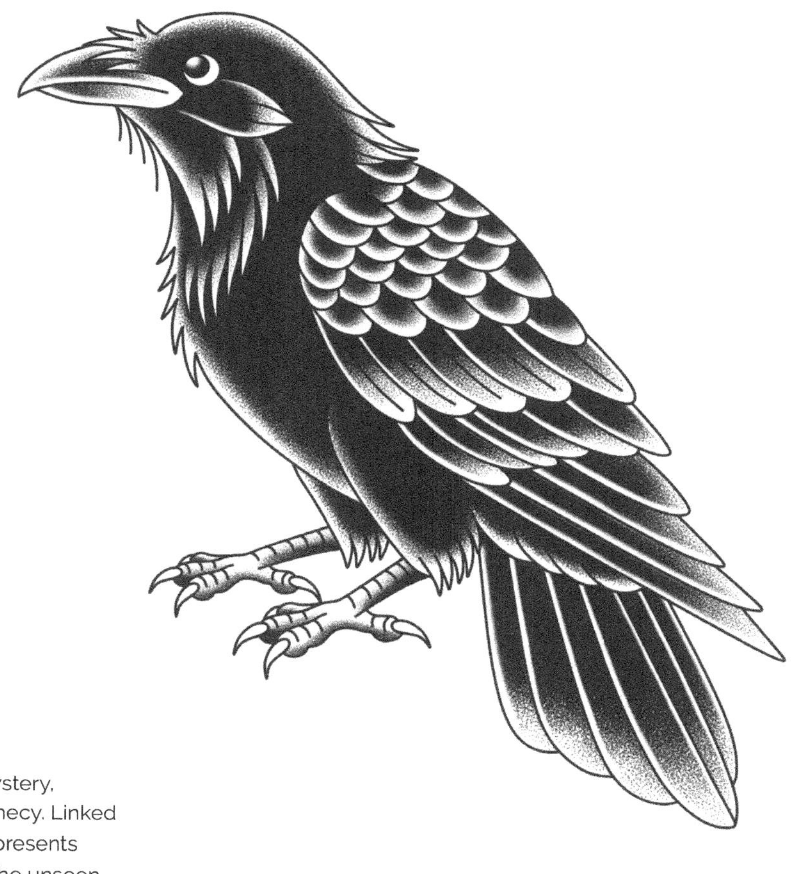

RAVEN

The raven symbolises mystery,
transformation, and prophecy. Linked
to death and rebirth, it represents
intelligence, magic, and the unseen.

01

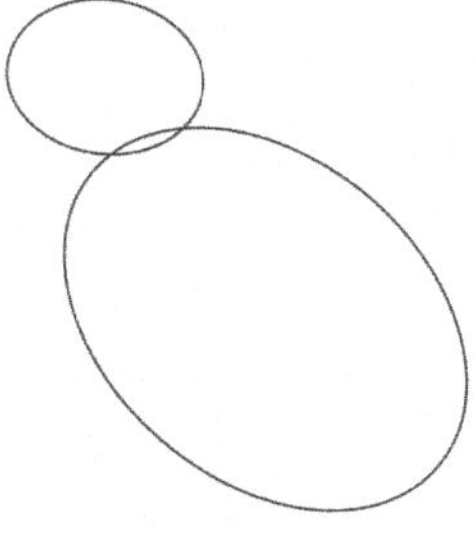

02

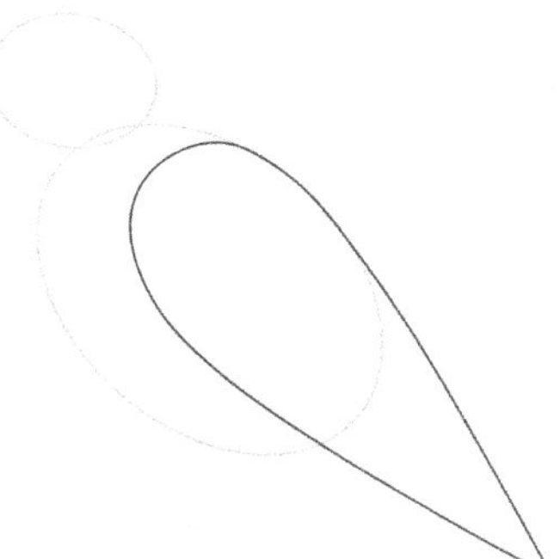

03

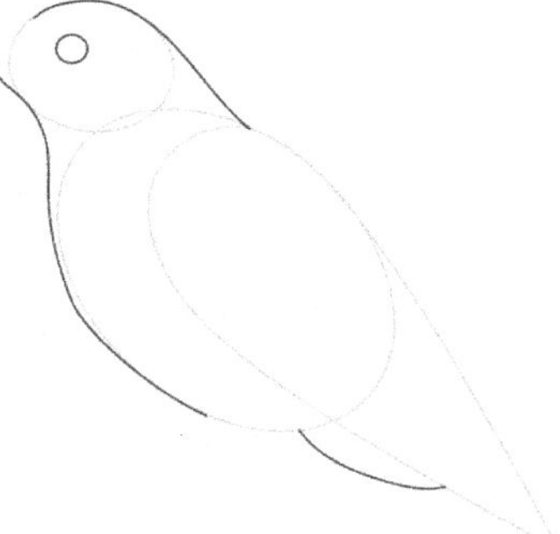

04

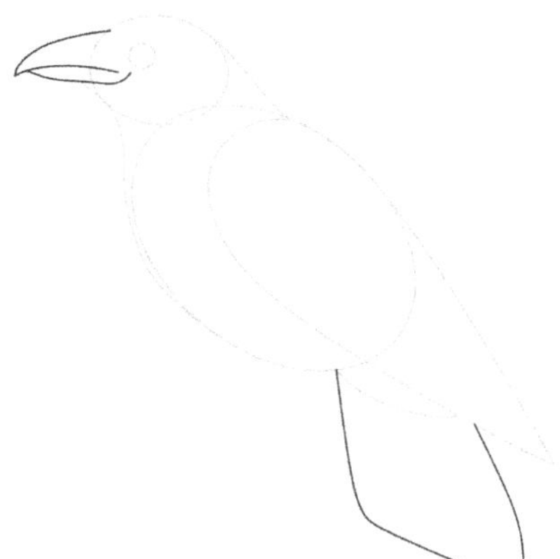

05

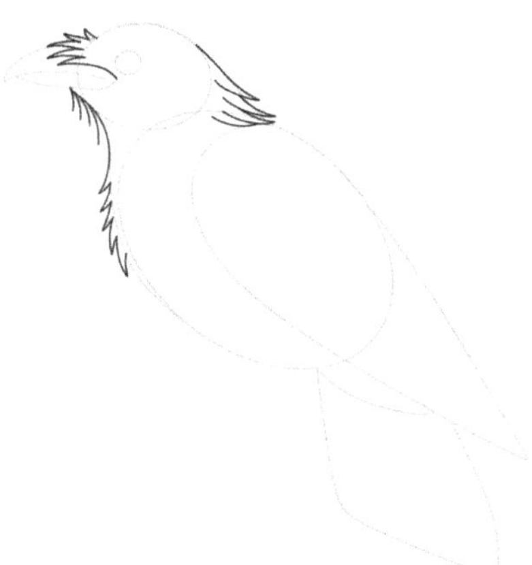

06

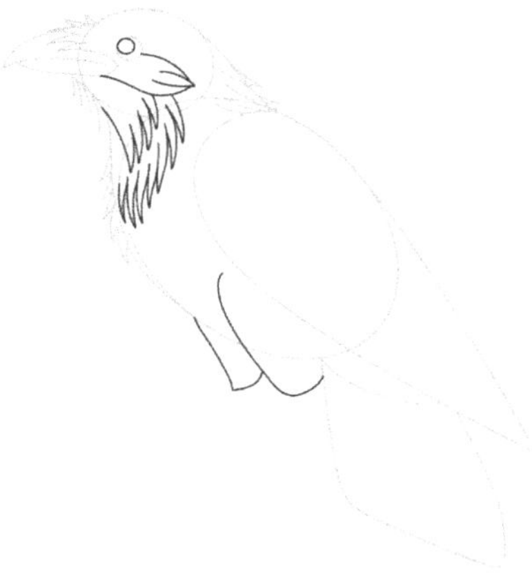

07

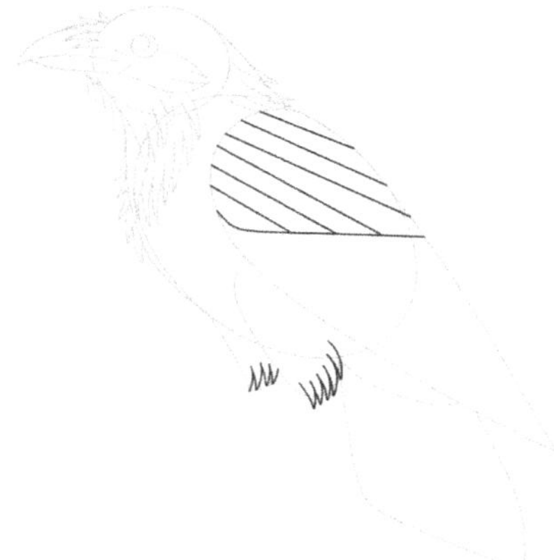

08

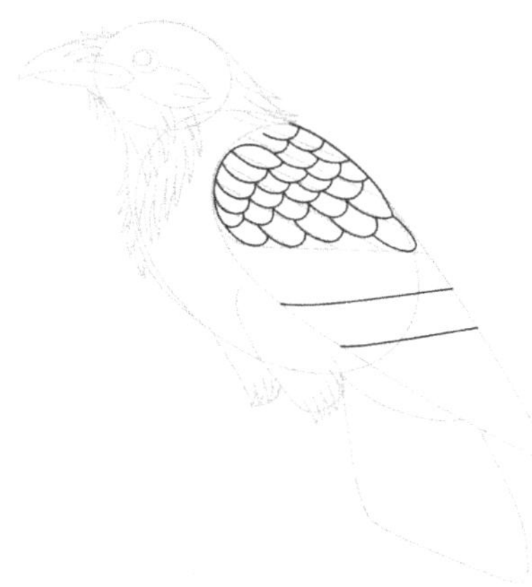

09

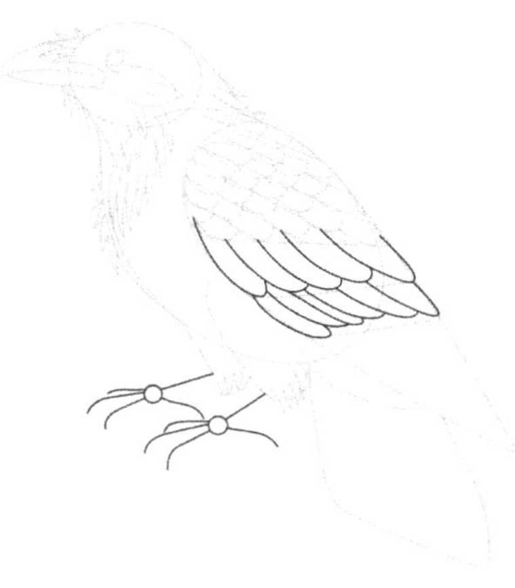

10

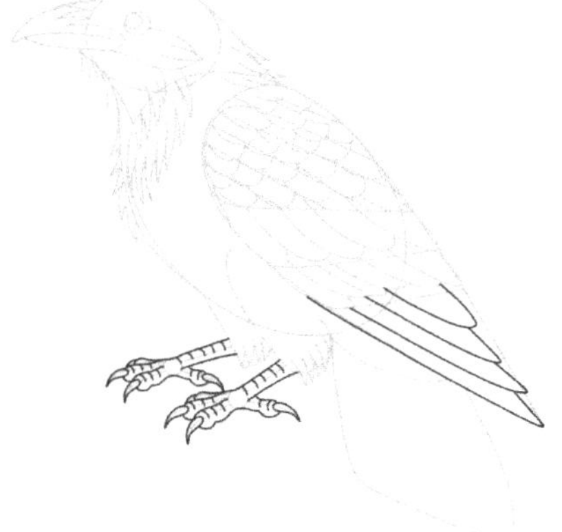

11

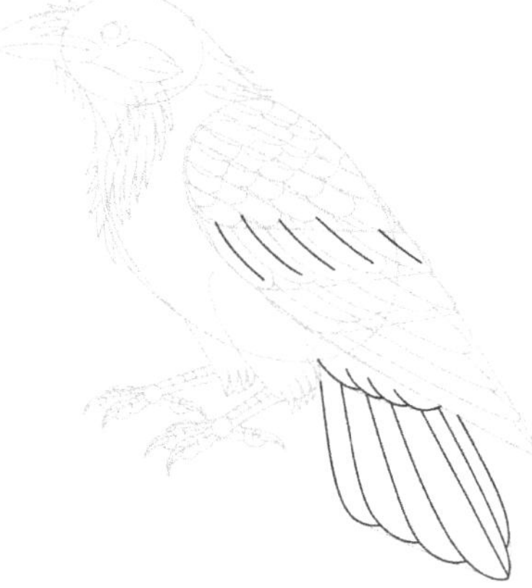

12

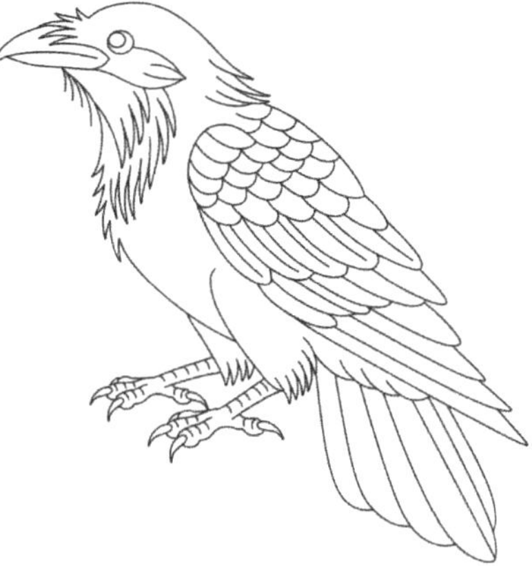

SCORPION

The scorpion symbolises protection, intensity, and resilience. Known for its deadly sting, it represents strength, survival, and a fierce, guarded nature.

01

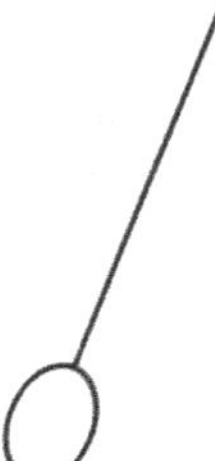

02

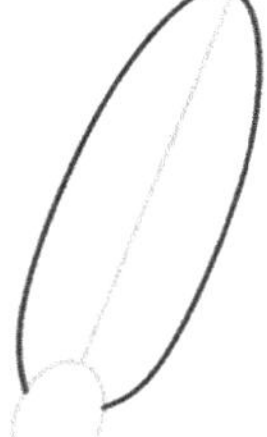

03

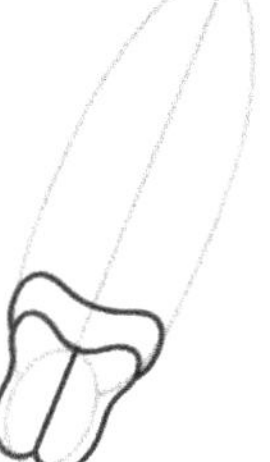

04

05

06

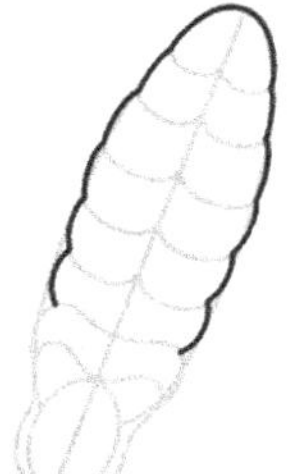

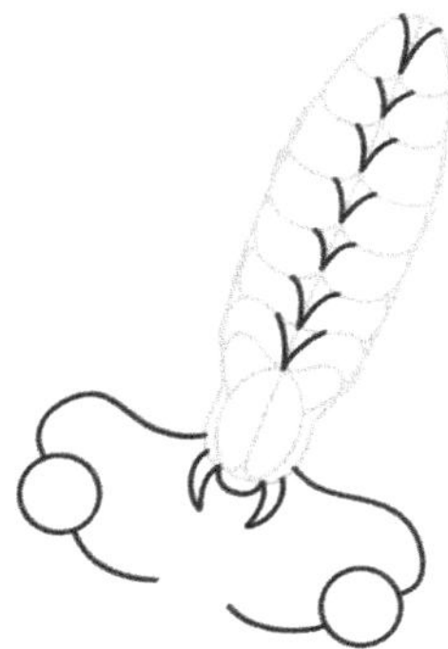

07

08

09

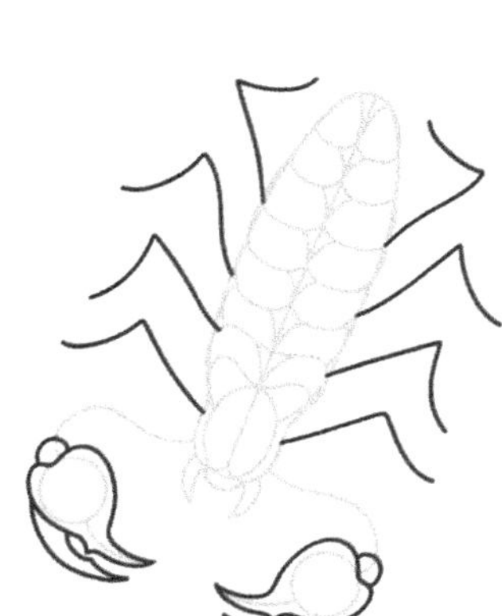

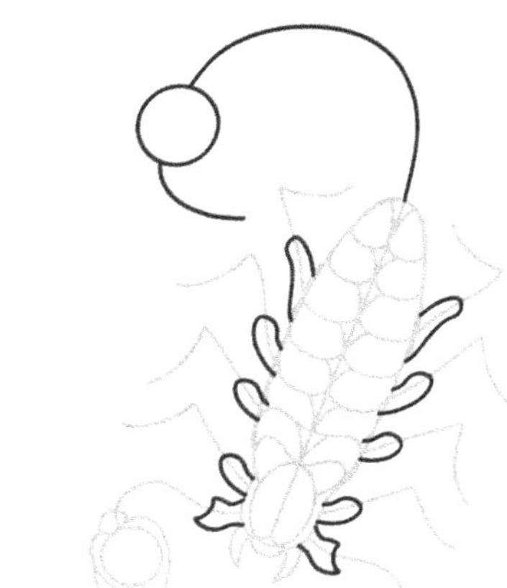

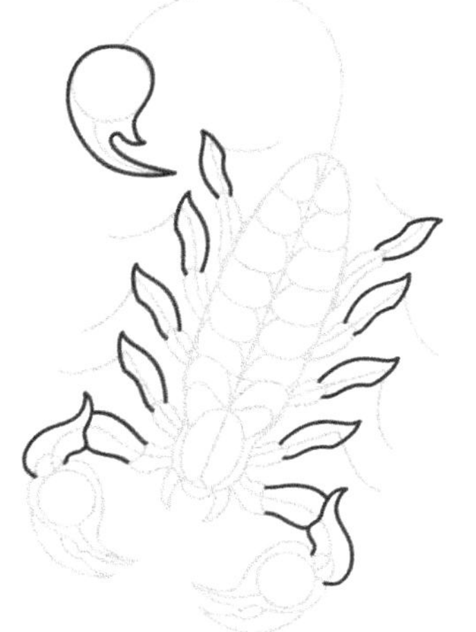

10

11

12

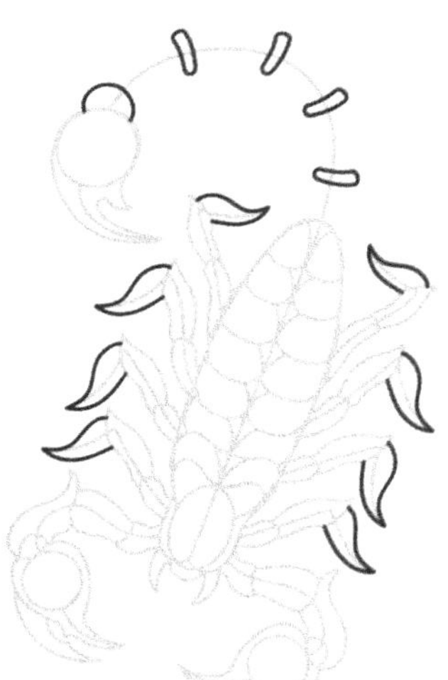

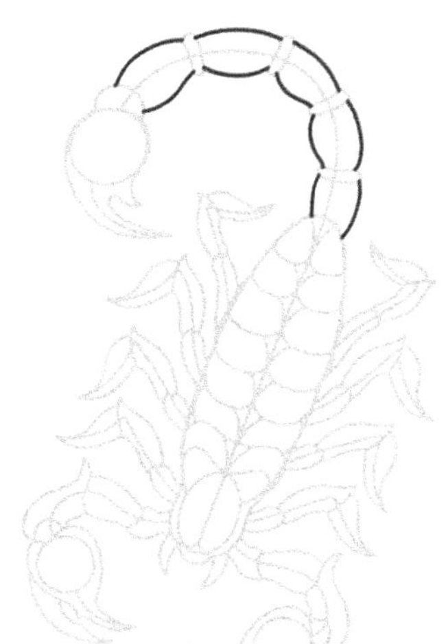

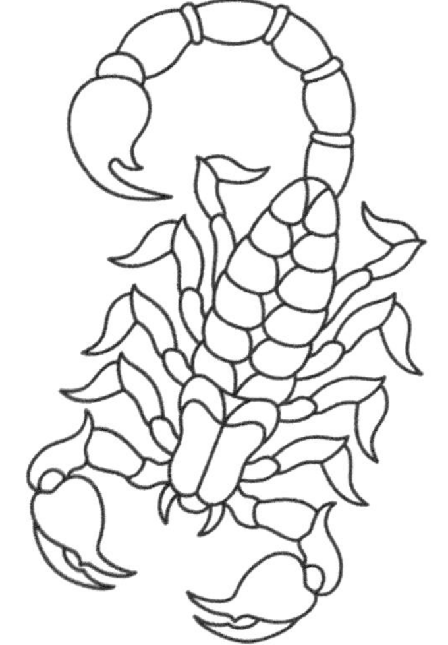

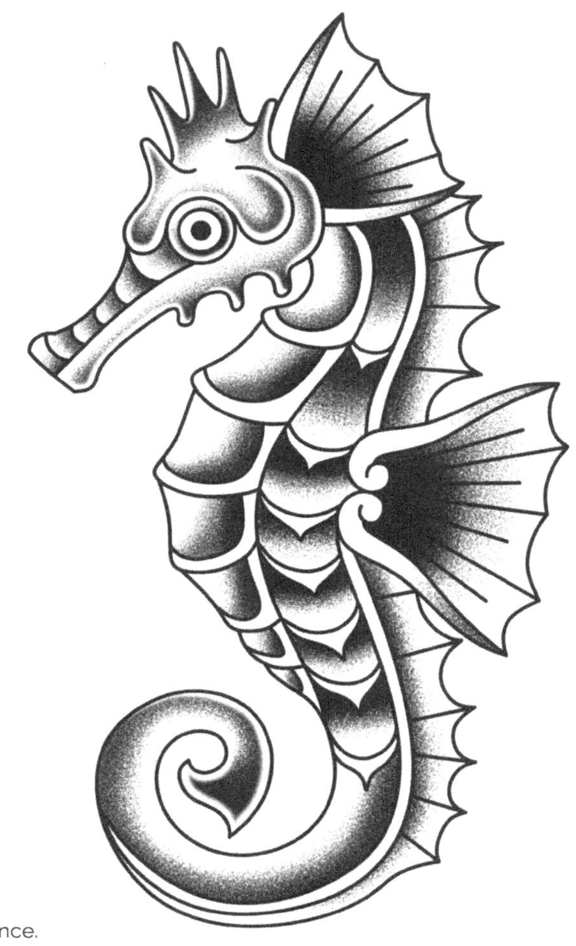

SEAHORSE

The seahorse tattoo symbolises
patience, tranquillity, and perseverance.
It represents gentle strength, protection,
and a connection to intuition and the sea.

01

02

03

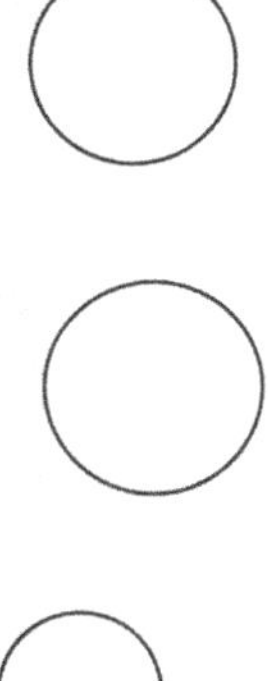

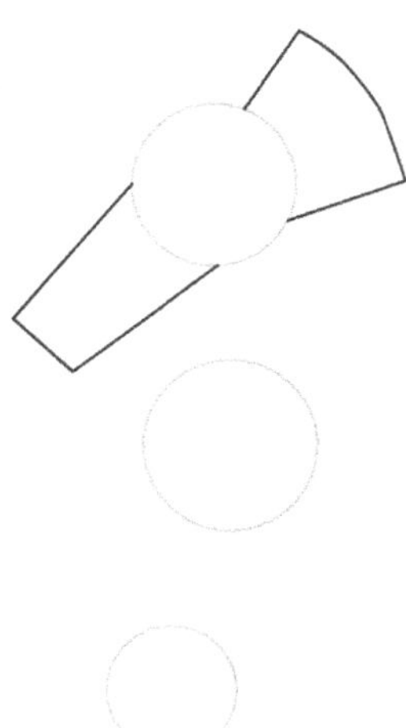

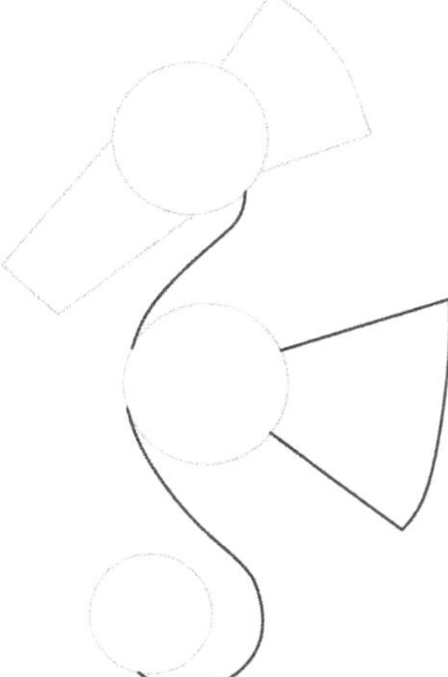

04

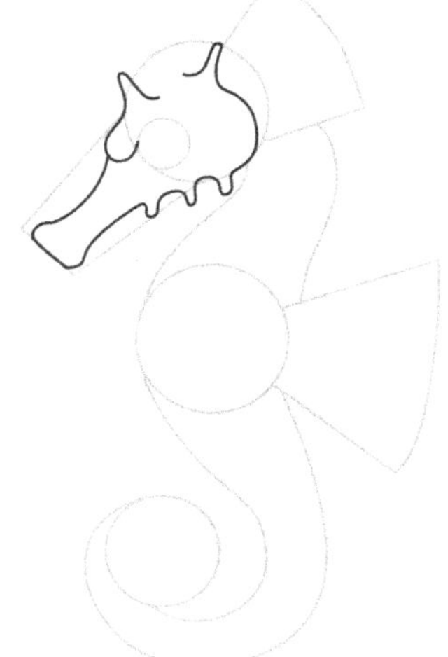

05

06

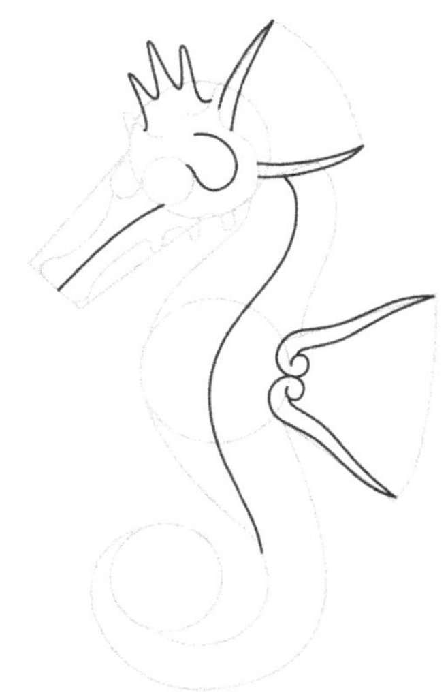

07

08

09

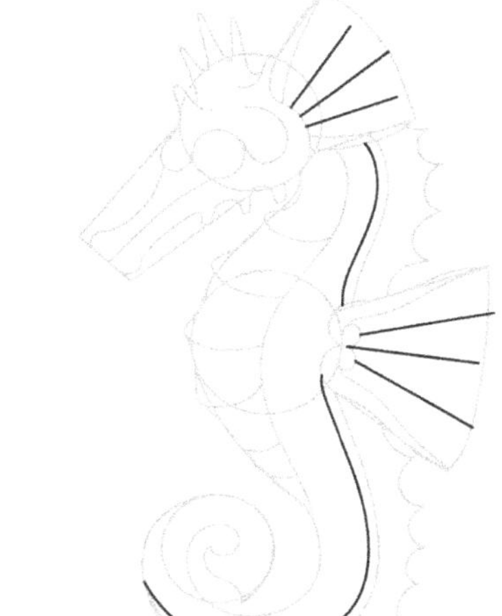

10

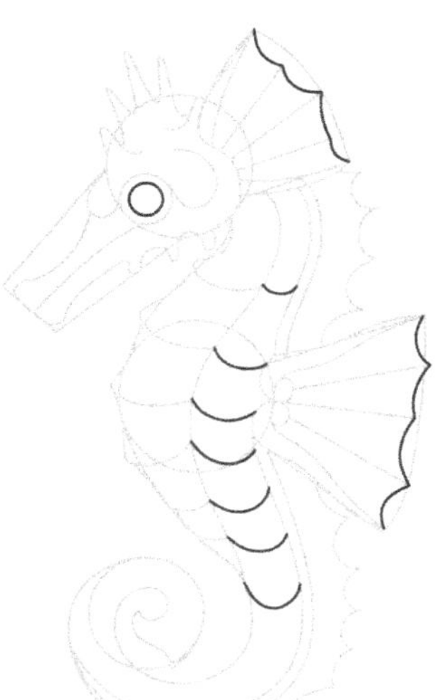

11

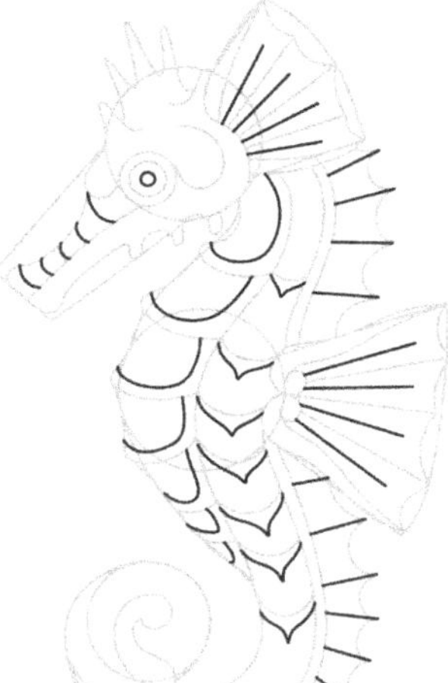

12

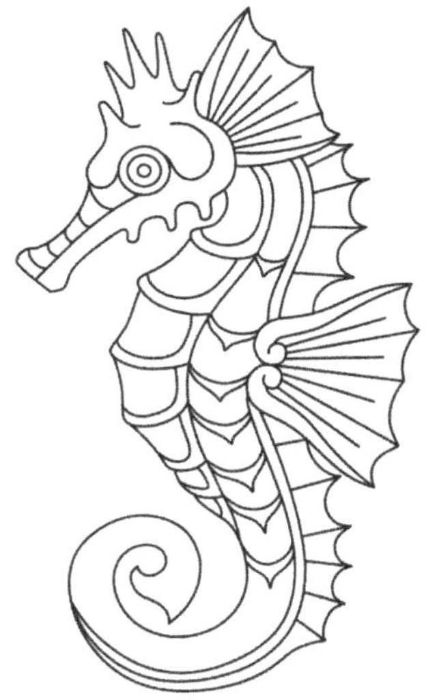

ANIMAL TATTOOS

SHARK & HARPOON

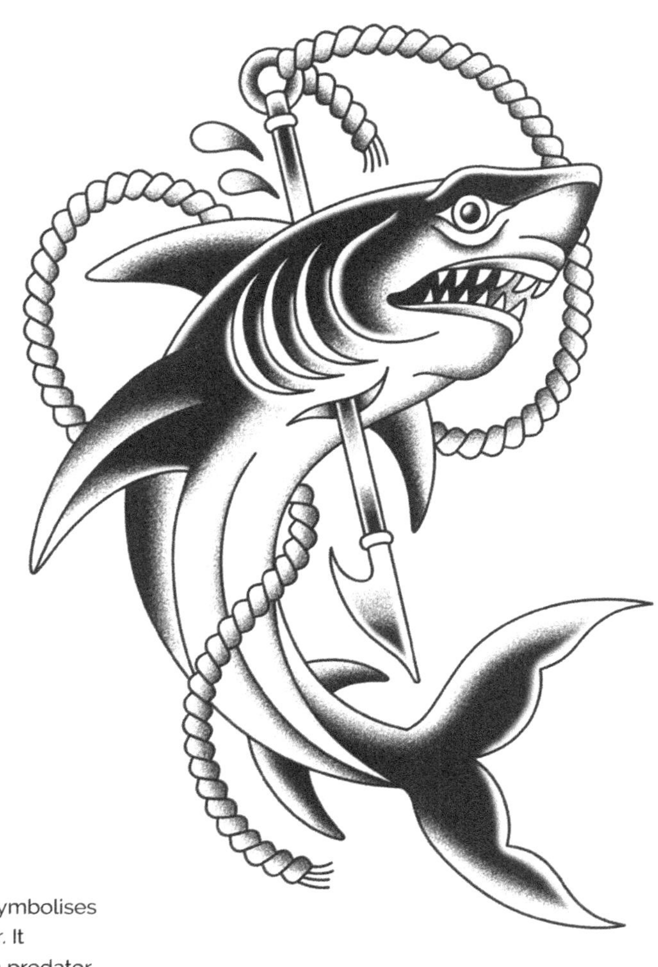

The shark and harpoon tattoo symbolises survival, conflict, and raw power. It represents the tension between predator and prey and the fight for dominance.

01

02

03

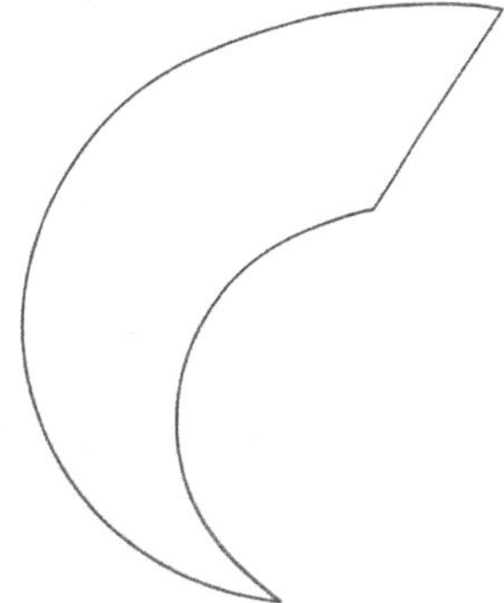

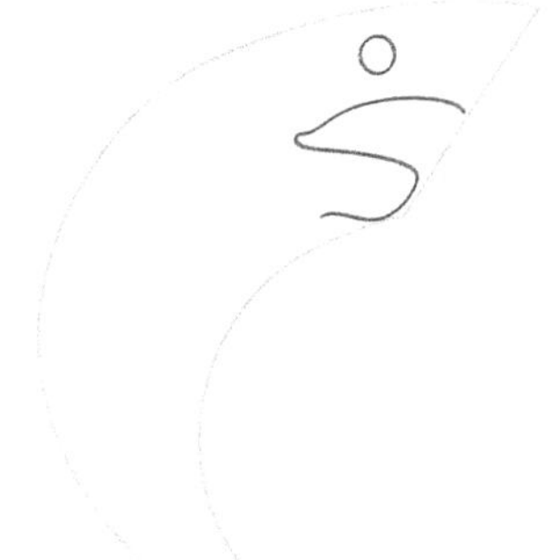

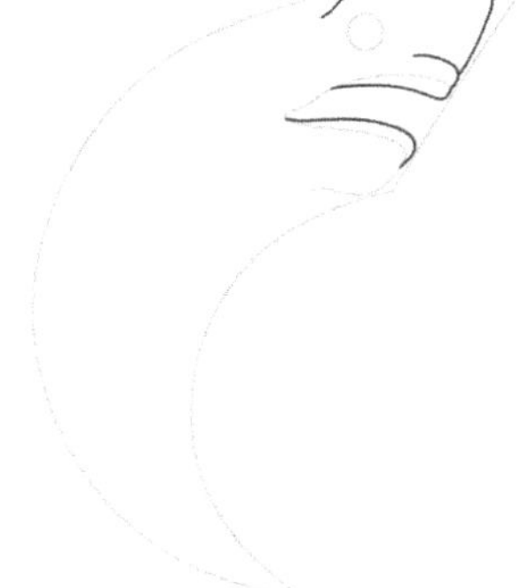

04

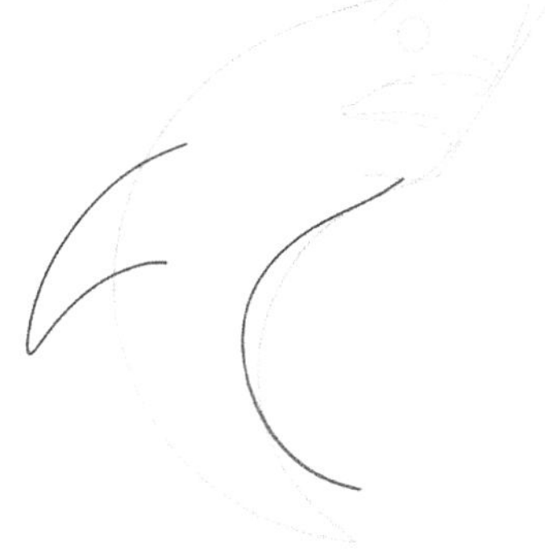

05

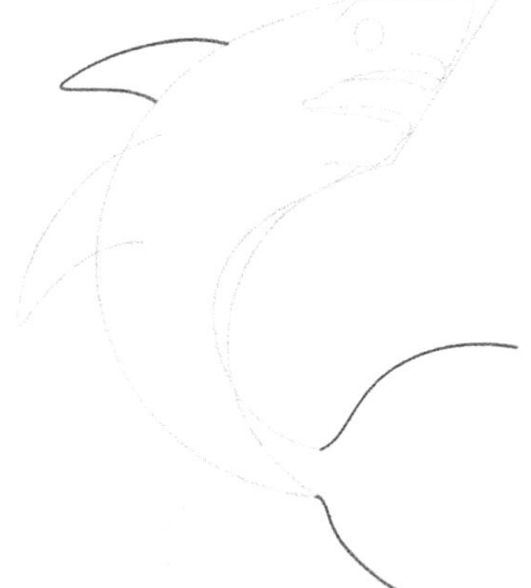

06

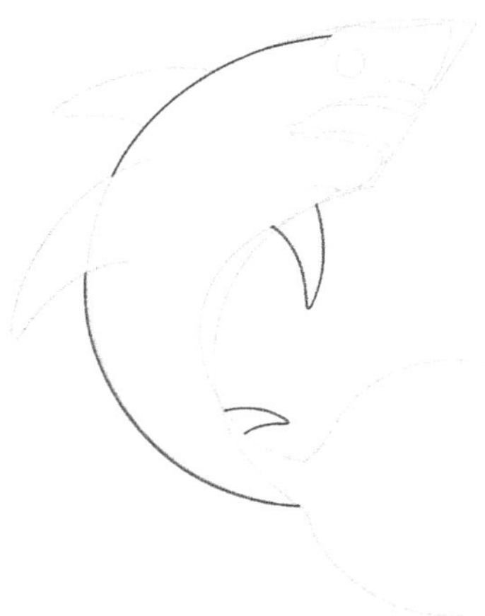

07

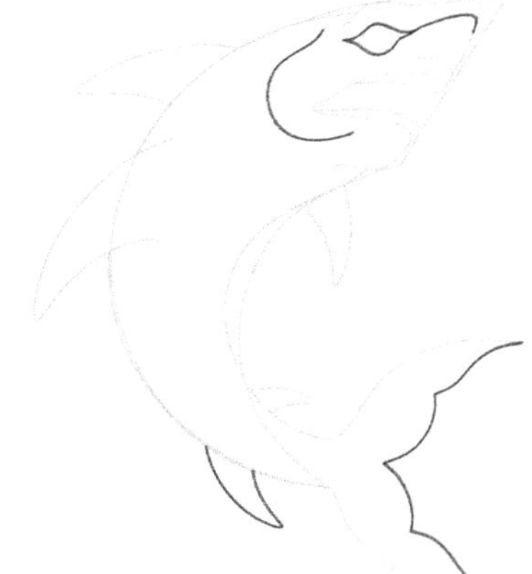

08

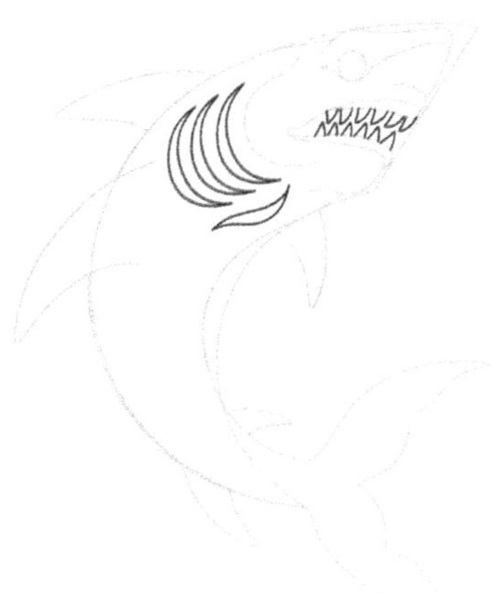

09

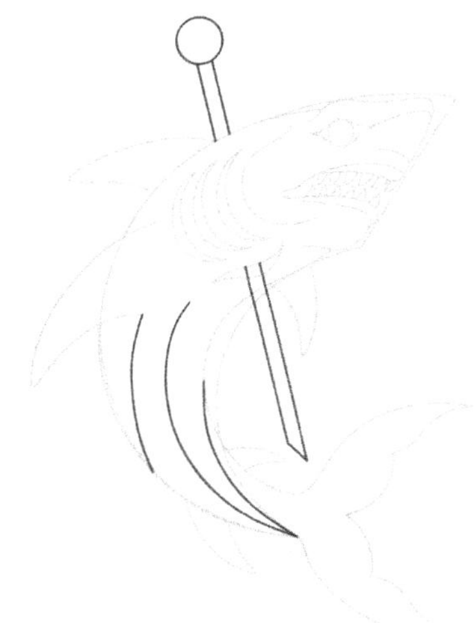

10

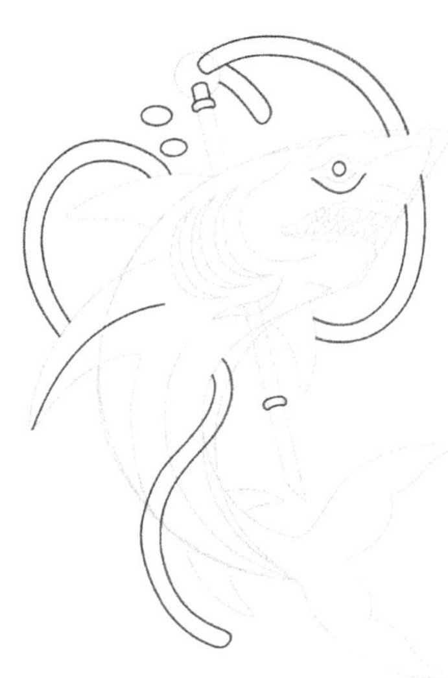

11

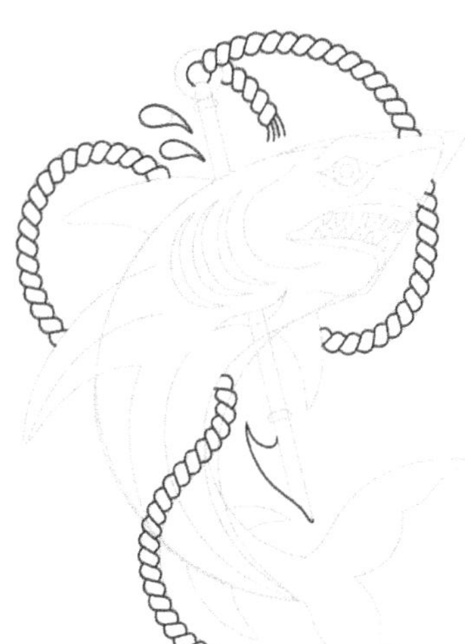

12

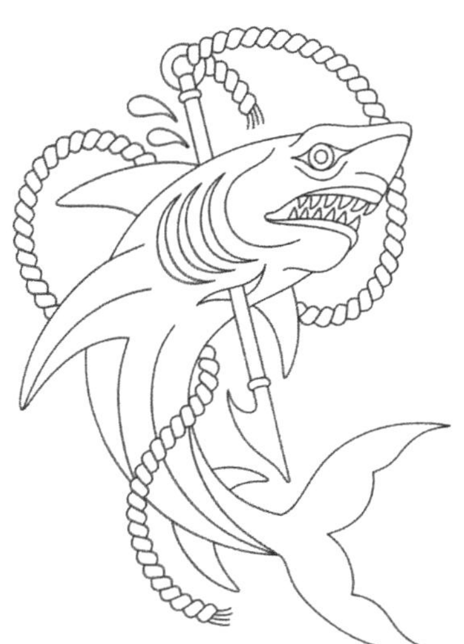

ANIMAL TATTOOS

SNAKE

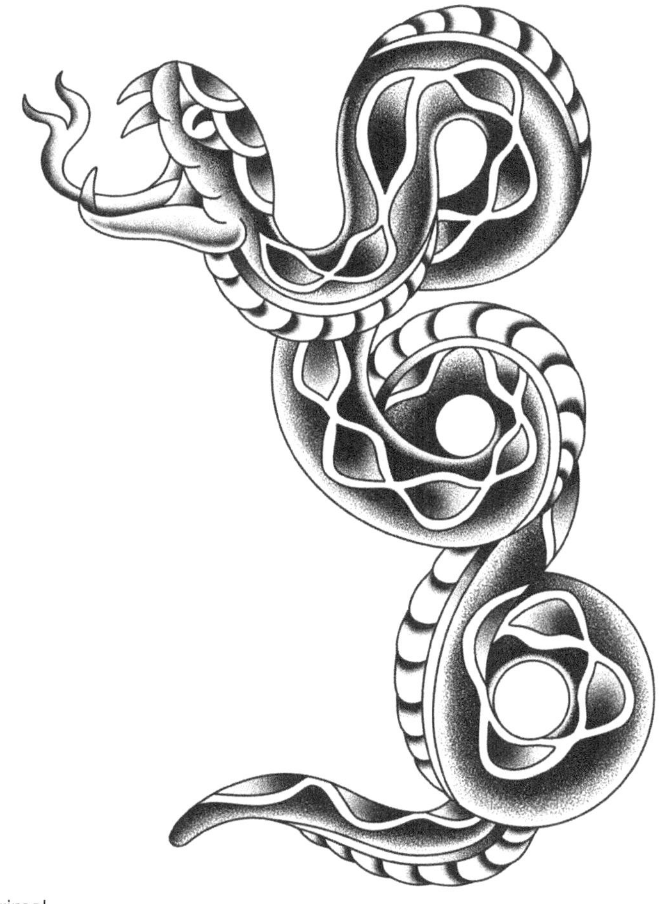

The snake tattoo symbolises transformation, rebirth, and primal energy. It represents wisdom, protection, and the cycle of life, death, and renewal.

01

02

03

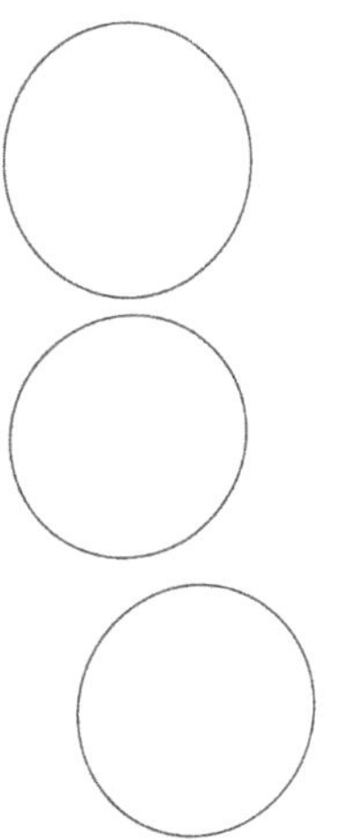

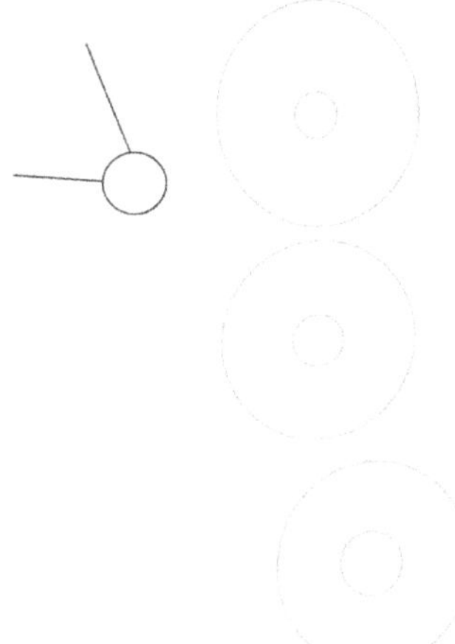

04

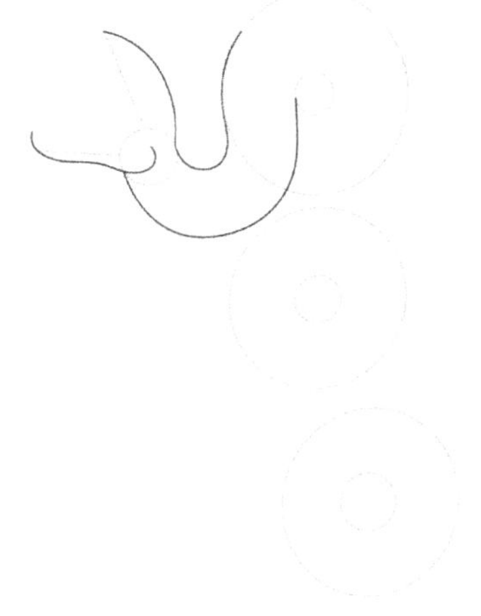

05

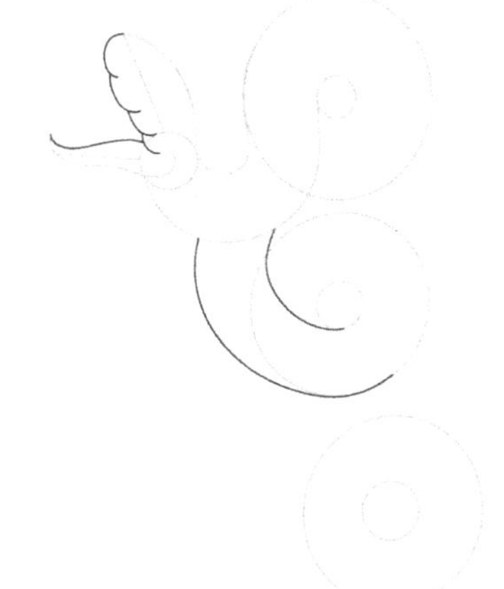

06

07

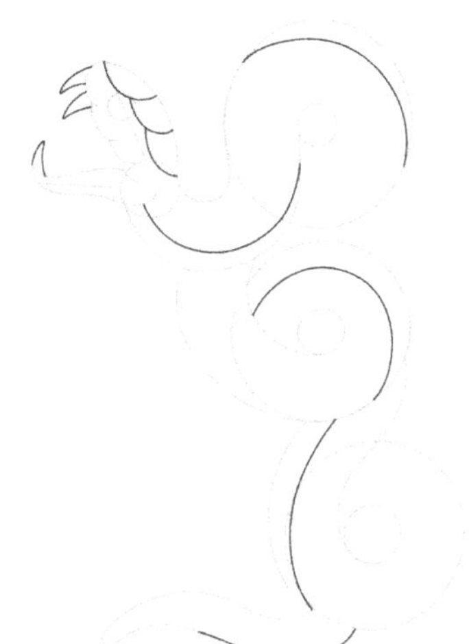

08

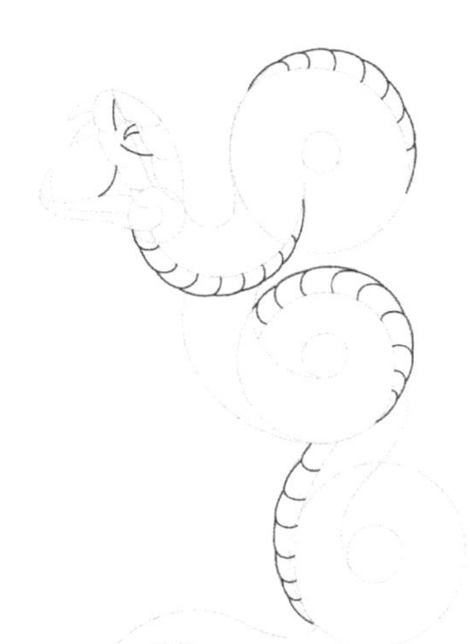

09

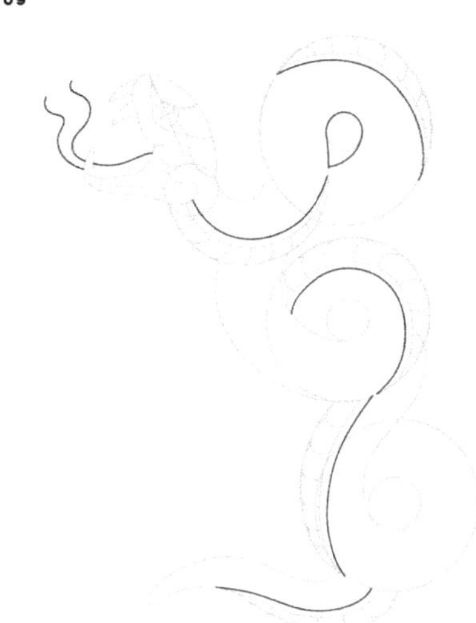

10

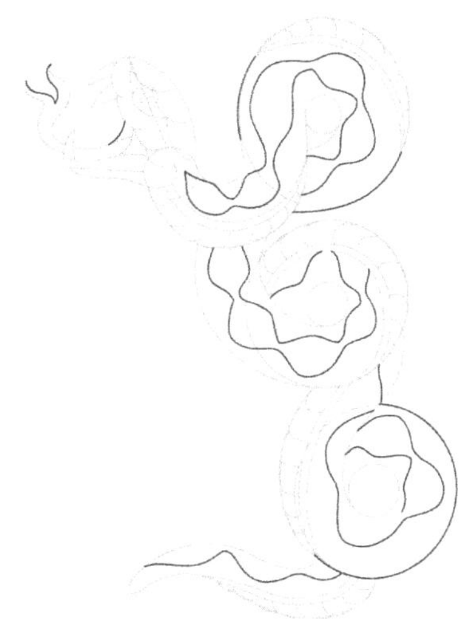

11

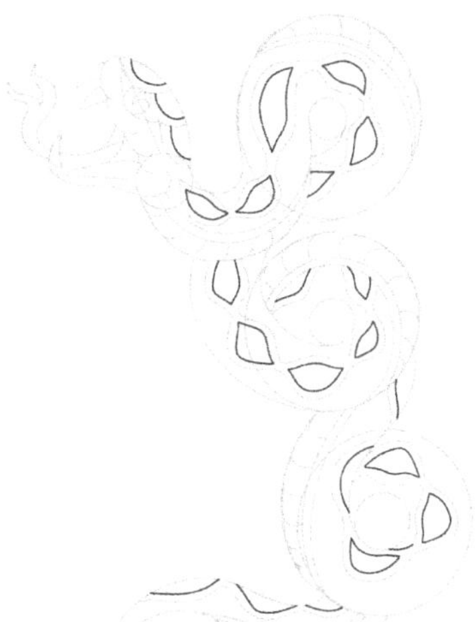

12

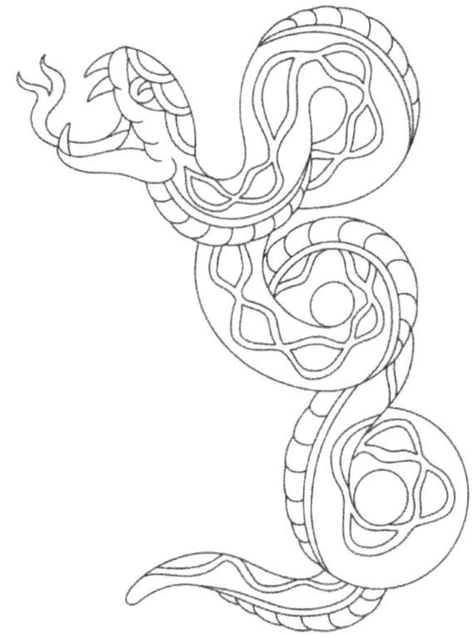

ANIMAL TATTOOS

SPIDER

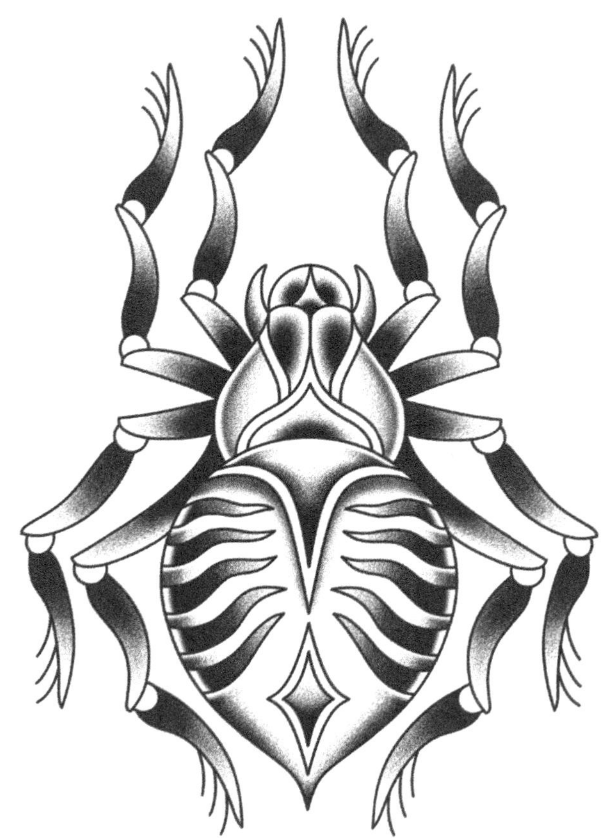

The spider tattoo symbolises creativity, patience, and fate. As the weaver of webs, it represents the power to shape one's destiny.

01

02

03

04

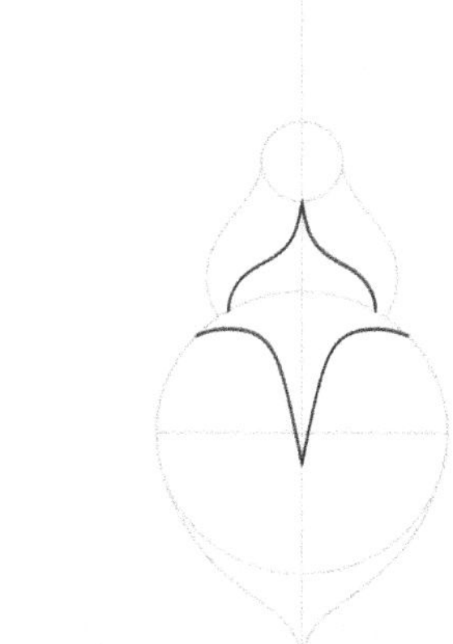

05

06

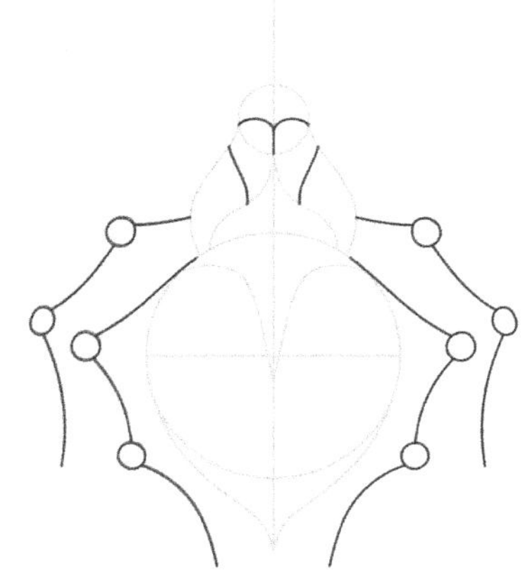

07

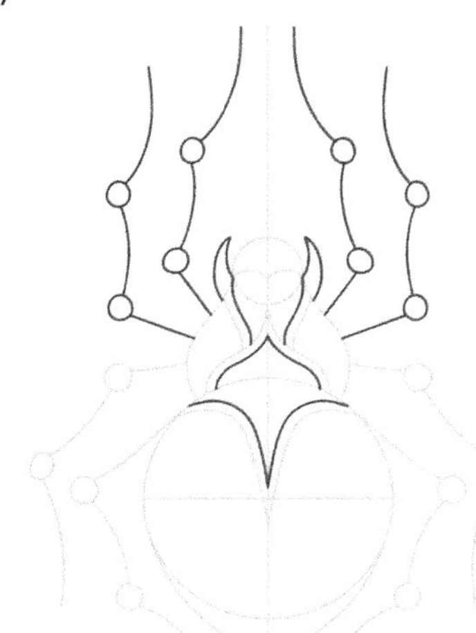

08

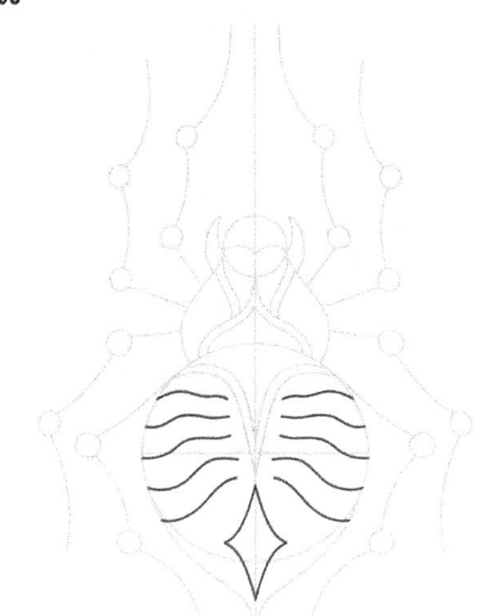

09

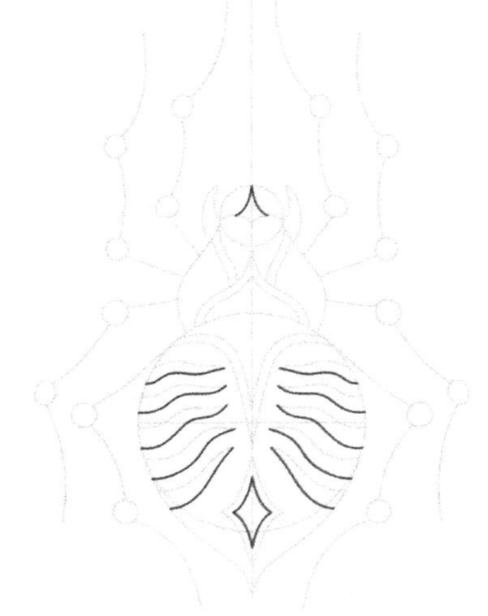

10

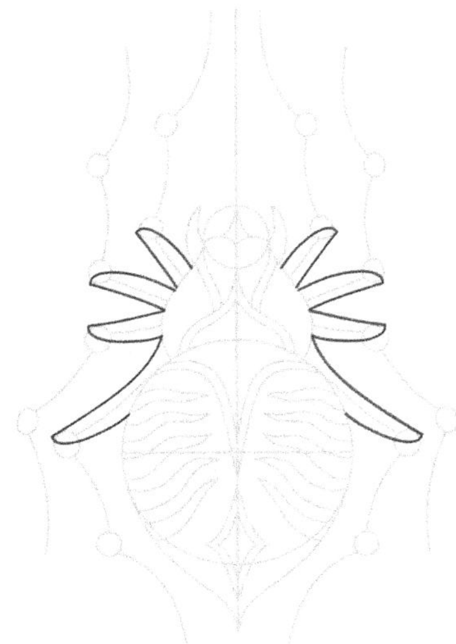

11

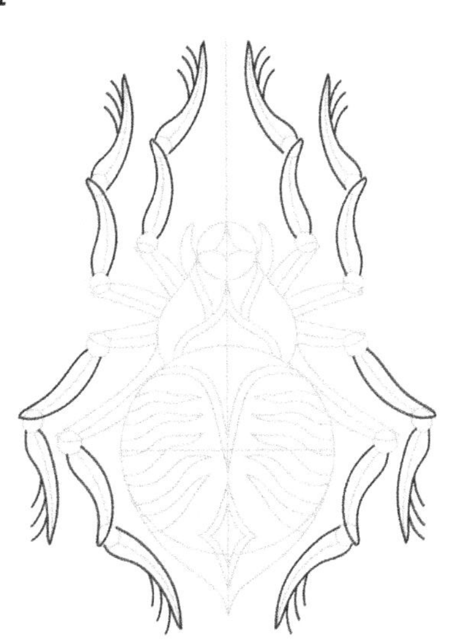

12

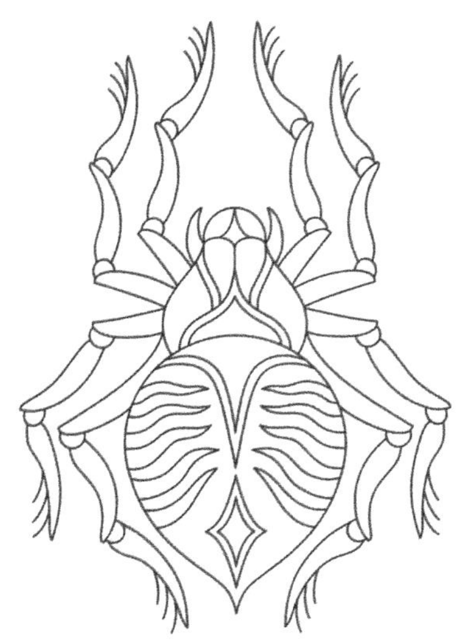

ANIMAL TATTOOS

STAG

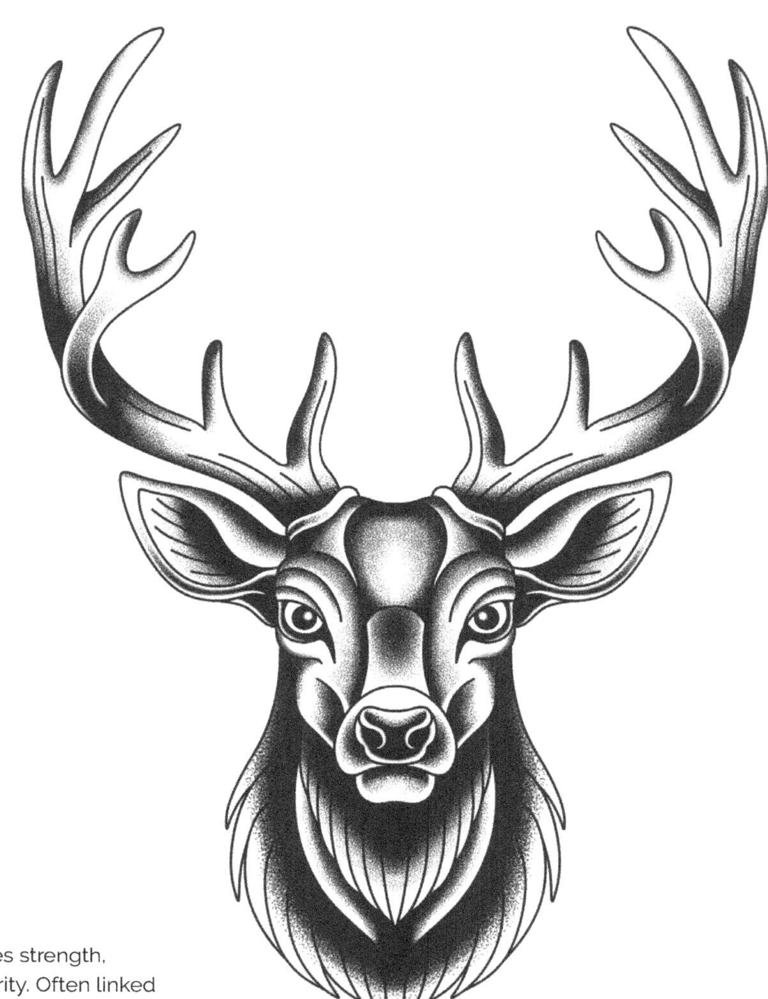

The stag tattoo symbolises strength, grace, and spiritual authority. Often linked to wisdom and connection with nature.

01

02

03

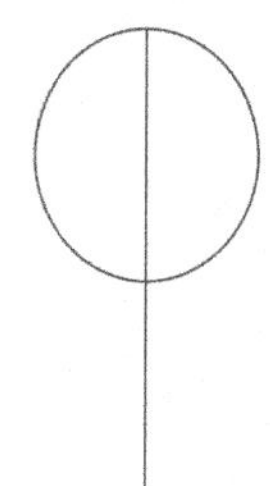

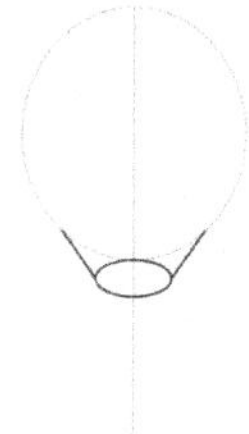

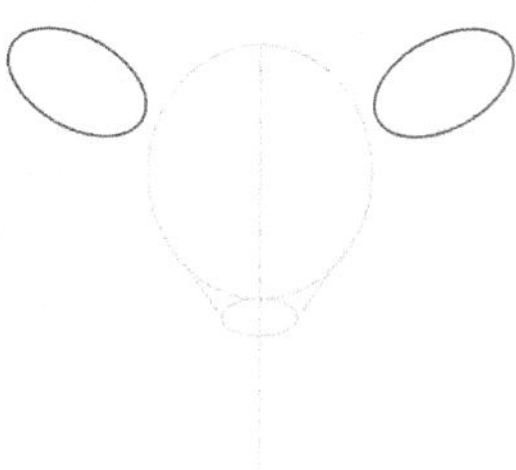

04

05

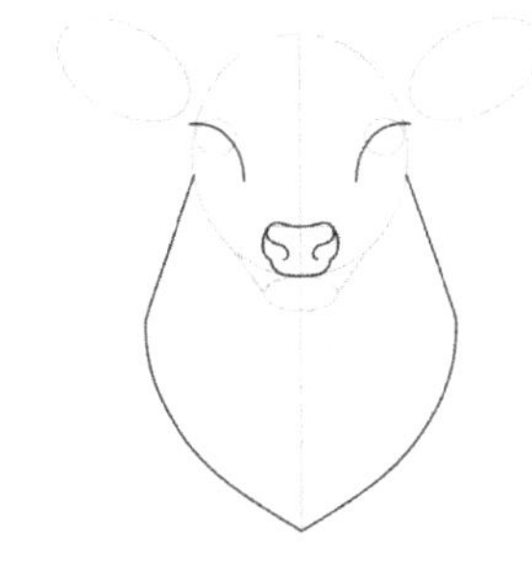

06

07

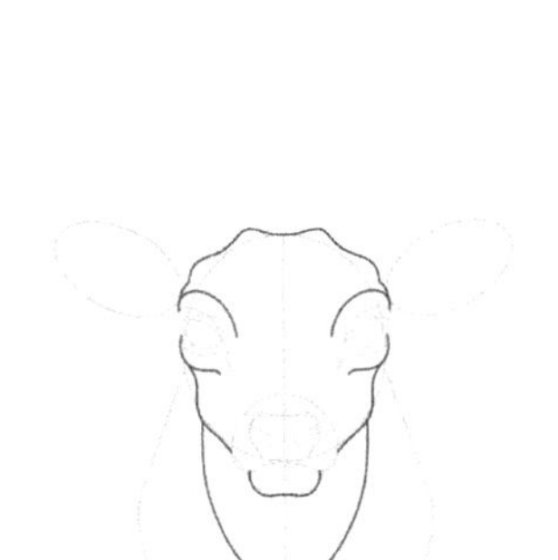

08

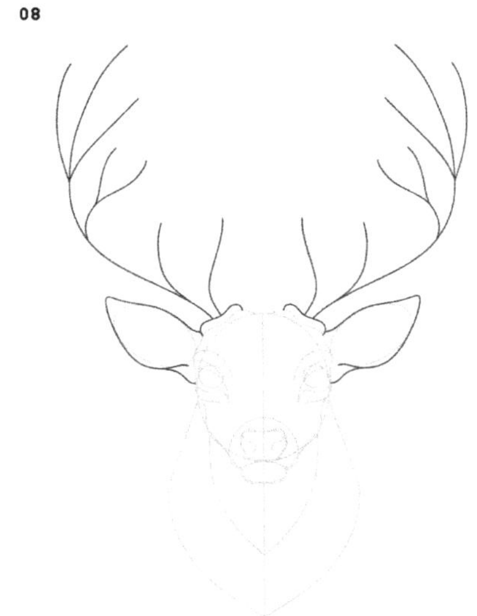

09

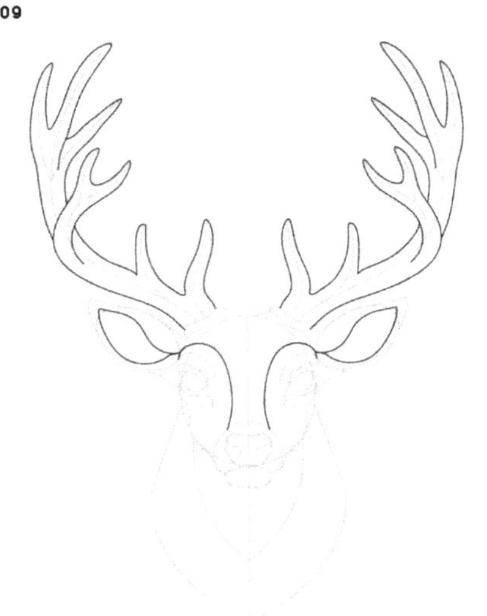

ANIMAL TATTOOS

10

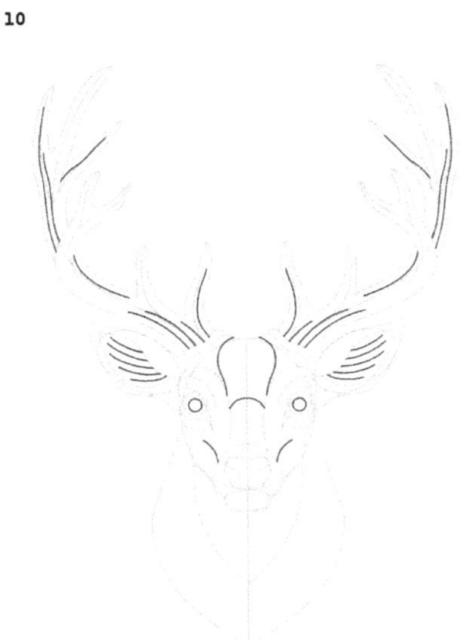

11

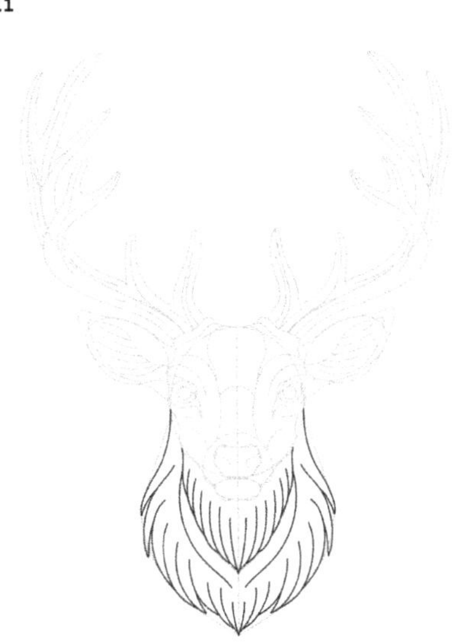

12

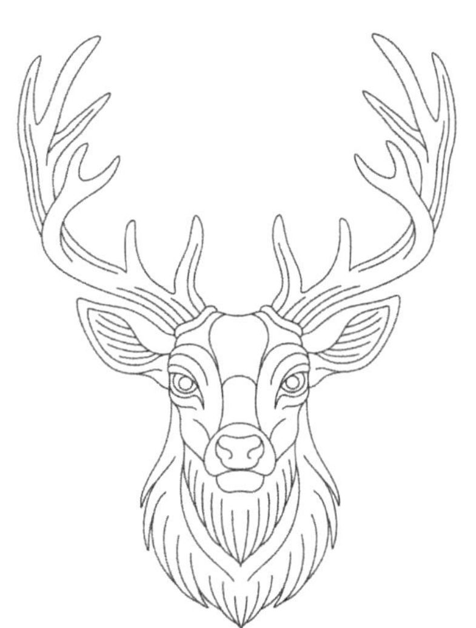

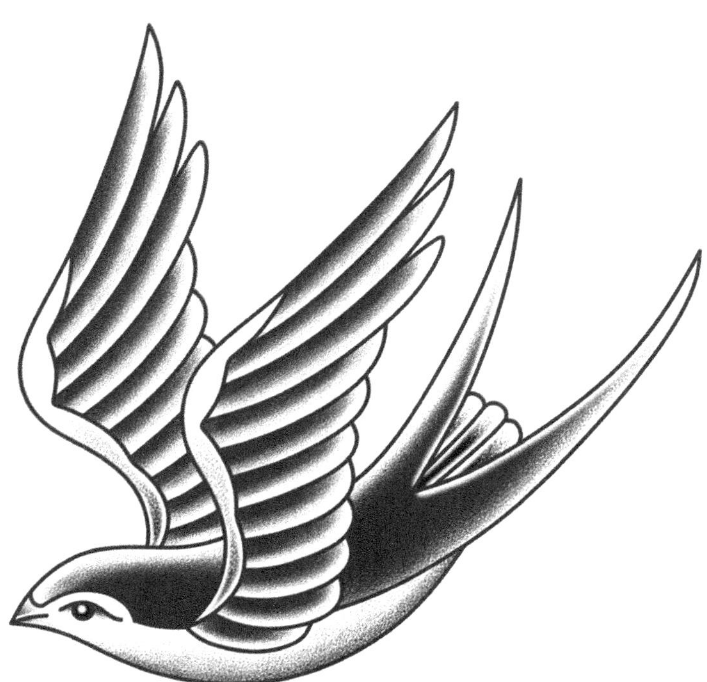

SWALLOW

The swallow tattoo symbolises
hope, safe return, and enduring love.
Traditionally worn by sailors, it represents
loyalty, freedom, and a journey home.

01

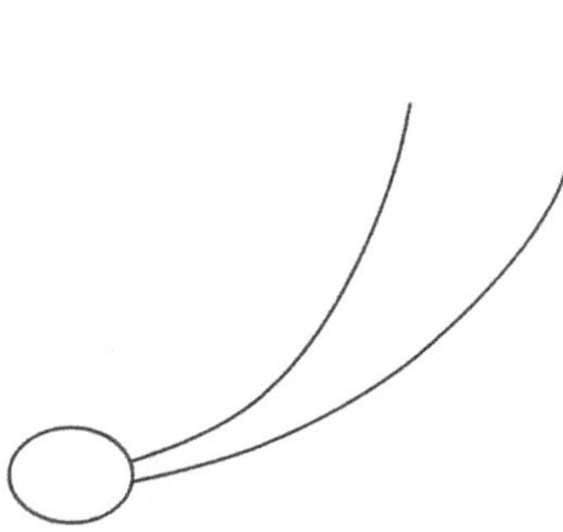

02

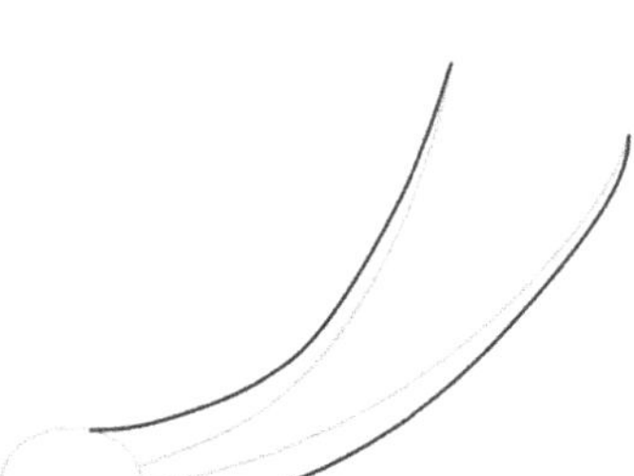

03

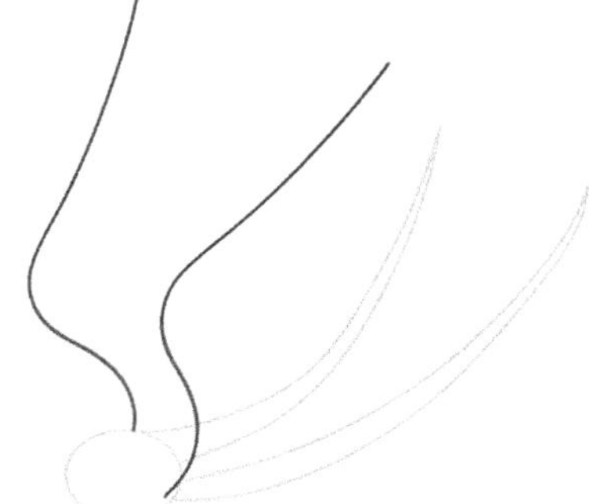

04

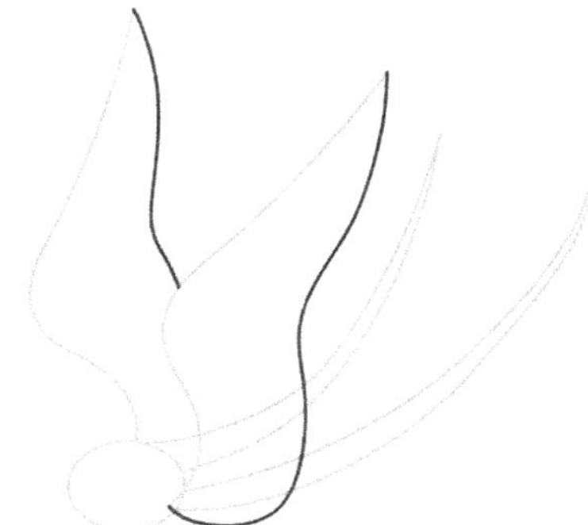

05

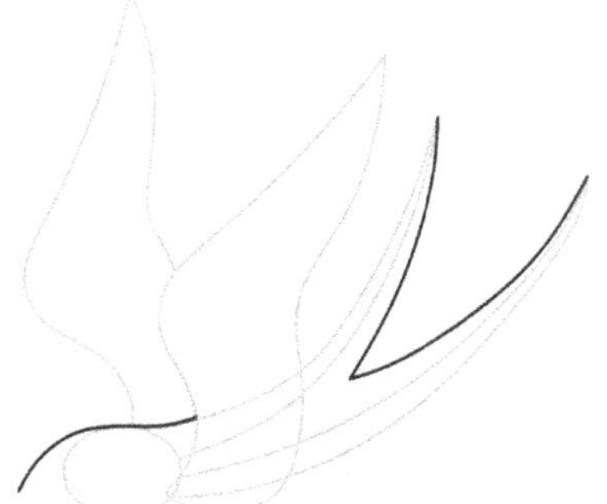

06

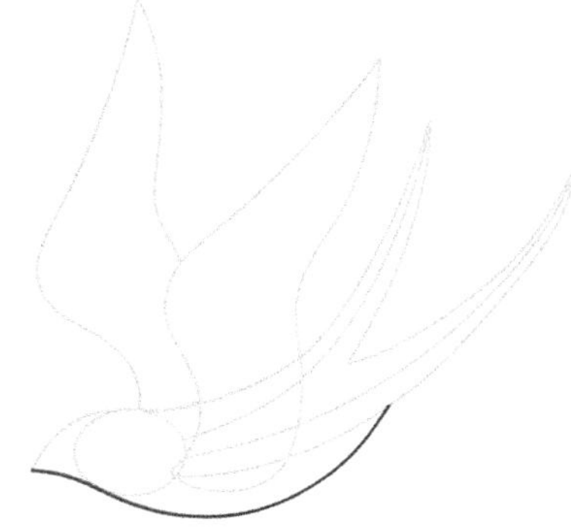

07

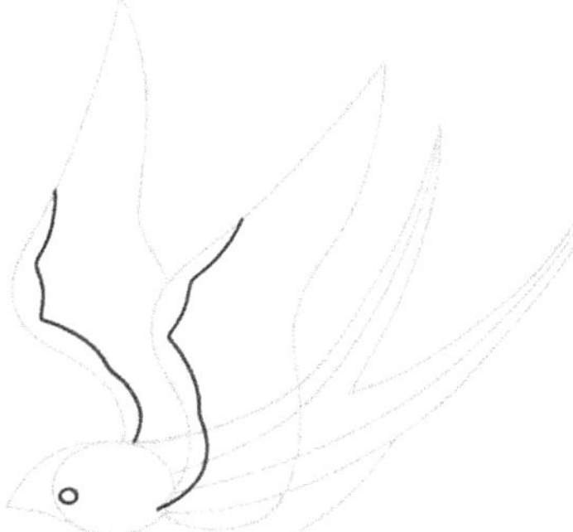

08

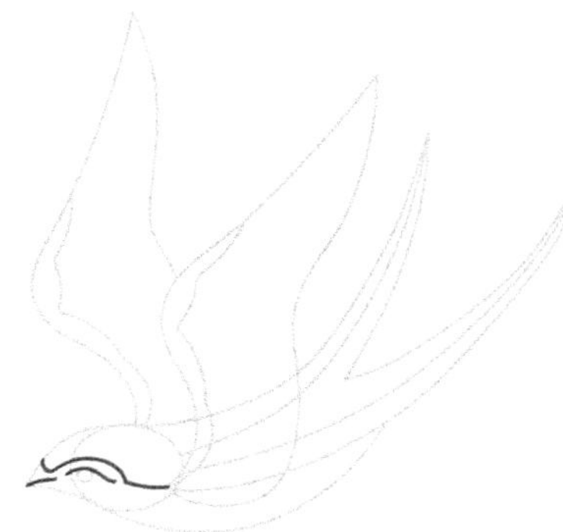

09

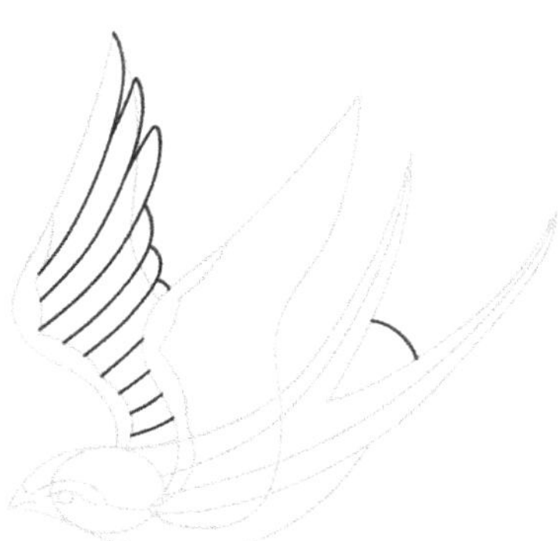

10

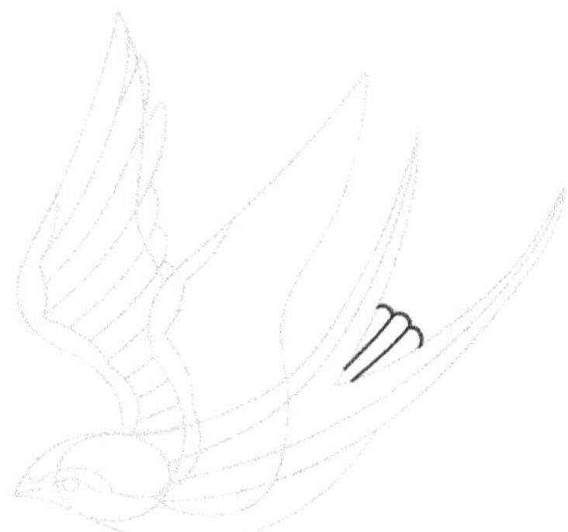

11

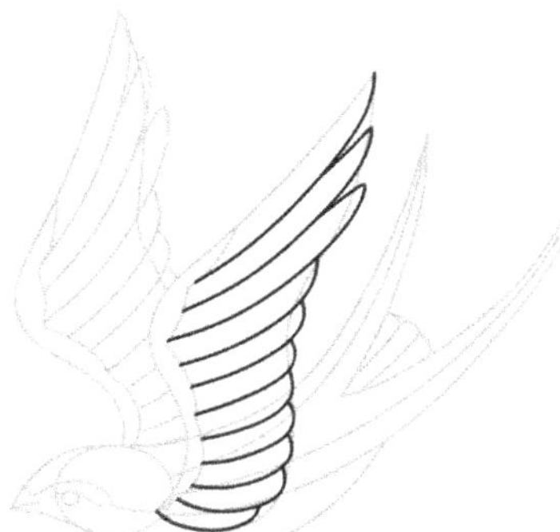

12

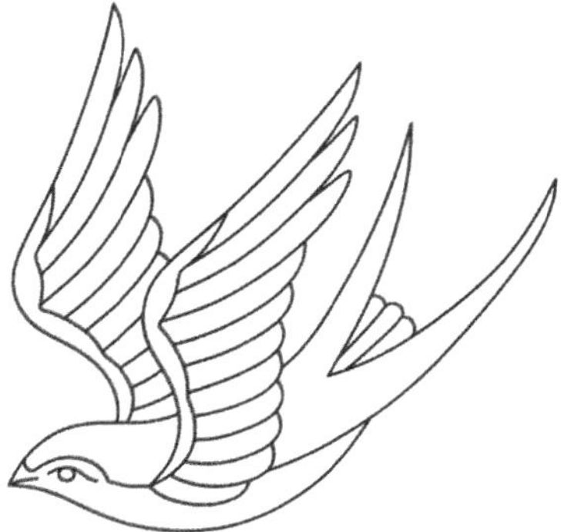

TURTLE

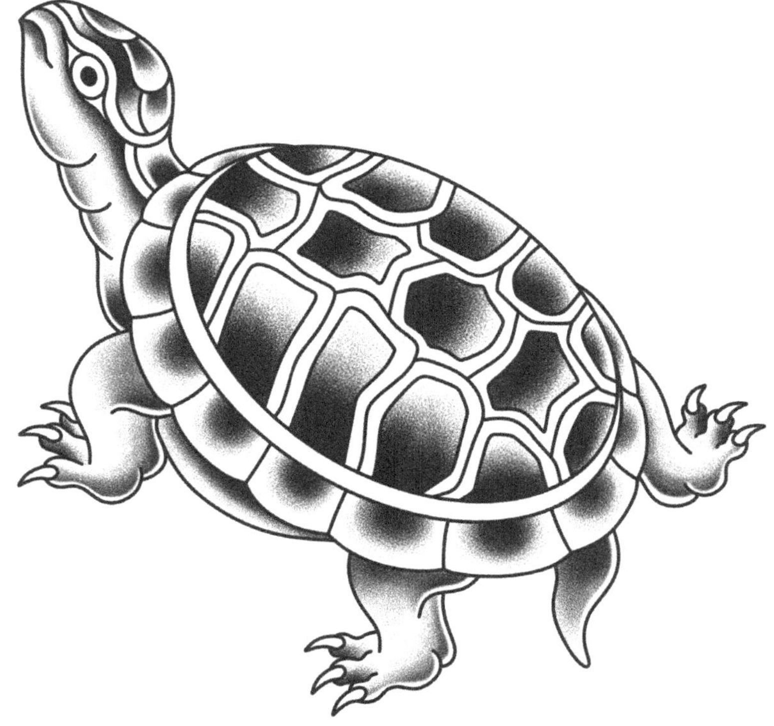

The turtle tattoo symbolises longevity, wisdom, and protection. It represents steady progress, resilience, and a deep connection to the earth.

01

02

03

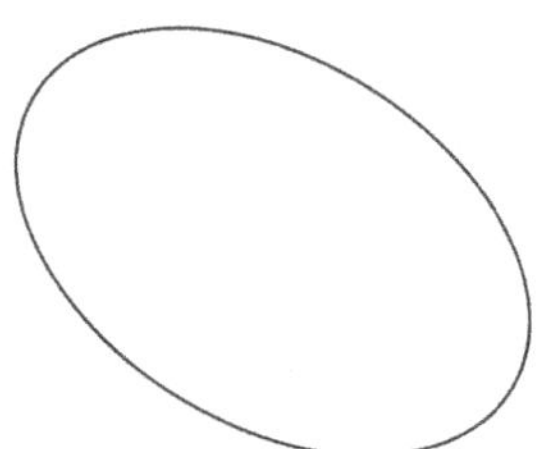

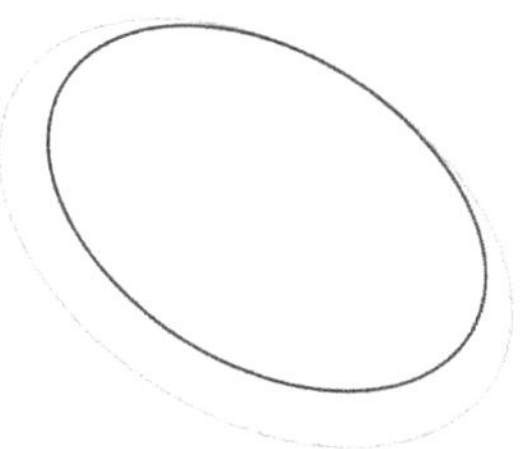

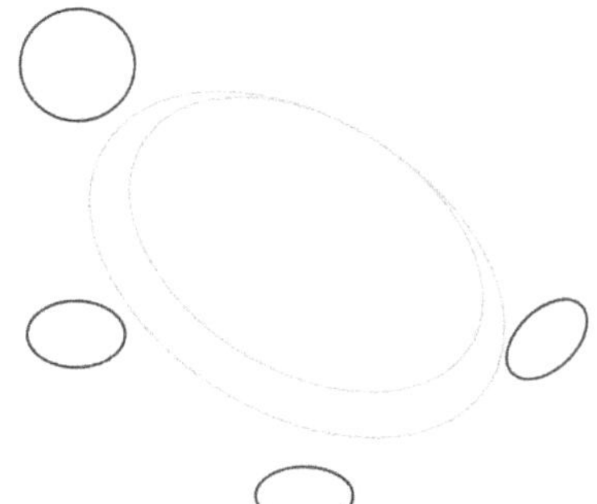

04

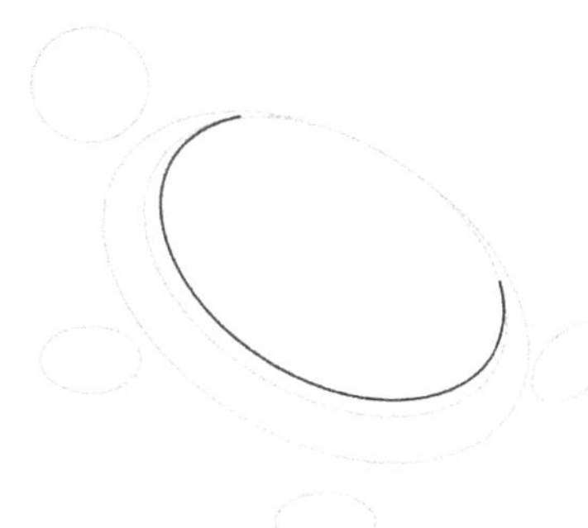

05

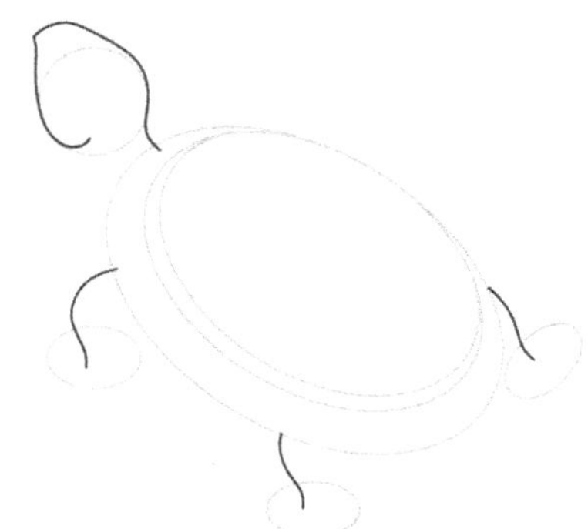

06

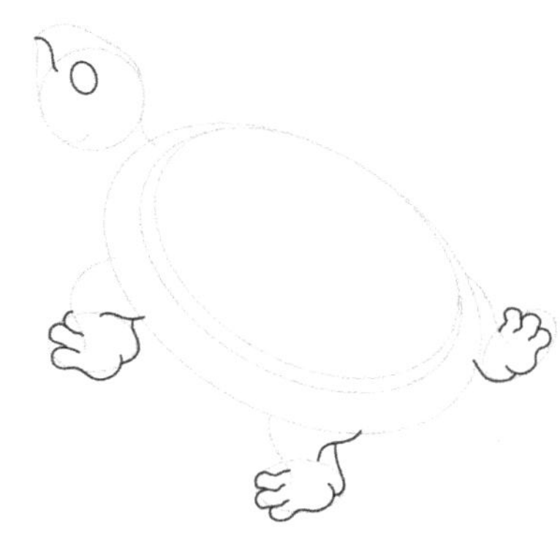

07

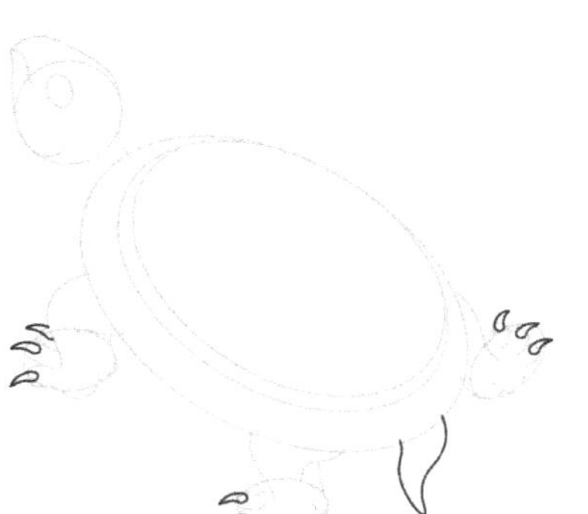

08

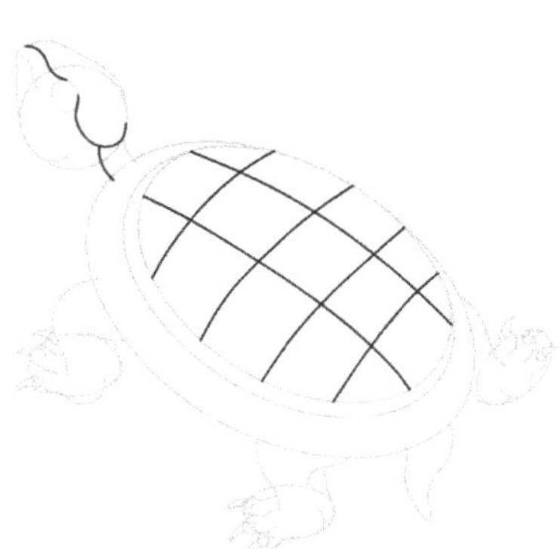

09

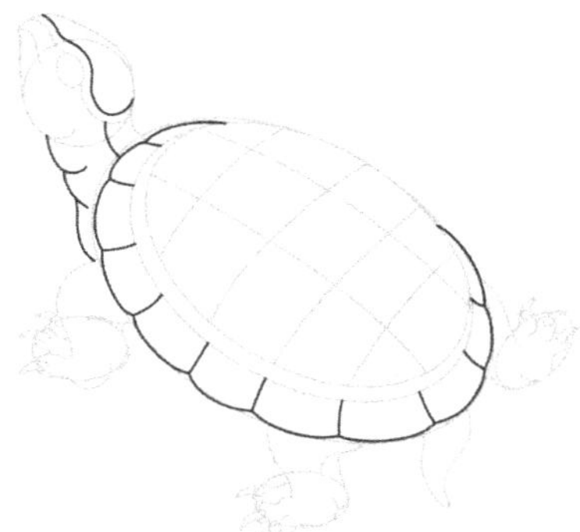

ANIMAL TATTOOS

10

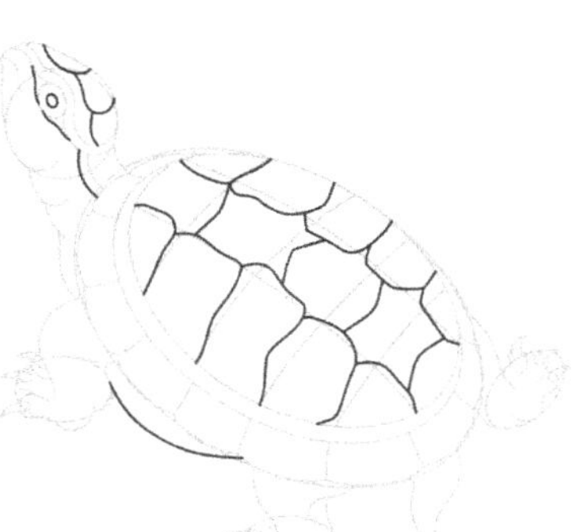

11

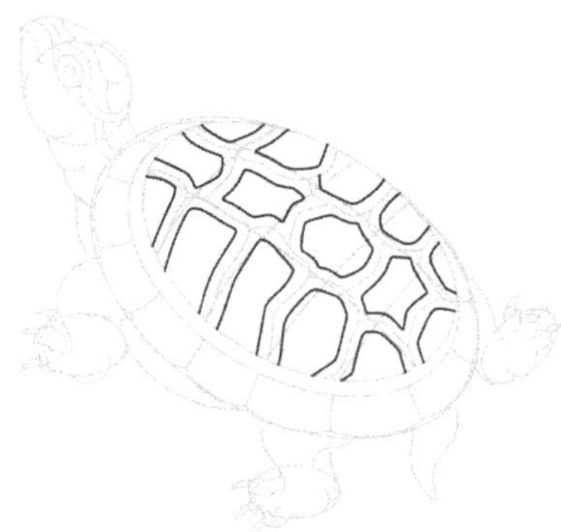

12

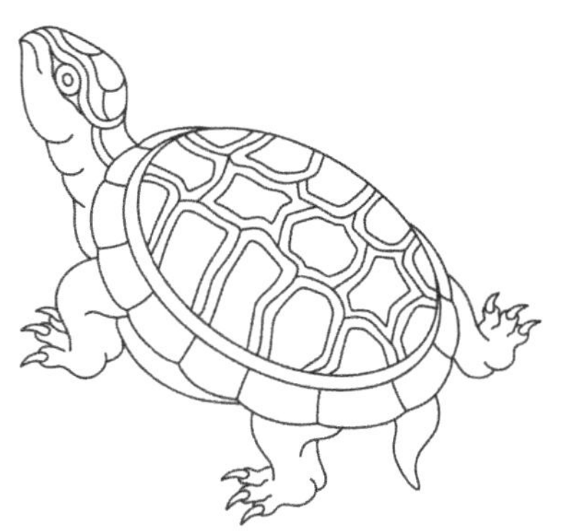

WHALE

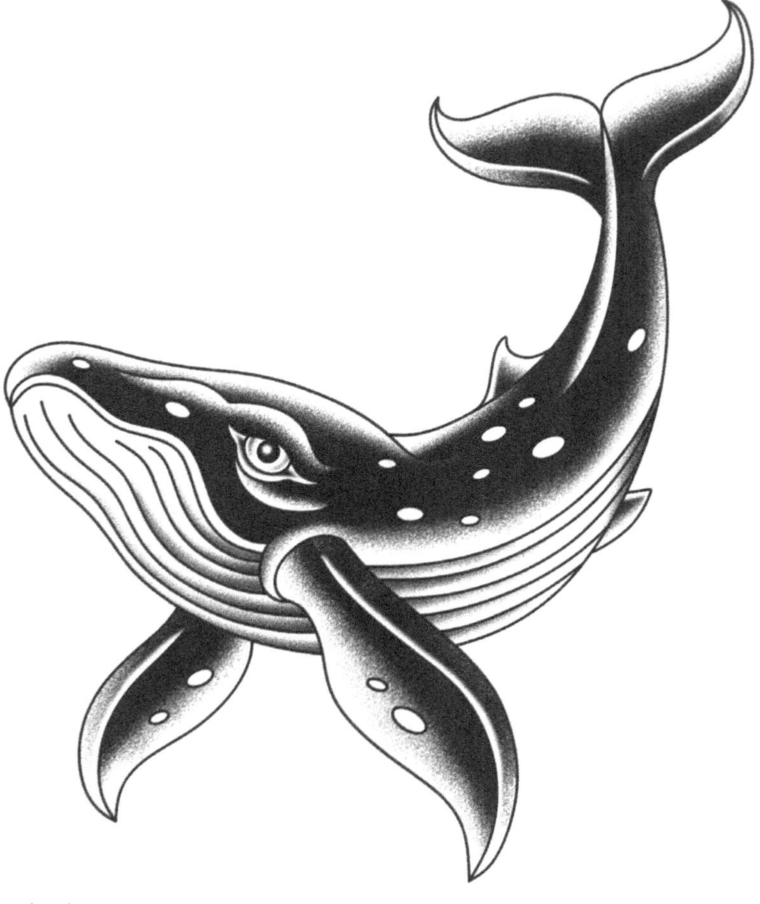

The whale tattoo symbolises depth, wisdom, and emotional intuition. As a guardian of the ocean, it represents spiritual journeys, ancient knowledge, and inner strength.x

01

02

03

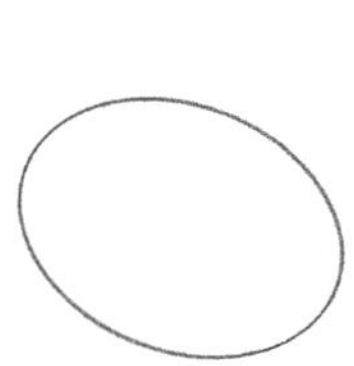

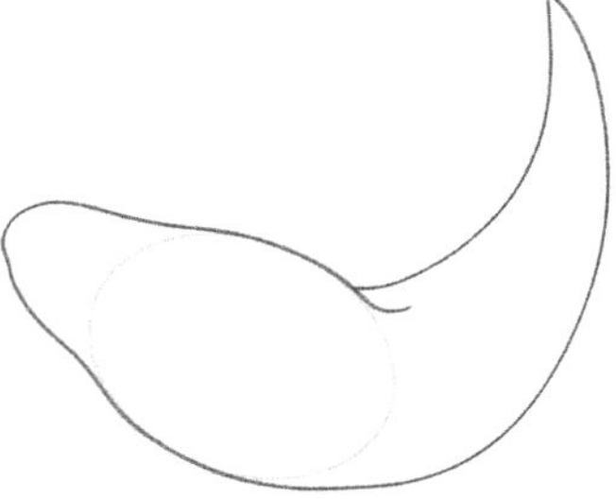

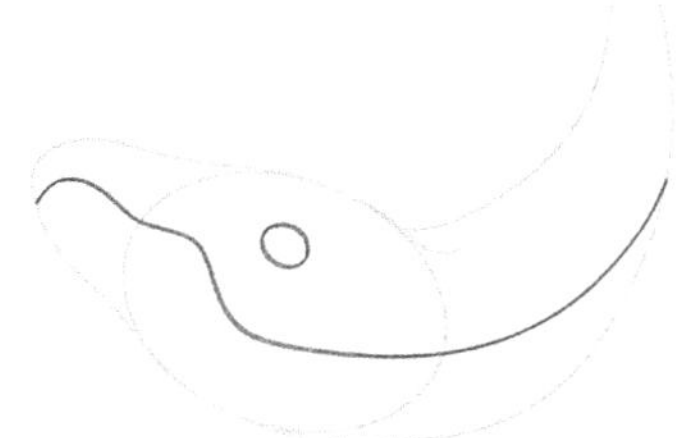

04

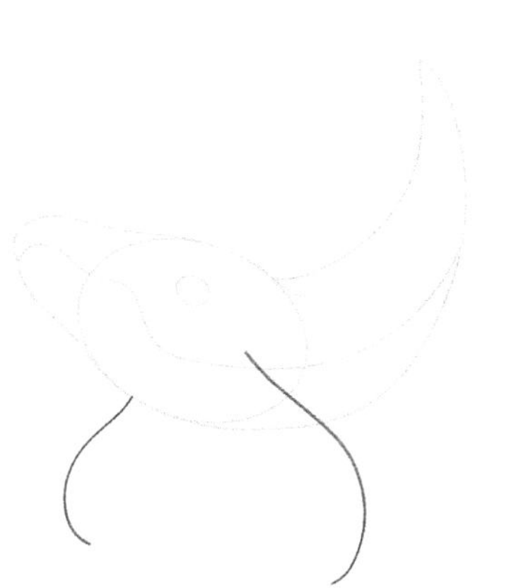

05

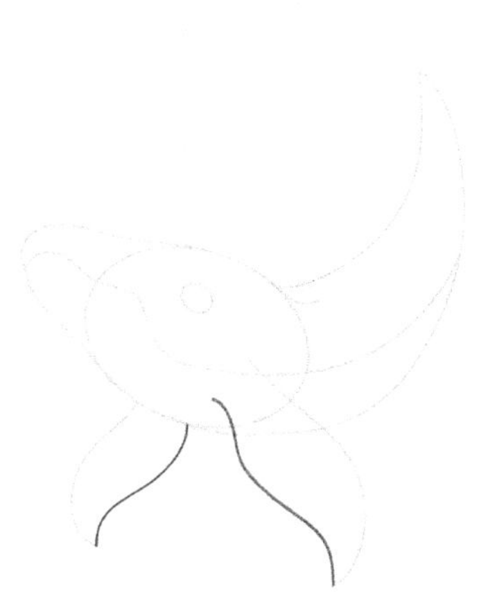

06

07

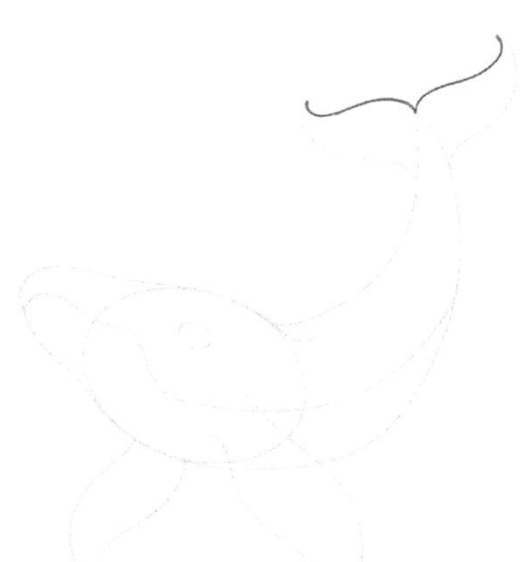

08

09

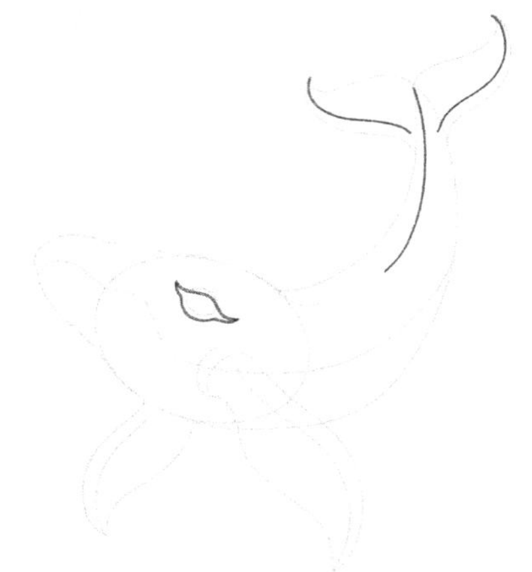

10

11

12

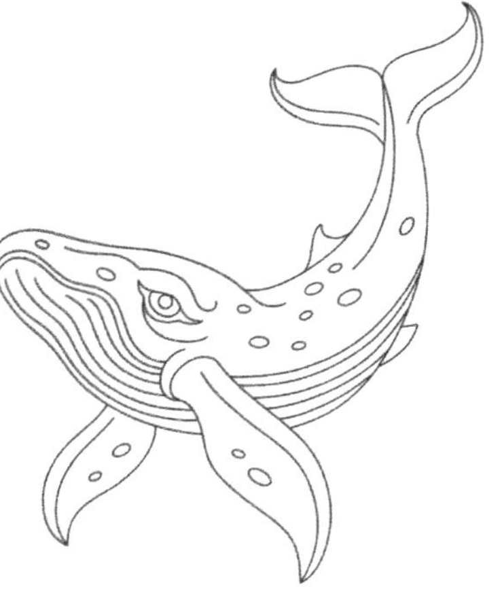

ANIMAL TATTOOS

VULTURE

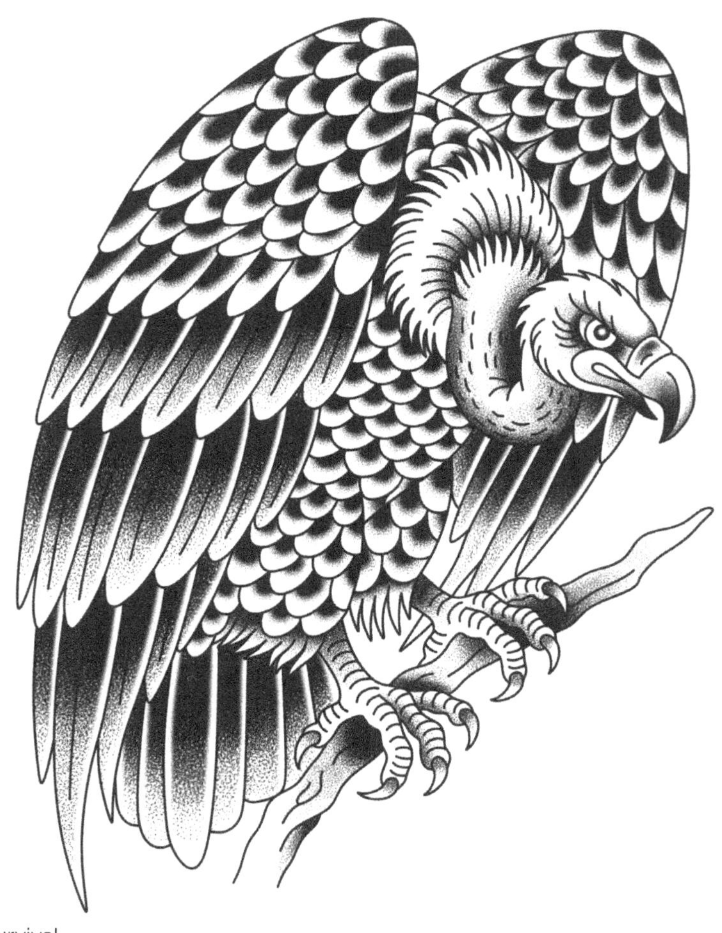

The vulture tattoo symbolises survival, purification, and transformation. Often misunderstood, it represents renewal, patience, and foresight.

01

02

03

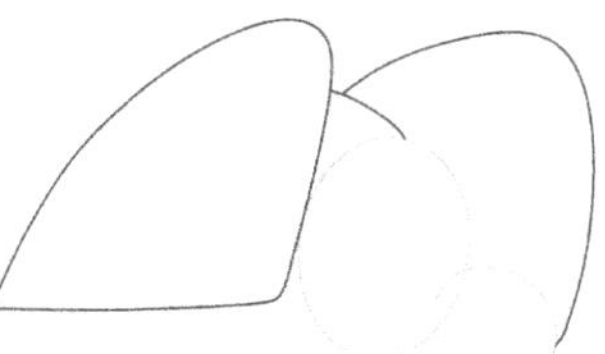

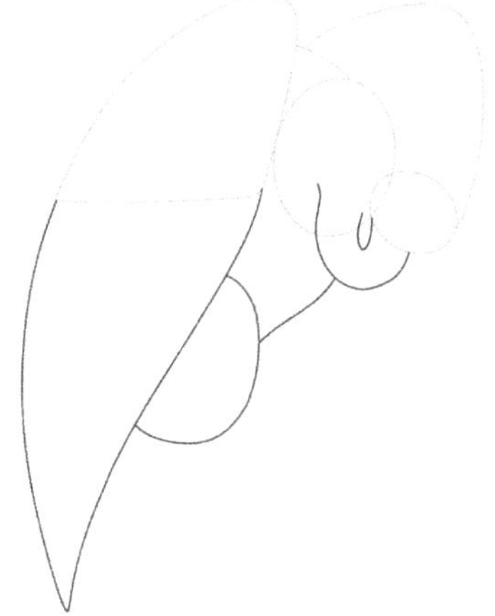

04

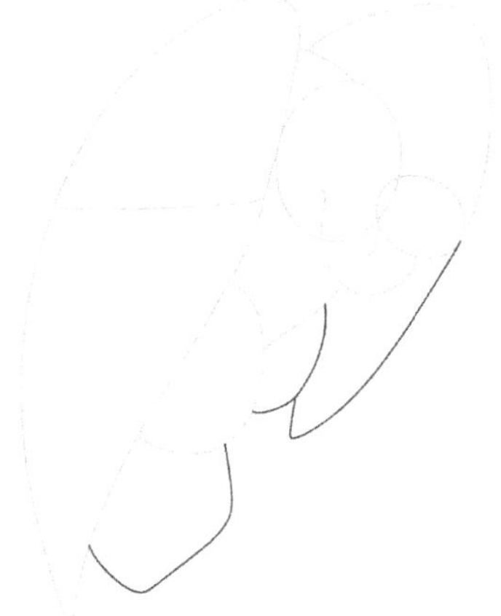

05

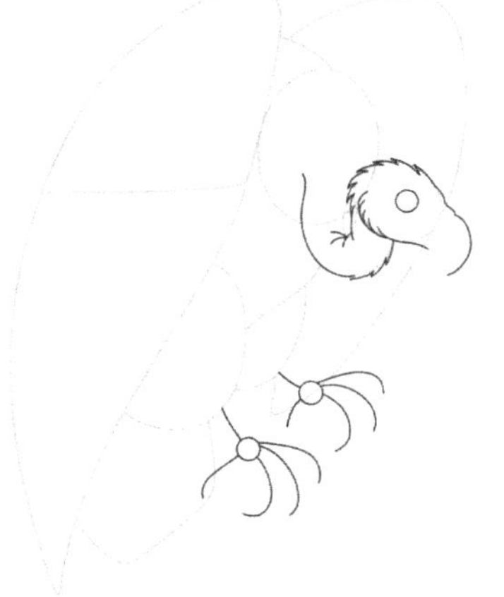

06

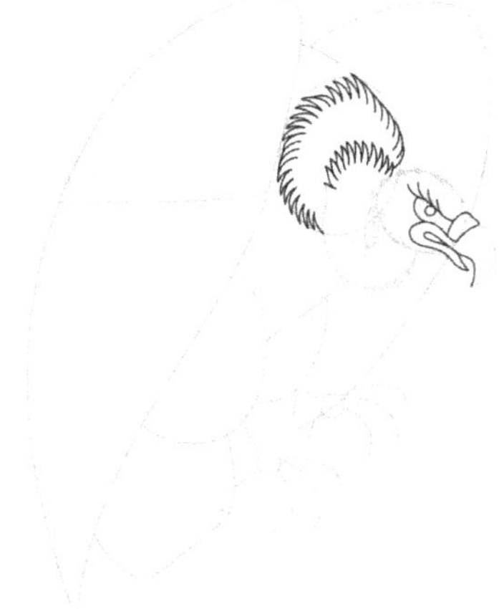

07

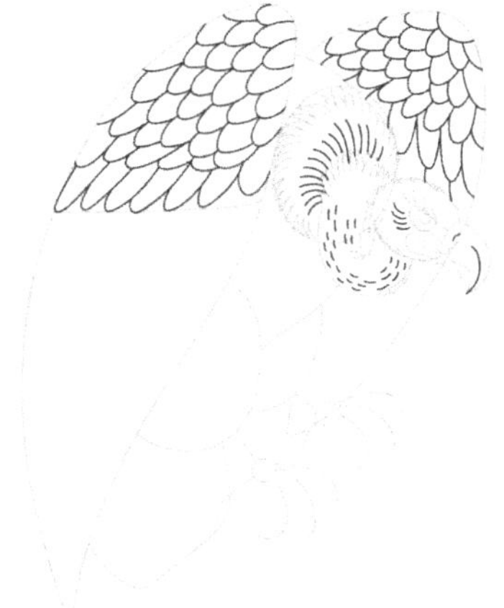

08

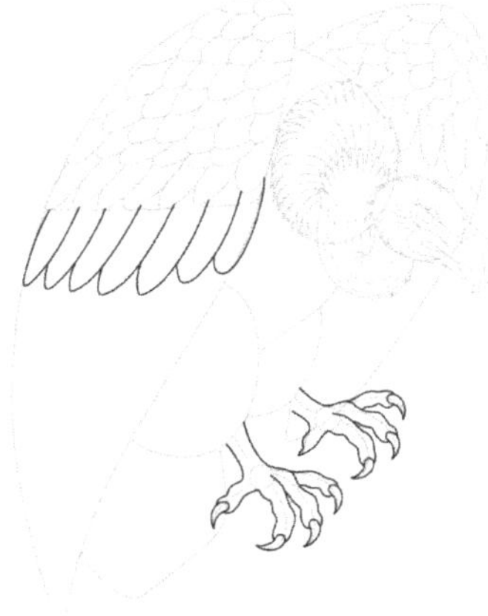

09

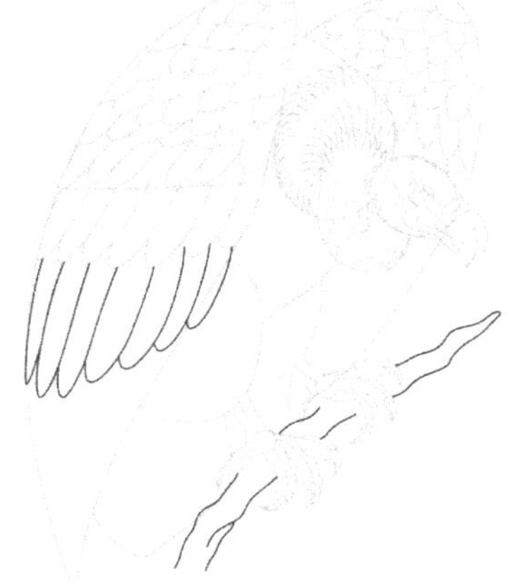

10

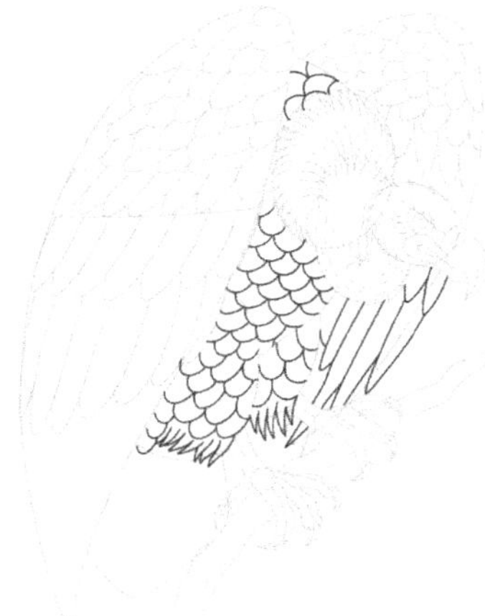

11

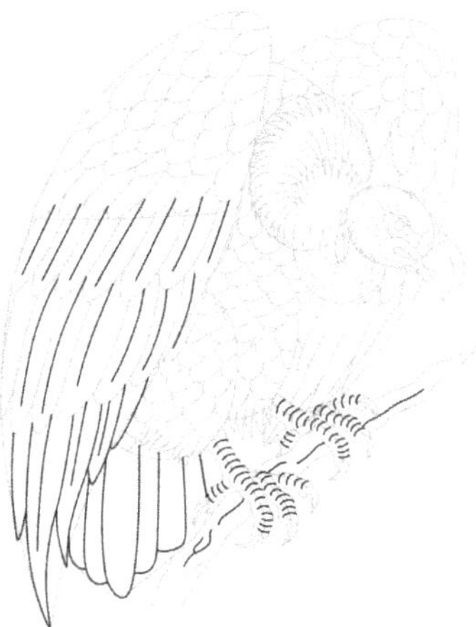

12

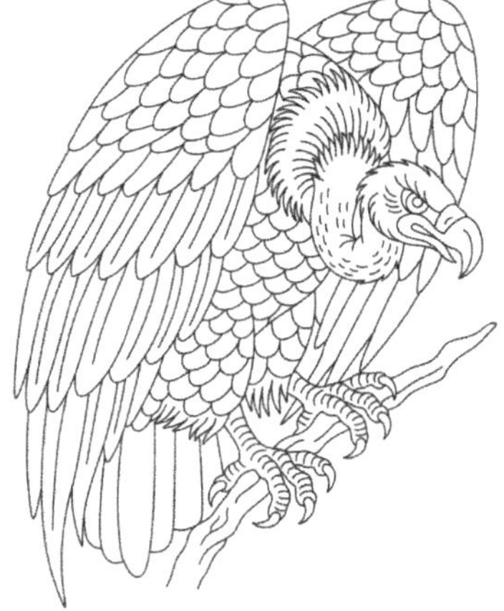

ANIMAL TATTOOS

PRACTICE MAKES PERFECT
TRD MRK

HOW TO DRAW
PRACTICE BOOK

PRACTICE MAKES PERFECT
TRD MRK

Vault Editions Ltd

CURATION AND RESTORATION SERVICES

LEARN MORE
VAULTEDITIONS.COM

HOW TO DRAW
PRACTICE BOOK

ANIMAL TATTOOS

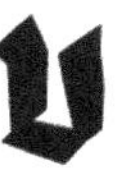
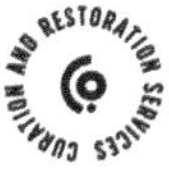

PRACTICE MAKES PERFECT
T R D M R K

HOW TO DRAW
PRACTICE BOOK

PRACTICE MAKES PERFECT
T R D M R K

ANIMAL TATTOOS

Vault Editions Ltd

CURATION AND RESTORATION SERVICES

LEARN MORE

VAULTEDITIONS.COM

PRACTICE
MAKES
PERFECT
T R D
M R K

HOW TO DRAW
PRACTICE BOOK

PRACTICE
MAKES
PERFECT
T R D
M R K

ANIMAL TATTOOS

HOW TO DRAW
PRACTICE BOOK

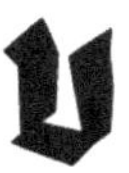
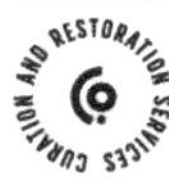

PRACTICE MAKES PERFECT
TRD MRK

HOW TO DRAW
PRACTICE BOOK

PRACTICE MAKES PERFECT
TRD MRK

ANIMAL TATTOOS

HOW TO DRAW
PRACTICE BOOK

ANIMAL TATTOOS

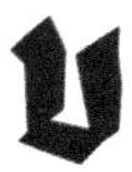
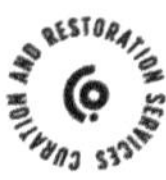

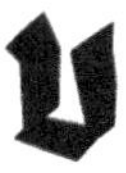
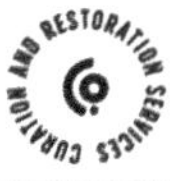

HOW TO DRAW
PRACTICE BOOK

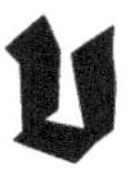
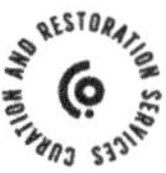

PRACTICE MAKES PERFECT
T R D · M R K

HOW TO DRAW
PRACTICE BOOK

PRACTICE MAKES PERFECT
T R D · M R K

ANIMAL TATTOOS

HOW TO DRAW
PRACTICE BOOK

ANIMAL TATTOOS

Vault Editions Ltd

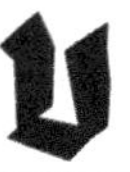
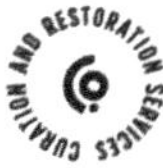

LEARN MORE

VAULTEDITIONS.COM

CONCLUSION

As you reach the end of *How to Draw Animal Tattoos*, you've not only sharpened your drawing abilities but also taken the first steps into a powerful visual tradition where animal imagery carries deep symbolic meaning. Each design in this book has offered a chance to explore how strength, resilience, freedom and transformation can be expressed through line, shape and composition.

Animal tattoo design is one of the most enduring and expressive forms in the tattoo world, a style rooted in both natural beauty and human storytelling. Whether you continue to refine these designs, begin developing your own interpretations, or simply take forward a deeper appreciation for the craft, the skills you've built here will serve as a strong foundation for your artistic journey.

Thank you for being part of this creative process. May your exploration of animal tattoo design continue to grow with confidence and curiosity.

ABOUT THE ARTIST

Abrom Rose, an accomplished artist with a remarkable talent for visual communication and instructional illustration, created the designs in this book. With a background in illustration and design, Abrom brings clarity, precision, and artistic sensitivity to every drawing he produces. His work is defined by confident linework, strong composition, and a deep understanding of form, qualities that make his illustrations both engaging and accessible to learners at all levels.

Abrom's approach to drawing is rooted in careful observation and a passion for traditional tattoo art, which he interprets with originality and technical skill. Whether guiding beginners or inspiring experienced artists, his ability to break down complex motifs into clear, teachable steps sets his work apart.

LEARN MORE

At Vault Editions, our mission is to provide the highest-quality reference materials for artists and designers, offering meticulously curated resources that inspire and empower creativity. If you've found value in this book, we invite you to explore more of our expertly crafted titles at vaulteditions.com, where you'll discover a world of visual inspiration and practical tools designed to elevate your creative work.

REVIEW THIS BOOK

As a family-owned and operated independent publisher, reviews are essential to the success of our business. Please leave an honest review of this book wherever you purchased it.

JOIN OUR COMMUNITY

Are you the creative and curious type? If so, you will love our community on Instagram. Every day, we share bizarre and beautiful artwork ranging from 17th and 18th-century natural history and scientific illustrations to mythical beasts, ornamental designs, anatomical drawings and more; join our community of 300K+ people today by searching @vault_editions on Instagram.

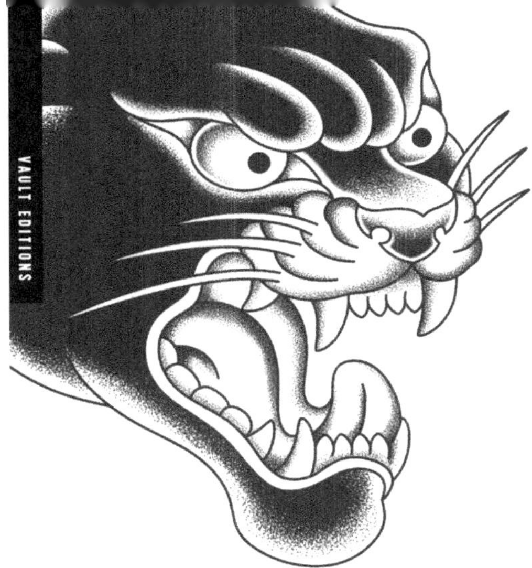

DOWNLOAD YOUR FILES

To enhance your creative journey, *How to Draw Animal Tattoos* comes with a digital PDF version of the book and a specially designed set of Procreate brushes. These resources are tailored to help you refine your skills and streamline your workflow.

The digital PDF provides easy access to the book's contents on any device, so you can reference the designs anytime, anywhere. It's perfect for artists on the go, allowing you to study and practice whenever inspiration strikes.

The custom Procreate brushes are designed to replicate the look and feel of traditional tattoo flash designs, from bold outlining to shading techniques. These brushes make it easier for digital artists to create authentic-looking designs in a digital medium, offering precision and flexibility as you sketch, refine, and finalise your artwork. Whether you're experimenting with new ideas or perfecting your final designs, these brushes allow you to bring your creations to life with the same iconic style that defines classic tattoo flash.

Download yours now and get creating!

STEP ONE

Enter the following web address on a desktop or laptop computer in your web browser.

vaulteditions.com/pages/htdb

STEP TWO

Enter the following password to access the download page:

htdb28466sxda

STEP THREE

Follow the prompts to access your high-resolution files.

CONTACT

For technical support, please email: info@vaulteditions.com

Copyright © 2025
Vault Editions Ltd

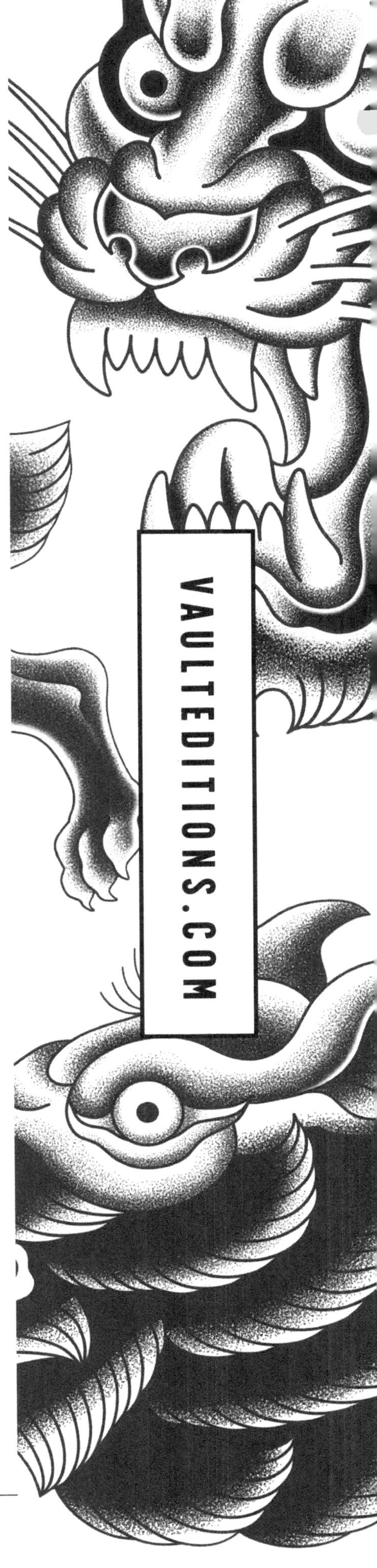

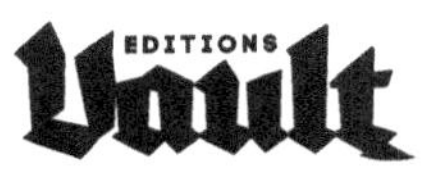

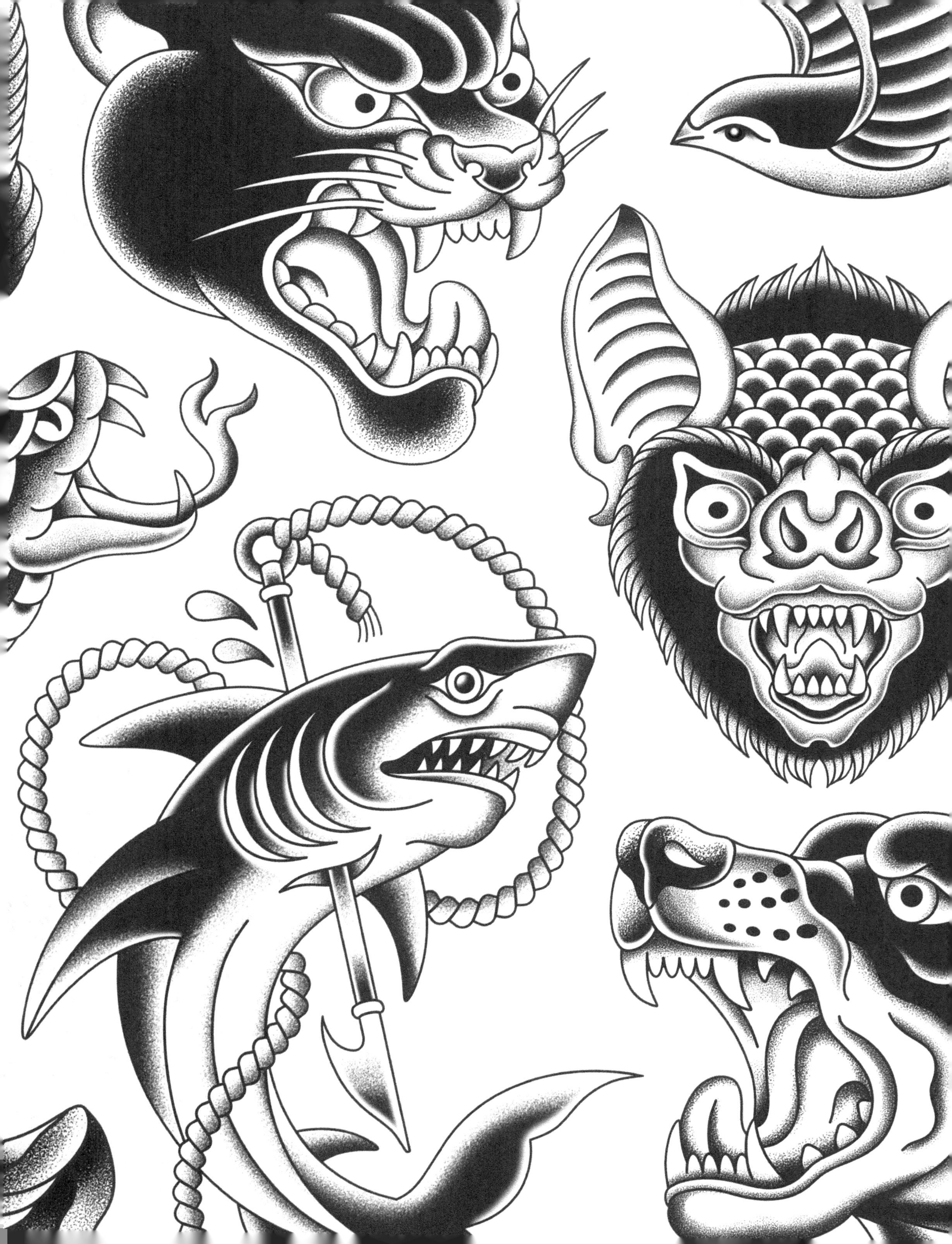